Graphology Explained

Graphology Explained

A Workbook

Barry Branston

SAMUEL WEISER, INC.

York Beach, Maine

First American edition published in 1991 by
Samuel Weiser, Inc.
Box 612
York Beach, Maine 03910

Library of Congress Cataloging–in–Publication Data

Branston, Barry
    Graphology explained / Barry Branston.
        p.   cm.
    Includes bibliographical references and index.
    1. Graphology.   I. Title.
  BF891.B713   1991
  155.2'82—dc20   91–23387
                                      CIP

ISBN 0–87728–735–X
MV

Printed in the United States of America

Contents

Acknowledgements

I am deeply indebted to Patricia Marne, President of the Graphology Society, without whose request, encouragement, help and guidance this book would not have been written. She also read my final draft and, with her useful observations, aided me in shaping the finished manuscript.

I am also greatly indebted to my close friend Olivia, now my wife, herself an advanced student of graphology, for her enthusiasm, painstaking attention to detail and command of the English language, for typing from my, at times, unintelligible scribble. I would have found it difficult to have undertaken this work without her dedicated, abiding and loving support. I am also grateful to her brother Dr Charles Warner for his valuable comments as a layman.

Finally, I extend my sincere thanks to those whose samples of handwriting appear in this book and also to another long-standing friend, John Freeman, for suggesting the title.

Note to the reader
Unless I have specifically used the words male or female, any references in the book may be taken as applicable to both.

Introduction

Handwriting is one of the most important ways in which civilised people communicate. It is used primarily for personal, rather than business, communications between person and person and for communications written to ourselves – reminders, lists, diaries and so on.

Our handwriting is the product of brain and hand, mind and body – thoughts expressed on paper using the muscles of the arm and hand, physical movements controlled by the brain. Not only brain and body are involved, however. Each time we write we are influenced by our inner feelings, by our emotions and moods of that moment. Worry, depression, optimism, elation, anger and passing thoughts will all be reflected in the writing we produce. It should be called 'brainwriting' rather than 'handwriting'.

A person's handwriting is as unique as their fingerprints and facial features. Even identical twins have slight differences. A trained graphologist is able to assess the personality of the writer – not only the way he wishes to be seen, his public face or *persona*, but also the inner person as he really is, the *ego*. We produce a portrait of ourselves as we write and this book will train you to translate this picture into a description of the personality of the writer.

'BUT MY HANDWRITING VARIES'
A person's writing will vary, depending upon the importance of the letter: for instance a note to the milkman is likely to be somewhat different from a letter of application for a job. But the basic structure does not change, nor does the size ratio of the upper and lower extensions. It must be made clear that the letter for analysis is representative of the writer's normal script.

WHAT GRAPHOLOGY CAN AND CAN'T DO
Handwriting cannot accurately reveal the age or sex of the writer. What it actually does is to indicate masculine and feminine influence which is present in both sexes. There are masculine women and feminine men. It will reveal maturity rather than actual chronological age. Nor can graphology predict happenings and future events. Some uninitiated people see it as a form of astrology and tea-leaf reading, which it is not. It can only point to a person's potential that may need to be brought out once they are made aware of it.

'I WRITE LIKE MY TEACHER'

This is another common objection to graphology's validity. Yes – some people may do so, but if they do then this in itself tells us something about them. We call this a copybook script and you will find out what *that* means later on. The teacher may not be a copybook writer, although most of them write clearly so that they can be easily understood by the class copying their instructions and information.

AN ART AND A SCIENCE

Graphology is both. The science lies in the recognition and evaluation of the several factors of handwriting that you will be learning about, while the art is needed in the bringing together (synthesis) of the traits and qualities of that particular personality to produce a portrait of them in words. Here you must use intuition and experience – all the knowledge you have gained in the past of people from all walks of life. This brings us to psychology.

PSYCHOLOGY AND GRAPHOLOGY

Along with the study and practice of handwriting analysis you do need at least a fundamental knowledge of psychology. By combining both you should be able to produce a full and objective picture of the whole personality in all its facets. This is the ultimate aim of this book.

THE USES OF GRAPHOLOGY

From the beginning you will be able to make use of graphology in your ordinary, everyday life. Through analysing the handwriting of those near and dear to you, you will gain a deeper understanding of family and friends and so be able to improve your relationships. This would also apply to people at work of course.

Who will be able to resist doing an analysis of their own handwriting? Graphology is a key to self-knowledge and, even if you only do this one analysis, the book will not have been wasted. If you don't understand yourself it is difficult to understand other people.

After gaining experience by practising analysis of your own writing and that of those near to you, you should eventually feel ready to start assessing the handwriting of strangers. Later still, you may become interested in one of the more specialised fields of graphology:

Vocational guidance

While graphology cannot point to a specific career on the basis of a handwriting sample, it can certainly point someone in the right direction, or away from the wrong direction, based on personality, abilities and inclinations. (More on this in chapter 31.)

Marriage guidance

A handwriting analysis of both partner can confirm compatibilities, point out potential trouble spots and help the couple to understand and accept each other's weaker points. (See chapter 31.)

Personnel

Graphology is being used increasingly by employers nowadays to help in personnel selection. It is especially useful at the short-list stage and to small businesses. Small companies, in particular, need to avoid friction and personality clashes between staff as well as getting the right person for the right job. Some candidates are better at interviews than at their job while others blow their chances through nervousness. A handwriting analysis can give a more complete picture.

Crime

'Handwriting experts' are professionals who are called in to examine documents suspected of having been forged. They are more concerned with technicalities such as the age of the paper and ink, rather than the personality of the writer. However, graphology can provide useful clues and the two skills can be combined. This work does demand an enormous amount of experience as well as the additional technical skills.

How to use this book

In addition to the book you will need:

1 *either* a file, paper and pen
  or an index box and cards

2 Sample(s) of handwriting

3 Some time

4 Somewhere to work (your knee will do – a table is better).

This is a practical workbook and I have designed it so that you can work through it, from start to finish, stage by stage. Some people prefer to start a book at the back or in the middle. This would prove difficult with this book as you need the knowledge of the first chapters before you can understand the later ones.

The book is in five parts. The first part gives you the basics. The next two parts take you deeper into the subject – then deeper. Then we reach the heart of the matter – speed and the all-important Form Level. In the final part we bring all the information together in a report or analysis.

Before beginning the first chapter you must have some samples of handwriting to work with. You may already have them if you look around – letters from family and friends tucked away in a drawer, for example. You will probably want to use your own handwriting too.

You will need a file of some kind, or you may prefer to use a card-index system. A word-processor would be another option, unless you – or it – are prone to 'losing' large chunks of information, as has been known.

Read the first chapter through to get the general meaning. Then, with your samples in front of you, work through it again, using the handwriting samples in the book to help you.

At the end of each chapter there is a sample chart – a mini-worksheet. For each of your samples, produce a similar chart. It is important that you do this at the end of each chapter, before moving on. If you don't, your information will be incomplete and the analysis inaccurate. You will see that in many cases there are positive and negative traits to choose from and your choice will often depend on knowing the Form Level or some other, as yet, unknown, factor such as pressure or connections. When this happens, leave the 'Interpretation' section and fill it in later when you have the missing information.

As you fill in the worksheets you are gradually building up a picture of each person's personality, point by point, and you will eventually produce your first complete worksheets.

By the time you reach the last section, you will have all the information you need to attempt the writing of your first analysis.

This book has far more handwriting samples than any other book on the market at the present time but every person's writing is unique. If you come up with a problem that the book does not seem to answer, there is an extensive bibliography which should help.

A NOTE ON MORALITY!

Whether or not you tell your first 'subjects' that their writing is going to be analysed is something only you can decide.

I hope you *will* tell them. Many people would feel that you were intruding on their private life unless you have got permission from them first.

CONFIDENTIALITY

If you have any reason to think that someone else may look at your work, then you should use some kind of code instead of the writer's name. This may sound a little MI5-like to you now but graphology is a profession, and it deals with sensitive issues – a person's inner, private being.

You must take responsibility for this from the very beginning, and ensure that the trust your writer places in you is never open to abuse. If you do not feel able to do this, for any reason, then restrict yourself to your own handwriting at first.

PART ONE

The basics

Chapter *1* | Size

The first thing we usually notice about a person's handwriting, or script, is the size, especially when it is particularly large or small. The size of the script can be seen as the writer's concept of space in relation to his own needs and demands.

LARGE WRITING
Large writing (fig 1) reveals a demand for freedom of expression and is associated with an outgoing personality. It is often to be found in the scripts of actors and people who enjoy the experience of projecting themselves in the public eye, where they can be seen and admired.

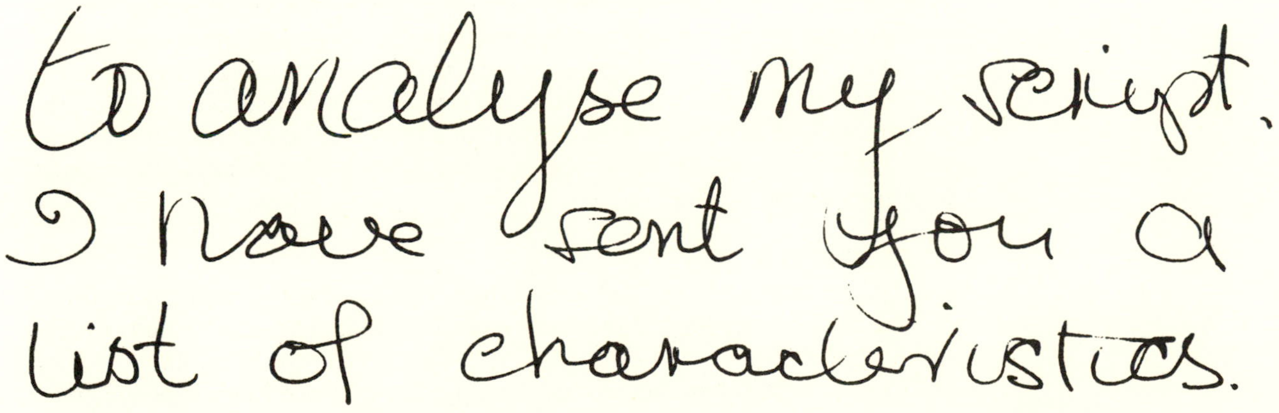

to analyse my script. I have sent you a list of characteristics.

Fig 1
Large script

SMALL WRITING
The small script writer (fig 2) is often found in the area of research, science and mathematics, computers and other fields or professions where concentration and exactness are necessary. These people are thinkers who keep themselves under strict control and usually accomplish whatever they set out to do.

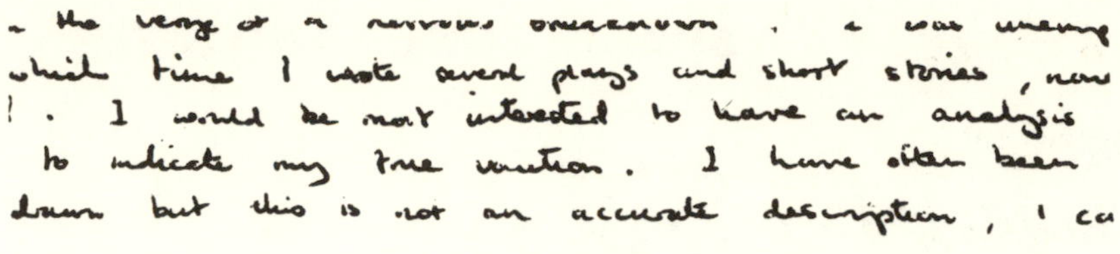

Fig 2
Small script

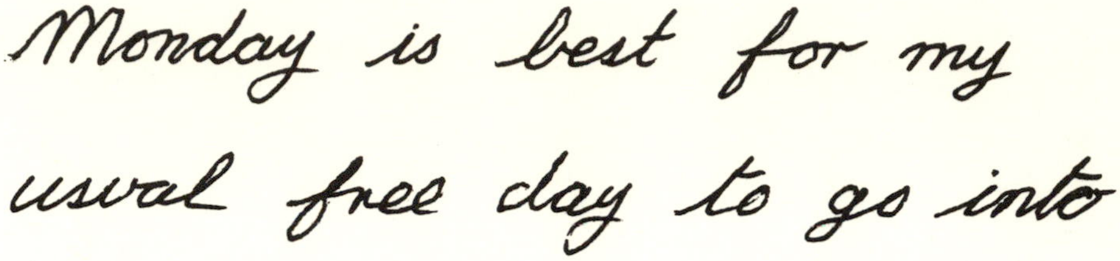

[handwriting sample – small script]

Fig 3
Normal copybook size

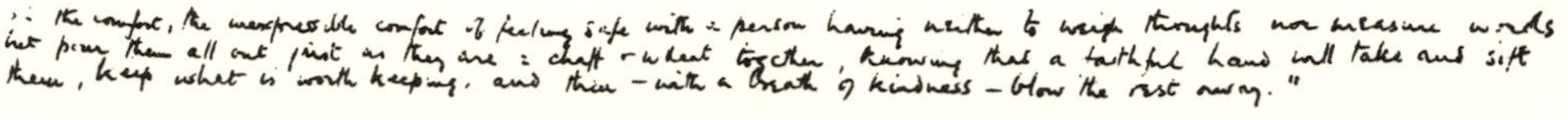

Monday is best for my usual free day to go into

Fig 4
Extremely small script,
very high standard of
writing (lady of 78
years)

[handwriting sample – extremely small script]

You must always remember that each separate factor of the script, while indicating certain traits, is influenced by what is called the Form Level, i.e. the overall quality of the handwriting. (The form level is fully explained in chapter 28.) For instance, the small writer with a very copybook type of letter formation (fig 3) – the style they were taught at school, with no originality – would be content to work in a very limited environment where initiative and imagination are unimportant. They are content to follow directions and orders rather than give them – i.e. they are followers, not leaders.

A high level of performance can be achieved by the small writer, who is rarely disturbed by outside interference (fig 4). A person with a large script, however, finds it difficult to concentrate for long periods, and is easily distracted. A word of warning is necessary here. Always make sure that the writing you are analysing is the normal size for that person and is not restricted or enlarged because of unusual conditions such as a postcard or computer print-out paper.

ASSESSING SIZE

When determining the actual size of the script use the following guidelines.

The British copybook size is considered normal at 9mm (⅜ inch) for the full length of the letter. The small 'f' is the only letter in the alphabet to have an upper, middle and lower loop occupying what are known as the three zones. Measurement can also be made from a combination of two letters – provided they are written in one movement only (fig 5), the measurement being made at 90% upright, regardless of the slant of the letters. This is known as the *absolute size*.

Under 9mm is considered small, and over 9mm large, in varying degrees, i.e. excessively large, large, moderately large, etc., or small.

The personality indications below are only for scripts where the letters measure over or under 9mm overall. In the normal writer (with a dominant absolute size of 9mm) it need only be noted that the size is 'normal'.

ABSOLUTE SIZE

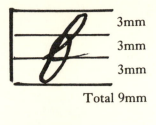

3mm
3mm
3mm

Total 9mm

Large writing (over 9mm):

Positive traits – *good quality Form Level*	*Negative traits –* *poor quality Form Level*
Active	Extravagance
Flexible	Lack of self-discipline
Sense of adventure	Attention easily distracted
Individual	Poor observation
Qualities of leadership	Vague, nebulous concepts
Enthusiasm	Accident-prone
Courage	Arrogance
Generosity	Conceit
Self-confidence	Pretentiousness
Self-reliance	Boastfulness
Good self-esteem	Pompous
Strong character	

Small writing (under 9mm):

Positive traits – *good quality Form Level*	*Negative traits –* *poor quality Form Level*
Realism	Pedantic
Prudence	Inferiority feelings
Accuracy	Temporary depression
Modesty	Inhibition
Ability to concentrate	Small fields of interest
Maturity	Self-limitation
	Submissive

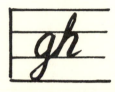

Fig 5
Absolute Size
is the upright
measurement of the
three zones together

Remember that these factors are just a starting point. They must be taken in combination with all the other features we have yet to explore.

Now make the first worksheet for your samples.

WORKSHEET FOR SIZE

Absolute size (all three zones)	*Interpretation*
e.g. between 6 and 16mm: average. 11mm large 2 and 10mm: average. 6mm small **Or** the size of the majority, i.e. if there are only eight under 9mm and 27 over 9mm, the writing is large.	(This will have to wait until the end when you establish Form Level)

The three zones

Chapter 2

Fig 6
Relative Size is the upright measurement of each zone

Total 9mm
Normal middle zone

Normal upper zone

Normal lower zone

In all three examples it should be noted that although they are not equal in the zone the measurements are normal absolute size as they total 9mm.

Having determined the absolute size, we can now go further and examine what is known as the *relative* size (fig 6). This is the measurement of each of the three zones – upper, middle and lower – as separate units, and in most cases you will find that the zones of a script are not of equal size.

The structure of the personality lies in the balance of these three zones, and they should be taken into consideration when showing where the strengths and weaknesses of the writer lie (fig 7).

When there is a disproportion between any of the three zones, the larger, or *dominant*, will point to the writer's over-enthusiastic response to that area (fig 8).

Upper Intellectual and spiritual limits

Middle Social relationships, the emotions and practical behaviour

Lower Sexual awareness and materialistic concern

Fig 7

6mm   Indicates exaggerated ambition

Fig 8

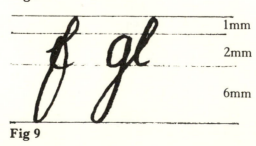

Indicates exaggerated sexual interest

Fig 9

A small middle zone between a large upper and lower zone indicates a gulf between a person's ideals and capabilities and therefore suggests a low achievement level due to reaching beyond capacity.

A very short upper loop will indicate a lack of spiritual values and awareness and also reveal a poor response to intellectual interests and very little ambition in that area.

In a writing in which the rhythm and regularity is poor, there can be a lack of regulating intellectual control over ethical values. You should bear this in mind when considering other factors on dishonesty in the appropriate chapter.

A dominant lower zone shows that the writer's interest is centred in the sexual and materialistic sphere (fig 9).

UPPER ZONE
The upper extensions or loops are written in varying degrees of size, the normal height being 3mm.

High upper zone (over 3mm):

Positive traits	*Negative traits*
Imagination	Lack of objectivity
Idealism	Extravagance
Intelligence	Pretentiousness
Enthusiastic response	Power-seeking
Spiritual awareness	Flights of fancy, not realistic
Good self-esteem	
Ambition (if not out of proportion)	
Generosity (if full loops)	

Low upper zone (under 3mm)

Positive traits	*Negative traits*
Self-reliance	Lack of intellectual ideas
Realistic concepts	Lack of religious spiritual awareness
Sociable attitude	Lack of ambition
Modesty	Lack of ethics (if very low)

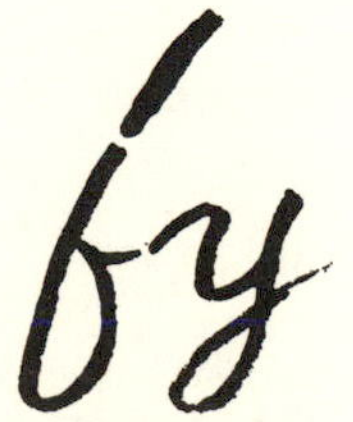

Any added extensions (touching up or an extra stroke) are usually compensation for inferiority feelings and anxiety (fig 10).

Fig 10
Extra stroke added

MIDDLE ZONE

In this zone we find all the small letters without upper or lower loops. These constitute a balance between the upper and lower zones. They relate to everyday experiences, emotions and social life.

A very large middle zone relates to a writer with an over-inflated ego, often a feminine feature (fig 11). This person will consider herself very important and will try to demand attention and expect others to adapt to her ways. She will be unable to hold a balanced view of reality, taking an extremely subjective attitude to personal matters, which to her are always the priority in her everyday functioning. Because their conception of reality is not usually fully developed, children often produce a large middle zone (fig 12).

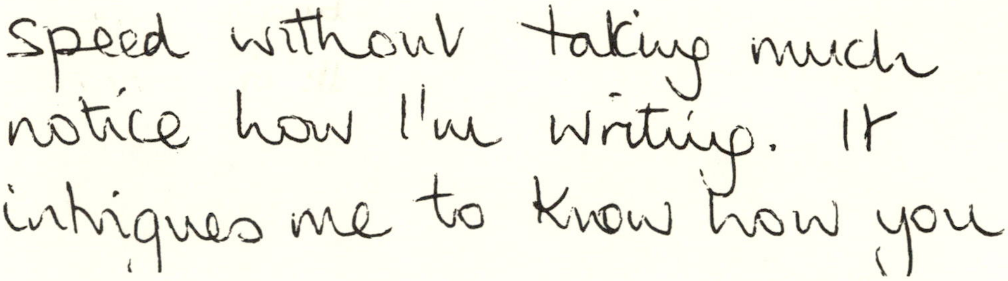

Fig 11
Dominant middle zone

Speed without taking much notice how I'm writing. It intrigues me to know how you

Fig 12
Dominant middle zone
(early teens)

watching television. I also enjoy listening to music.

Always when there is an extra large upper and/or lower zone (especially if inflated like a balloon), with a reduced middle zone, there is a personality strain in the everyday social and emotional sphere of the writer (likened to an elastic band being stretched) (fig 13). This person would allow his personal life a very small range, with little concern for emotional outlets and their expression. An extra large upper zone often indicates a high Form Level writer whose intellect and mental capacity is on a high level (fig 14). A poor Form Level script, with a dominant upper zone, indicates a writer who seeks power but does not have the ability to attain it (fig 15).

Fig 13
Dominant upper and
lower zones

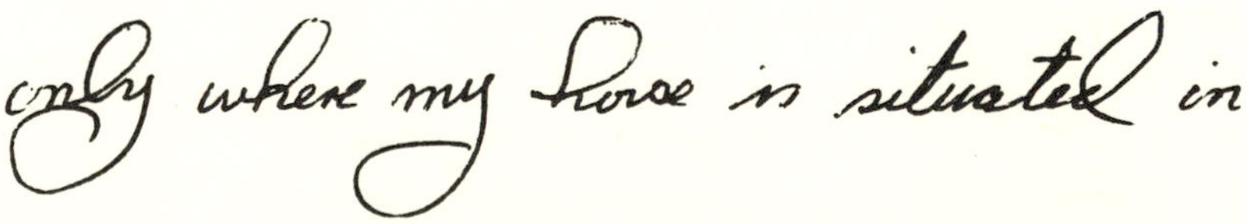

only where my horse is situated in

Fig 14
Small middle zone

In respect to the multiplier effect.

Fig 15
Dominant upper zone

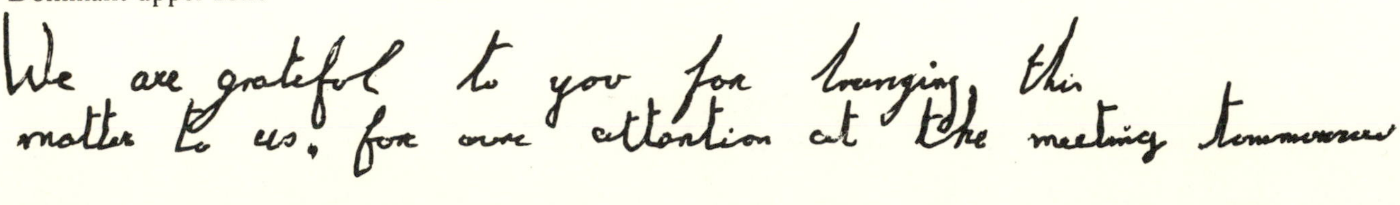

We are grateful to you for bringing this matter to us, for our attention at the meeting tomorrow

As explained in chapter 16 on Regularity (see pages 134–8), the middle zone size can be subject to change. Only people with a stable disposition and never-changing self-confidence are invariably able to maintain a consistent middle zone height (fig 16). Excessive fluctuation in the zones can, depending upon other factors such as varied slant, reveal inconsistent mood levels and problems in coping with difficulties and obstacles in general life. This unstable disposition can result in troublesome relationships (fig 17).

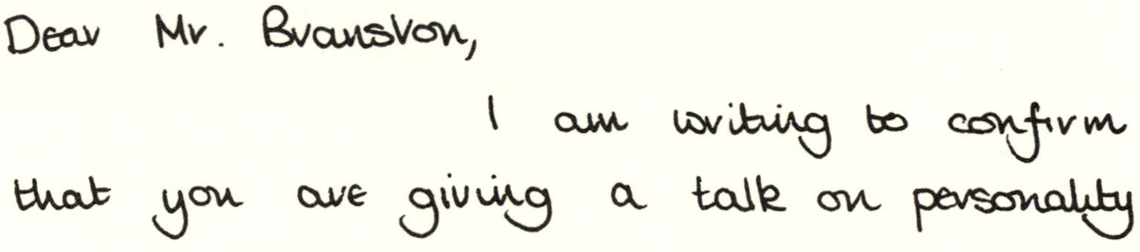

Dear Mr. Branston,

I am writing to confirm that you are giving a talk on personality

Fig 16
Consistent zones

Expanded middle zone (over 3mm)

Positive traits	*Negative traits*
Social enthusiastic response	Self-concern
Desire for recognition (do-gooder)	Need for comfort
Self-assurance	Presumptuousness
Strong emotional feelings	Eccentric ideas
Strong likes and dislikes in daily life	Subjective attitude
	Conceit (over-compensating inferiority complex
	Poor sexual drive, dissipated into social activity
	Low on ethical values

Small middle zone (under 3mm)

Positive traits	*Negative traits*
Ambition and intelligent planning	Pettiness
Careful attention to detail	Narrow-mindedness
Sedate manners	Indifference
Modesty	Personality strain caused by whichever is the dominant full zone
Contentment	Emotional feelings kept to a minimum
	Lack of enthusiasm
	Lack of interest in social life

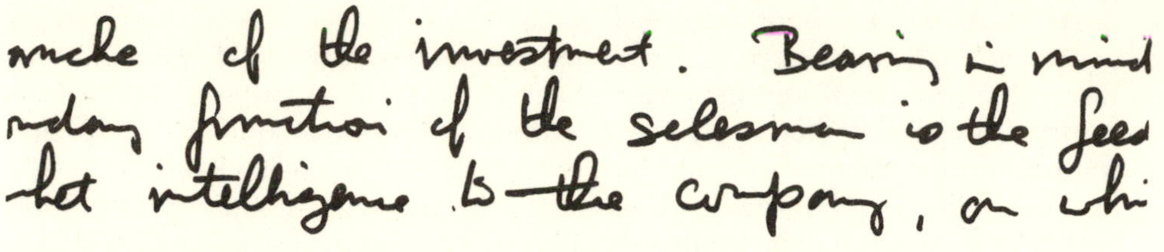

Fig 17
Fluctuation in the
zones

[handwriting sample]

LOWER ZONE

This is the area of instinctive sexual drive and materialistic concern.

The lower zone comprises the lower loops of the letters g, j, p, q, f, z, g and y (fig 18). The personality indication depends upon the *length* and *width* of the loop, and the *pressure*, which must always be considered (fig 19).

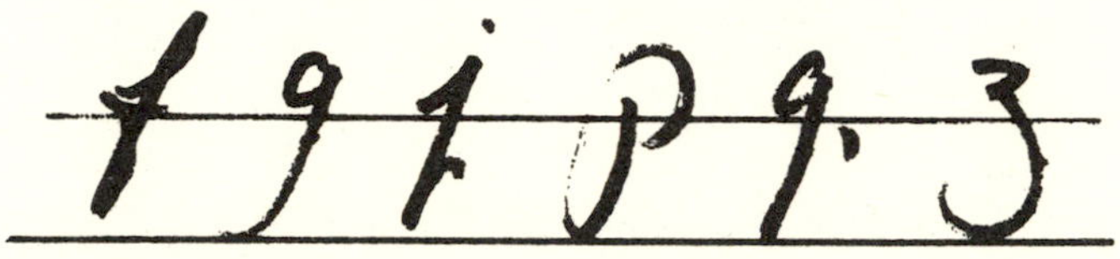

Fig 18
Lower zone comprising
the lower loops of
letters f, g, j, p, q, z.

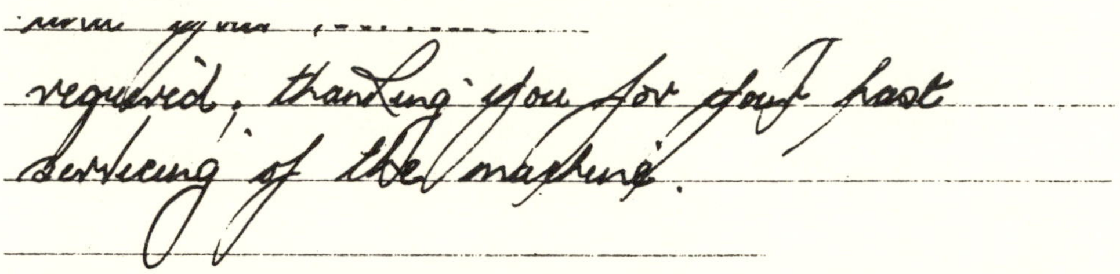

[handwriting sample]

Fig 19
Dominant lower zone,
light pressure

[handwriting sample]

The long lower stroke belongs to a person over-concerned with materialistic success and pleasure. He is dominated by his security needs and survival instincts. Control over these impulses will depend upon the writer gaining a realistic concept of balanced drives in order to maintain his natural expressiveness without over-indulgence.

When the pressure is fairly heavy (fig 20), the writer will be physically active. A very heavy pressure will indicate the energy is being distributed into the sexual sphere with little regard for the other areas of life, probably resulting in a clumsy approach. The fuller the loop, the greater the degree of fantasy a writer displays. Whether this is realistically constructive depends upon the Form Level of the writing (fig 21).

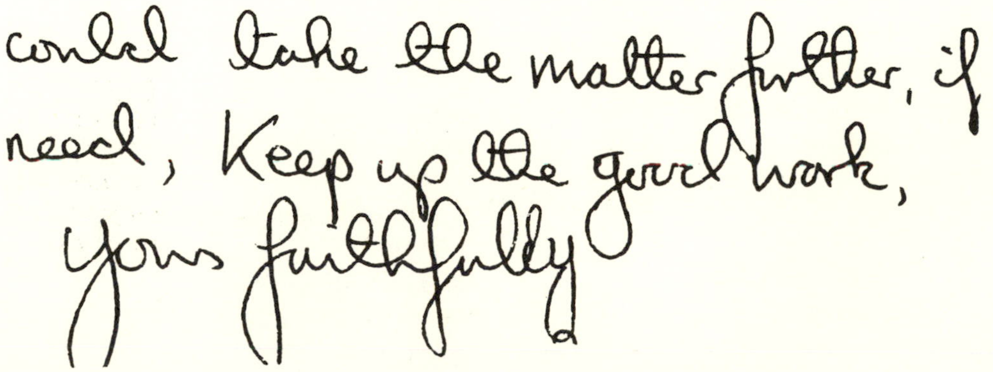

[handwriting sample]

Fig 20
Lower loops showing
physically active person

A money-minded attitude is prevalent with the long lower stroke writer who shows no 'return' loop and has weak to normal pressure. These writers are to be found in banking, insurance and accountancy; their absolute writing size is usually small (under 9mm) and the dominant zone is the lower (fig 22). I do not want to suggest that this type of writer is uninterested in sexual matters – it is just that he is motivated by money as a way of life, which can put a strain on his married life and restricts his emotional response to sexual matters.

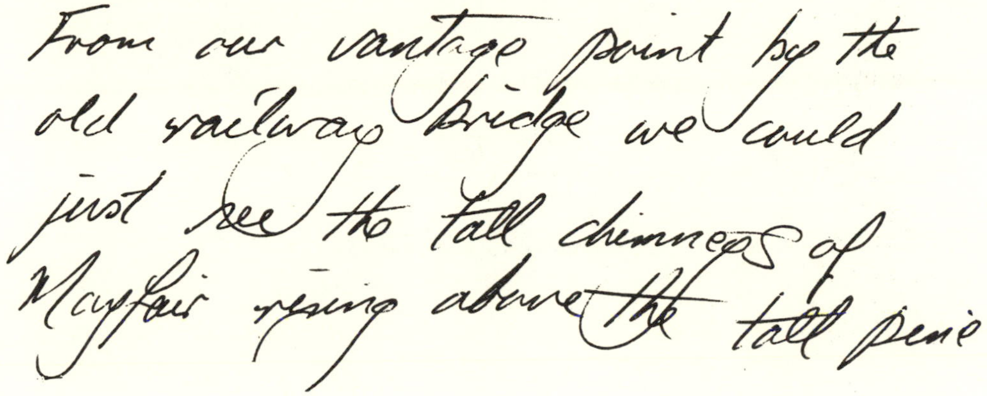

Fig 21
Fantasy loops of a very intelligent writer

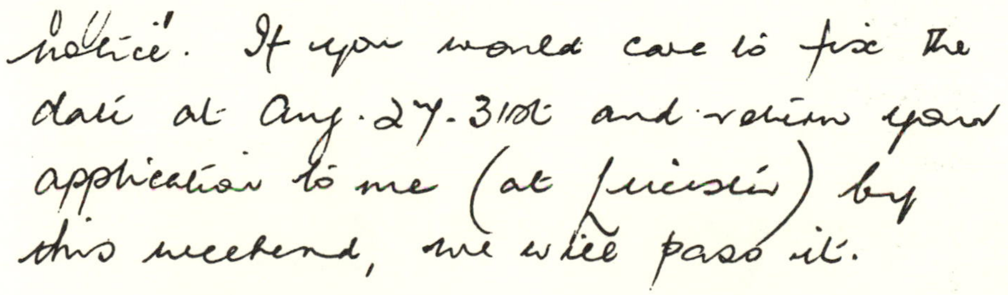

Fig 22
Lower zone showing business-minded writer

Long lower loop *with pressure*	
Positive traits	*Negative traits*
Practical inclination	Clumsiness (heavy-handed)
Physically active	Sensually dominated
Perseverance	Materialistic
Sexual gratification needs	Slow-starting
Strong security instincts	Pedantic
Strong material desires	

Long lower loop *with light pressure*	
Positive traits	*Negative traits*
Business-minded	Money complex
Sensitive	Sexual indifference
	Petty-mindedness

> **Lower loop neglected** (fig 23)
> Lack of realistic outlook
> Sexual uncertainty and little active involvement
> (possibly due to fear of failure)
> Low self-preservation instinct

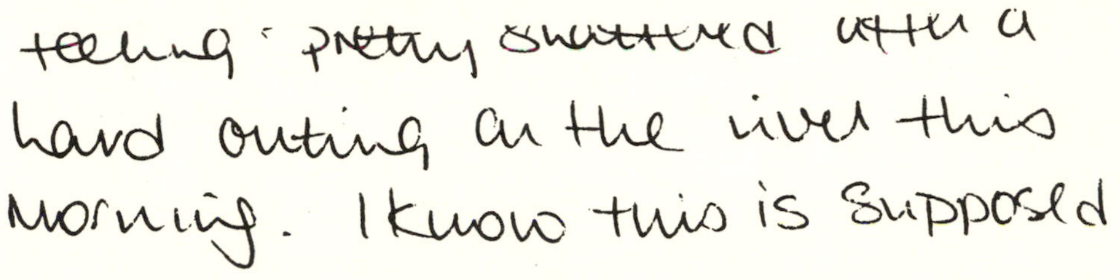

Fig 23
Neglected lower zone

feeling pretty shattered after a hard outing on the river this morning. I know this is supposed

The pivot of the personality structure is the middle zone and, taking into account that we are not machines, a moderate proportional balance should be maintained throughout the script if the writer is to indicate a stable balance between intellect and ideals, materialistic and security values and rational reasoning in daily routine and personal relationships. Such a well-balanced personality structure will maintain an interesting lifestyle.

MORE ON UPPER AND LOWER ZONE LOOPS

Where the upper and lower zone extensions are even in size (i.e. regular) the interests relevant to that zone are kept within controlled limits.

If the size ratios are uneven (irregular) then there could be much excitement and, in the case of very uneven lengths, there may be a lack of control over excitement threshold – a negative effect and likely to be unconstructive because it is unrealistic.

You should also note whether the lines of writing are clear, or do the extensions mingle into one another? (See line spacing, examples 19 and 21.) Mingling shows a writer who likes variety and change, but often there is a confusing element in the writer's mind as to which area is the dominant. The low Form Level writer tends to become restless and muddled; the medium to high Form Level writer is aware of his sexual fantasies in this sphere but is able to co-ordinate them with his general understanding of life's forces and can relate them accordingly.

The proportions of the zones in writing are a very individual feature and are difficult to alter deliberately while retaining the natural fluidity of the movements, as many a forger has found to his dismay. (Try to alter your own zonal ratios and you will be aware of the tension imposed.)

In dealing with the symbolic movement in the formations of the loops (particularly in the letters 'g' and 'y'), here are some factors you should take into consideration:

Wide loops = Emotional; a sensitive dreamer

Compressed loops = Repression of desires and inhibited response to stimuli

High loops = Idealism; power-seeking

Long, with heavy pressure = Materialism; physically active

Short loops = Practical

Short with lack of pressure = Lack of physical activity

Short with very heavy pressure = Physical inertia. Clumsy co-ordination

Loops of monotonous regularity = Dull temperament; over-controlled

With marked irregularity = Excitable. Lack of strict self-control

Elaboration of loops = Self-conscious; compensation for inferiority complex

Upper Loops

1 Tall and narrow = spiritual inspirations (light pressure); intellectual aims (irregular). Secret desire for recognition and power.

2 'l' crossed like a 't' = lack of attention
'l' crossed like a 't' in confused writing = confused mind; defective speech functions

3 'l' broken at the top = physical weakness.

4 With square top = aggressive tendencies.

5 With no loop, normal height 2–4mm = uncluttered mind. Good judgement; intelligent

Lower Loops ('g' and 'y')

The downstroke represents the energy, the loop the imagination

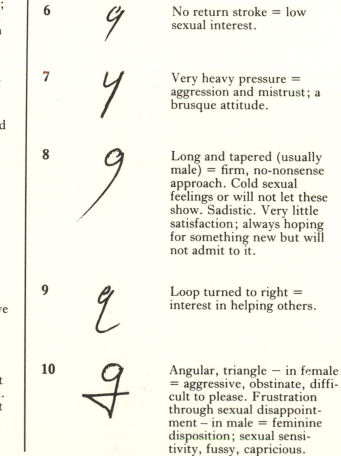

6 No return stroke = low sexual interest.

7 Very heavy pressure = aggression and mistrust; a brusque attitude.

8 Long and tapered (usually male) = firm, no-nonsense approach. Cold sexual feelings or will not let these show. Sadistic. Very little satisfaction; always hoping for something new but will not admit to it.

9 Loop turned to right = interest in helping others.

10 Angular, triangle – in female = aggressive, obstinate, difficult to please. Frustration through sexual disappointment – in male = feminine disposition; sexual sensitivity, fussy, capricious.

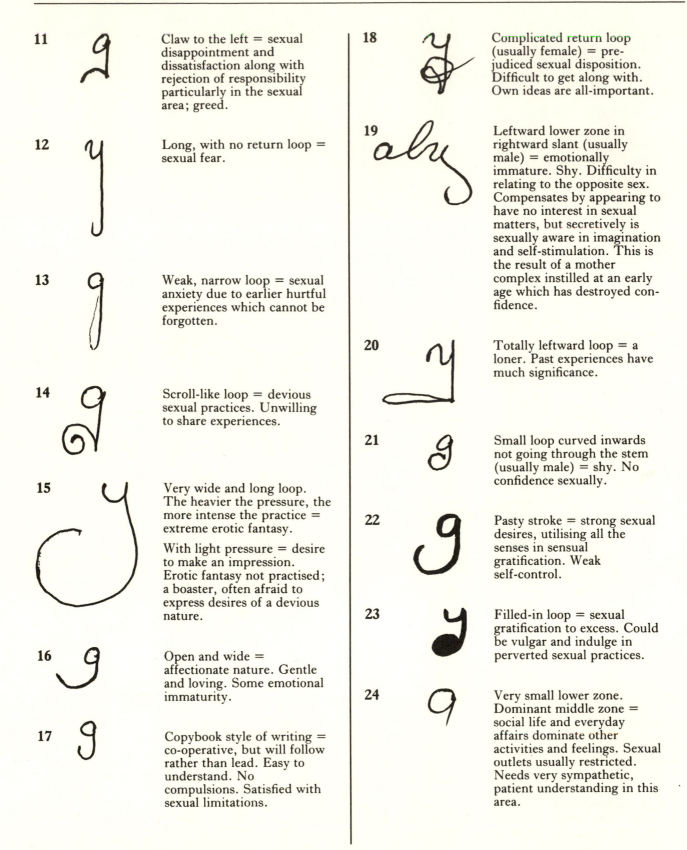

11 Claw to the left = sexual disappointment and dissatisfaction along with rejection of responsibility particularly in the sexual area; greed.

12 Long, with no return loop = sexual fear.

13 Weak, narrow loop = sexual anxiety due to earlier hurtful experiences which cannot be forgotten.

14 Scroll-like loop = devious sexual practices. Unwilling to share experiences.

15 Very wide and long loop. The heavier the pressure, the more intense the practice = extreme erotic fantasy.

With light pressure = desire to make an impression. Erotic fantasy not practised; a boaster, often afraid to express desires of a devious nature.

16 Open and wide = affectionate nature. Gentle and loving. Some emotional immaturity.

17 Copybook style of writing = co-operative, but will follow rather than lead. Easy to understand. No compulsions. Satisfied with sexual limitations.

18 Complicated return loop (usually female) = prejudiced sexual disposition. Difficult to get along with. Own ideas are all-important.

19 Leftward lower zone in rightward slant (usually male) = emotionally immature. Shy. Difficulty in relating to the opposite sex. Compensates by appearing to have no interest in sexual matters, but secretively is sexually aware in imagination and self-stimulation. This is the result of a mother complex instilled at an early age which has destroyed confidence.

20 Totally leftward loop = a loner. Past experiences have much significance.

21 Small loop curved inwards not going through the stem (usually male) = shy. No confidence sexually.

22 Pasty stroke = strong sexual desires, utilising all the senses in sensual gratification. Weak self-control.

23 Filled-in loop = sexual gratification to excess. Could be vulgar and indulge in perverted sexual practices.

24 Very small lower zone. Dominant middle zone = social life and everyday affairs dominate other activities and feelings. Sexual outlets usually restricted. Needs very sympathetic, patient understanding in this area.

25 Loop with fine light pressure ('money bag') = economic and material possessions take precedence.

26 Heavy angle in slow script = untrustworthy.
Note: There must be at least four other indications of dishonesty. See Chapter 26, page 184.

27 Angle in a crude formation – in male = aggressive behaviour in an immature, petty and irritating manner. Attitude is ceremonious.

In female = not easy to live with. Sexually disappointed and fussy; capable of emotional blackmail. This also applies to illustration 26.

For further study of lower loops refer to the book *Crime and Sex in Handwriting* by Patricia Marne.

WORKSHEET FOR THE THREE ZONES

Zones (relative size) Examples:	*Interpretation*
Upper Zone Between 1 and 5mm; the average is 3mm, indicating a normal size upper zone	
Middle Zone Between 1 and 3mm; the average is 2mm, indicating a small middle zone	
Lower Zone Between 2 and 8mm; the average is 5mm, indicating a large lower zone NB Pressure See note at foot of page	
Zones (Loops = formation of) *Upper Zone* *Lower Zone*	

Note: In writing being analysed, should there be only two letter parts (whatever zone) at 1mm, and only one at 7mm, but, for example 46 at 2mm, then the mean size is not taken between the 1mm and the 7mm, because this would indicate the size as large, which would be misleading. The majority in this example is 46 at 2mm, which, in this case, would give a finding of small for that particular zone.

Chapter *3* | Layout

The arrangement of space between each word and between the lines indicates a writer's aesthetic sense and how he or she organises their life in general. Good spacing would indicate orderliness, the ability to think and speak clearly and to arrange life intelligently, with economical planning and expenditure of mental, physical, emotional and spiritual resources. It can also show how well the writer integrates his experiences and how he shares experience with others.

You should therefore begin by making a general assessment of the layout and spacing. It is worth pointing out that occasionally there may be poor spacing in the writing of a person with literacy problems caused, for example, by childhood illness and interrupted schooling.

Good spacing	Poor spacing
Organized	Disorganized
Thinks clearly	Fuzzy thinking
Communicates well	Problems in communicating
Aesthetic sense	Poor aesthetic sense
Planning	Lack of planning
Balance	Wastes resources
Integrated personality	

1 Margins

The first spatial feature to consider in more detail is the margins, which can be likened to a frame in which the handwriting is the picture. The margins are usually formed subconsciously and depend on the writer's motivation to reach the desired goal – the end of line. They can also indicate the extent to which a writer is held back in life by past experiences.

LEFT-HAND MARGIN

The left margin represents the past and its influence on the writer and also the way the writer's resources are utilised.

Fig 24
Very narrow left margin

Fig 25
Widening left margin

Narrow left-hand margin

A *very* narrow left margin (fig 24) is symptomatic of a writer who would not seek personal social contact (unless the right margin is also very narrow) and this (i.e. a narrow left-hand margin) would be confirmed by a narrow leftward slant script, indicating an insecure person whose fears stem from experience in early life. Such people will often try to hide their intentions and are afraid of being influenced by others; they therefore over-react in their resistance to changes of any kind.

Left margin	*Narrow*
Wide	Thriftiness
Generosity	Fear of the past
Pride	Informality
Reserve	Lack of organisation (if with cramped letters)
	Desire for popularity

Widening left-hand margin (fig 25)

Often in a spontaneous script written at a fast speed, the left margin widens with each new line, the writer being carried away impulsively. Each line is therefore started a little more to the right than the previous one.

These writers are impulsively motivated to save time – often at the expense of accuracy. This can also show excitement in, for instance, a new project in which the writer finds a welcome release from mundane activities.

There is a tendency for such people to lose control – for example, after deciding to be more careful with money they may indulge in a spending spree.

More rarely, a writer may become aware of the widening margin and pull himself back into line each time he starts a new paragraph. In this way he is controlling his impulsive nature (fig 26).

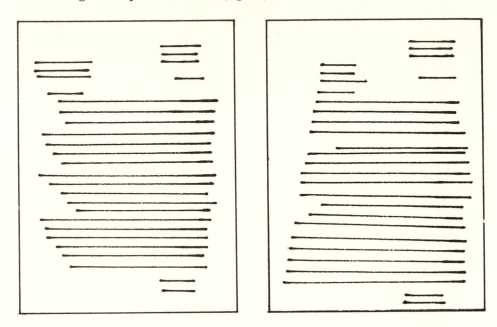

Fig 26
Paragraph formation
left margin

Fig 27
Narrowing left margin

Narrowing left-hand margin (fig 27)
This is fairly rare and shows the writer curbing his spontaneity by slowing down and allowing his margin to be more consciously formed, with each line moving a little more leftward.

This leftward pull can be accompanied by a leftward slanting writing, pointing to a person who, after an initial show of friendship or enthusiasm, will retreat into the background rather than commit himself any further. These people are shy and reserved and, while they may try to overcome this, they probably don't succeed. They feel safer in their own company and in doing things their own way.

Left margin	
Widening	*Narrowing*
Impatience	Fear of others
Haste	Caution
	Shyness

HAPHAZARD LEFT-HAND MARGIN
Usually found where the writer is unaware of aesthetic values, mostly through lack of education; or they are not accustomed to letter-writing generally. This is not very often encountered professionally because those

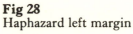

Fig 28
Haphazard left margin

Fig 29
Very regular left margin

writers are not in a position in which their handwriting is submitted for analysis.

Haphazard left-hand margin
> A disorganised person
> No artistic awareness
> Poor education
> Lackadaisical attitude

RIGHT-HAND MARGIN

Obviously, some irregularities in the right-hand margin are natural. When reaching the end of a line we have to make a decision as to whether a word will fit into the space without having to be crammed in and distorted or hyphenated. General planning ability, or the lack of it, is reflected here.

If the right-hand margin is *too* regular (fig 29) it has probably been contrived to create a pretentious effect, in which case you should look for other indications of artificiality in the script itself – for example, large capital letters with ornamentation, slowly written script, calligraphic style.

Many people who have received office and secretarial training make an effort to control their margins as they would when using a typewriter (fig 30).

A person who is artistically aware might produce a more regular right-hand margin too. This would be confirmed by very regular letter height and line spacing.

In the case of a slowly written script with regular right-hand margins, a rather slow, self-conscious thinker is indicated – not the dynamic personality who is prepared to take a risk for the sake of expressive involvement. (See chapter 27 on speed.)

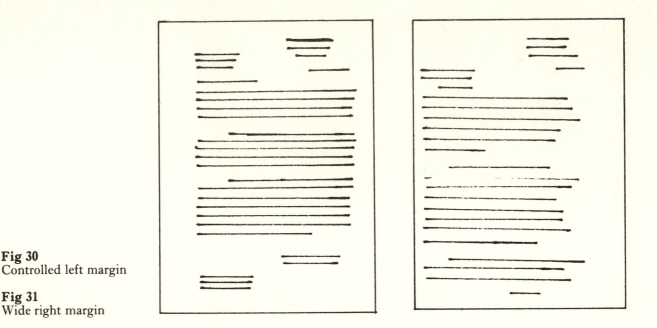

Fig 30
Controlled left margin

Fig 31
Wide right margin

Wide right-hand margin (fig 31)
This suggests a person who is wary of becoming personally involved in any-thing progressive – this would be confirmed by a leftward slanting script. They are likely to be standoffish due to suspicion of others' motives. This could indicate a person whose profession demands some secrecy, and in which they reveal only facts and suggestions to their own benefit (e.g. politicians).

Narrow right-hand margin
Always an indication of a positive factor. The writer wishes to communicate and to be involved in the environment and its affairs.

From left to right is a bridge of communication – from 'I to you': therefore the further rightward the script progresses the more positive it becomes, pro-vided the end words are not squeezed to fit. If they are, this indicates a lack of organisation.

Narrow right-hand margin
Willing to relate to others
Will face life's problems
Good vitality
Willing to co-operate
Often talkative
Can be gregarious (with close word spacing)
A healthy respect for the future

Right margin

Wide	*Narrow*
Reserve, shyness	Communicative
Fear of the future	Desire for involvement
Suspicion (if narrow word spacing)	Talkative

Right and left-hand margins widening (fig 32) (rare)

A complex situation in which the beginnings of the letter being written is normal in margin spacing; but as the writer continues, his attitude alters from one of normal respect for the past and future and being unafraid of people to one of trepidation where he is unsure of his intentions and purpose. He then pulls in from the left (past) and is reluctant to approach the right (future). As he very quickly tires of any writing task and needs to get it over with quickly, the writing rapidly deteriorates into an illegible scrawl.

With slow tempo	*With fast tempo*
Afraid of being isolated from the happenings of life	Lack of willpower to control situations
A fear of people, indicating conflict	Excessive haste to finish a task

Wide left-hand, narrow right-hand margins (fig 33)

These writers are outgoing. They are not unduly influenced by the past and are not fearful of the future.

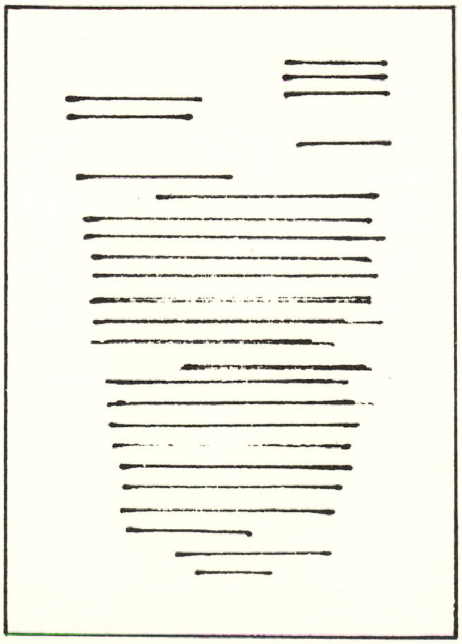

Fig 32
Both margins widening (rare)

Fig 33
Very wide left margin, narrow right margin

UPPER MARGIN

Narrow upper margin
In a letter, a cramped address and very narrow top margin would be a sign of a poor educational background and poor planning ability (fig 34). A poor Form Level (see chapter 28) would also be evident.

Wide upper margin
If this is combined with a cramped lower margin it indicates poor planning ability (fig 35). This writer gives very little thought to the future.

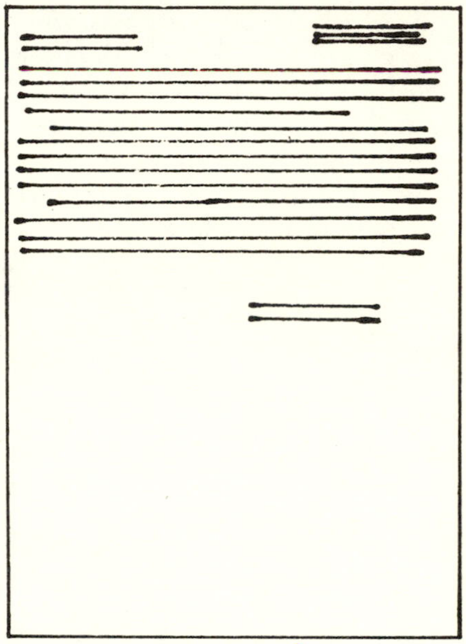

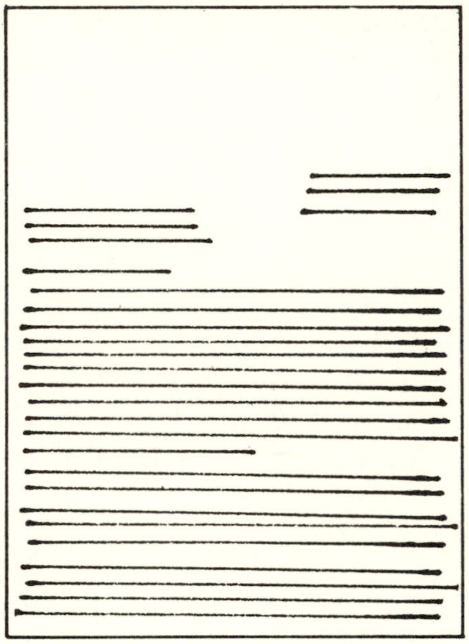

Fig 34
Narrow upper margin

Fig 35
Wide upper margin
with cramped lower
margin

Upper margin

Wide	*Narrow*
Respectful	Informal
Formal	Obtrusive
Reserved	Lack of respect
Artistic appreciation	Lack of artistic appreciation

Lower margin

Wide	*Narrow*
Aesthetic sense	Communicative
Reserve	Materialistic
	Indecisive

LOWER MARGIN
The lower margin depends largely on the writer's planning ability to visualise at the start of the letter how much space he will use and what is left in the

lower margin and signature area. It is therefore better to form an opinion by viewing an intermediate page.

Where the complete letter is written on one page there should be adequate room left for the ending, 'Yours faithfully' etc. The top of the letter should be normal, relating to the writing space taken up.

ALL FOUR MARGINS

Clear, equally spaced margins (fig 36)
This shows consistency in manner with constancy of purpose. It often indicates a person who needs to be clearly understood verbally. This could also be produced by someone with a commercial background or by an artistic person, in which case there would be a fairly fast rhythm tempo (see chapter 17).

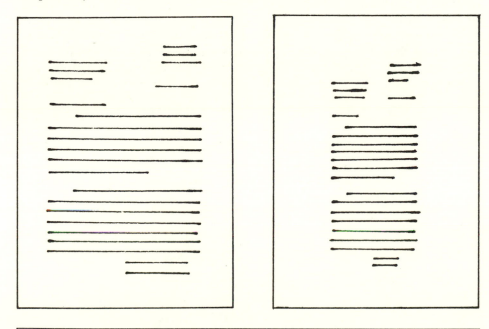

Fig 36
Equally spaced margins

Fig 37
Very wide margins

Equal margins
Aesthetic sense (when normal size)
Reserve
Pride
Commercial awareness
Over-formal
Consistency of purpose
Clarity of expression

Very wide margins all round (fig 37)
These writers show vanity in trying to create an impression of importance and lavishness along with a false culture which they do not, in reality, possess – a snobbish and pretentious personality.

However, in a natural-looking script with a high Form Level (chapter 28) and rhythmic tempo (chapter 17), the writer could be talented in the visual arts.

Wide margins all round

Positive traits	*Negative traits*
Good design sense	Isolated
Independent	Capricious
Good colour sense	Vain, pretentious, snobbish
Artistic sensitivity	Possible phobic fear

Absence of margins (fig 38)

In this case you should take into account the spacing of the letters and words, and the slant.

No margins with narrowly spaced letters and words and with a rightward slant would show a gregarious person who needs to be wanted and admired as one of a team – possibly a compulsive talker and apt to cling to relationships.

No margins and leftward slant would point to miserliness.

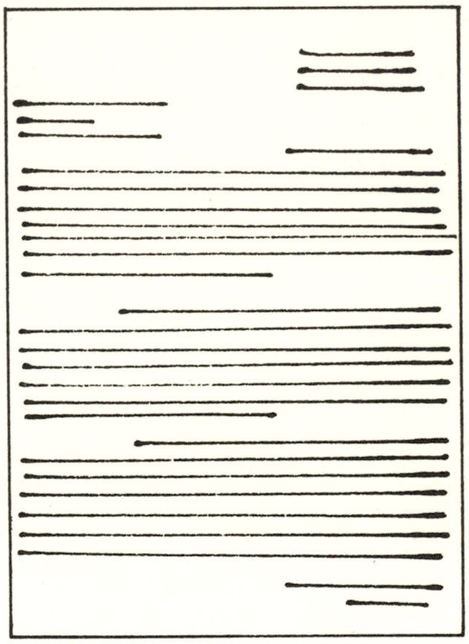

Fig 38
Absence of margins

No margins

Good word spacing	*Poor word spacing*
Desire for total expression	Lack of reserve
Ready to help others	Lack of good taste
Sincere interest in people	Morbid curiosity
(with right slant)	Tactless
	Obtrusive
	Pedantic views

2 Line Spacing

The next thing to look at is line spacing.

GOOD LINE SPACING (figs 39, 40)
Practised writers subconsciously relate their letters to an imaginary baseline and can produce a straight line of writing on plain paper without using a guideline underneath (but see the next section on the direction of the lines.) They space the lines so that the loops do not touch or mingle with those of the lines above or beneath.

Such writing reflects an organised mind, a sense of direction, firmness and the ability to maintain a personal drive towards a goal, without being sidetracked by inner or outer disruptions.

Good spacing *(In proportion to the size of the script)*

Good organisation of time and effort

Constructive thinking

Sense of direction

Irregular line spacing *(loops mingling)*

Poor judgement

Careless attitude

Lack of method

Inability to express ideas clearly

Lack of concentration

POOR LINE SPACING
(*Irregular line spacing*), perhaps with the loops mingling, points to a lack of rational control, willpower or physical co-ordination.

Fig 39
Line spacing showing organised mind

Fig 40
Sense of order shown with ability to organise routine

NORMAL SPACING

Normal spacing but with loops mingling show that the writer can manage ordinary routine tasks but can be unreliable in emergencies.

Length of stroke It is the longer than normal (i.e. 3mm) upper or lower stroke which is defined as 'long'.

With long lower zone strokes – strong instincts

Long lower zone strokes, wide loops – daydreaming

Long lower zone strokes, wide loops and heavy pressure – highly erotic sexual needs and strong sexual fantasy

Tall upper zone strokes – an indication of the writer's scope for intellectual interests, ideals, and spiritual awareness. Whether realistic or not depending on the zonal balance, Form Level, and degree of fullness.

WIDE SPACING

Wide line spacing may be produced by writers who are very concerned about the clarity of their thinking and the clear communication of their ideas.

Wide line spacing (fig 41)

Positive traits	*Negative traits*
Clear, factual, expressive organisation of facts	Lack of spontaneity
Objective thinking	
Analytical mind (with angles)	
Logical thought processes	
Strong sense of justice	
Cultured	
Considerate	

Fig 41
Line spacing showing logical order of effort

Fig 42
Excessive exaggeration of distance between lines to avoid disorder etc

> **Excessively wide line spacing** (fig 42)
> > Fear of making a mistake
> > The urge to over-organise
> > Mental strain

NARROW SPACING

Narrow line spacing will, of course, suggest qualities which are the opposite of the above. However, even when the loops are mingling, the general Form Level of the writing (see chapter 28) should be taken into account.

Narrow line spacing

Good, original Form Level	*Medium to poor Form Level*
Lively	Confused thinking
Active	Poor judgement
Creative	Hastiness
	Lack of reserve

COLUMNING

Columning (fig 43) is when each word is deliberately written underneath another. It is usually found in the writing of young children who are in need of reassurance, special care, love and attention.

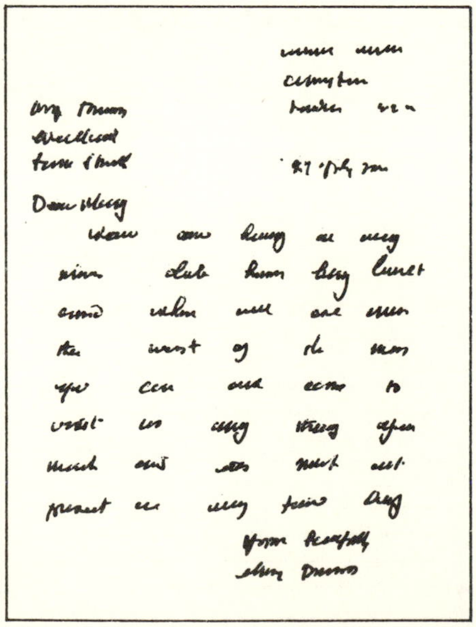

Fig 43
Columning

In adult writing it shows an immature compulsion to allay anxiety and feelings of insecurity by the use of excessive control and is usually found in conjunction with wide line spacing.

Columning	
Children	*Adults*
Insecure	Anxiety
Needing love and attention	Insecurity
	Excessive control

LINED PAPER AND GUIDELINES

Lined paper (fig 44) – **rigid line spacing** (fig 45)
A sample written on lined paper should not be accepted for analysis unless you can confirm that the writer always uses lined paper or puts a guideline underneath (fig 44). The use of a guideline can usually be detected by an over-rigid spacing and is often accompanied by a copybook script.

Lined paper – rigid line spacing (*guideline used*)
Needs a crutch to lean on
Likes to follow orders
Doesn't like making decisions
Lacks self-confidence

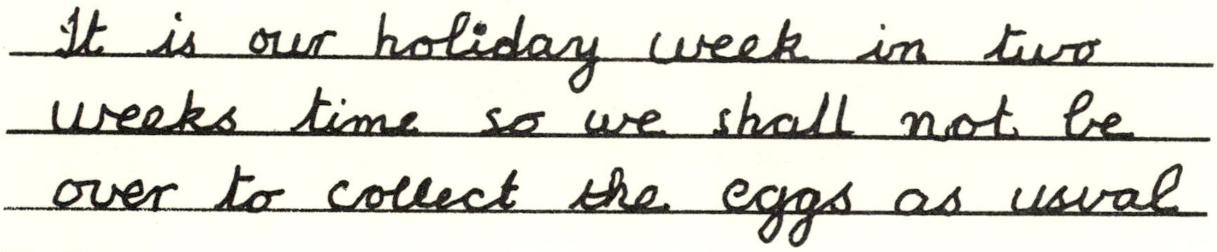

Fig 44
Spacing compulsively rigid – writer needs crutch to lean on throughout life

Fig 45
Spacing too rigid

Lines drawn beneath the writing (fig 44)
> Exaggerates the above tendencies

Guidelines used but deviated from (fig 46)
(Writing riding above or below the guidelines)
> Needs help and support but rejects it
> Mistrust

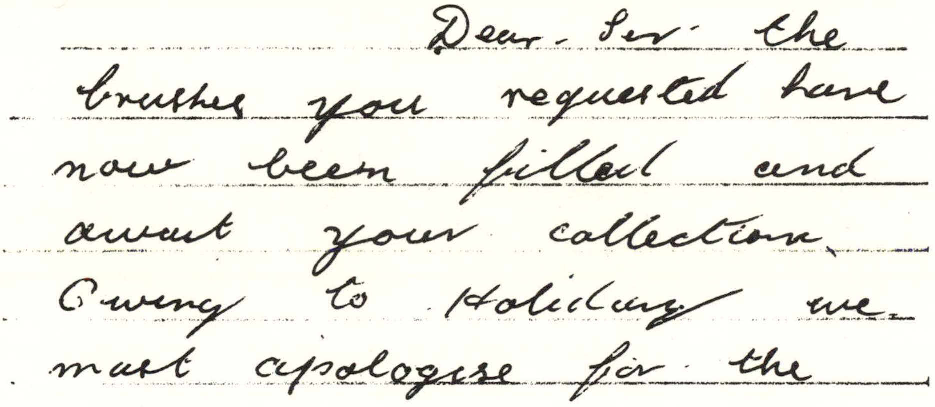

Fig 46
The script riding above
the guideline

CROWDED SPACING

Crowded line spacing at the bottom of the page (fig 47)
This shows a writer with poor organising ability who cannot think ahead and who tends not to make a decision until a crisis point is reached.

Fig 47
Crowded line spacing
at the bottom of a page

When these traits become compulsive they may even write around the margins too. These people will find that most of their efforts in planning and construction are ruined by an over-done effect. They don't know when to stop. This is the person who, when making a wooden box, would put in thirty screws instead of the ten that are needed.

**Crowded line spacing at the bottom –
writing in the margins**

        Poor planning ability

        Lack of organisation

        Needs a crisis before making decisions

        Doesn't know when to stop

---

3 The direction of the lines

STRAIGHT LINES

We have already mentioned that constantly straight lines of writing on plain paper are an indication of good line spacing. However, all positives can turn to negatives when they become too rigid and so the rhythm of the writing (see chapter 17) should be taken into account too.

Straight lines

Good rhythm	*Rigid rhythm*
Reliable	Over-control
Orderly	Dullness
Methodical	Inflexibility
Responsible	Lack of emotional response
Constancy of purpose	Defensive attitude
Self-control	

RISING AND FALLING LINES

In popular theory, rising lines indicate optimism and falling lines pessimism. However, you must always take other aspects of the writing into account and with rising and falling lines you should always consider:

(a) *Temporary conditions* such as illness, for example: arthritis, fatigue or depression, all cause the arm muscles to slacken and drop towards the body, resulting in falling lines.

(b) *The mood of the writer.*

(c) *The pressure, rhythm, regularity, speed and connections.*

Rising lines (fig 48)

Rising line

Optimism

Ambition

Initiative

Devotion to a purpose

Willing to co-operate with others

Strong response to new ideas

Not easily discouraged

Extreme rising line

Over-ambitious

Impractical

Exuberant elation

Excitable

Restless moods

Agitated pace of speech

Fig 48
Rising lines

Fig 49
Falling lines (see also fig 50)

Falling lines (figs 49, 50)

Falling line

Depression (heavy pressure)

Pessimism

Apathy (slow script)

Anxiety

Fatigue

Illness or old age –
shaky stroke (ataxia)

Grief (temporary state)

Emotional hurt (temporary state)

Extreme falling line (fig 51)

A serious depressive state

Excessive self-concern

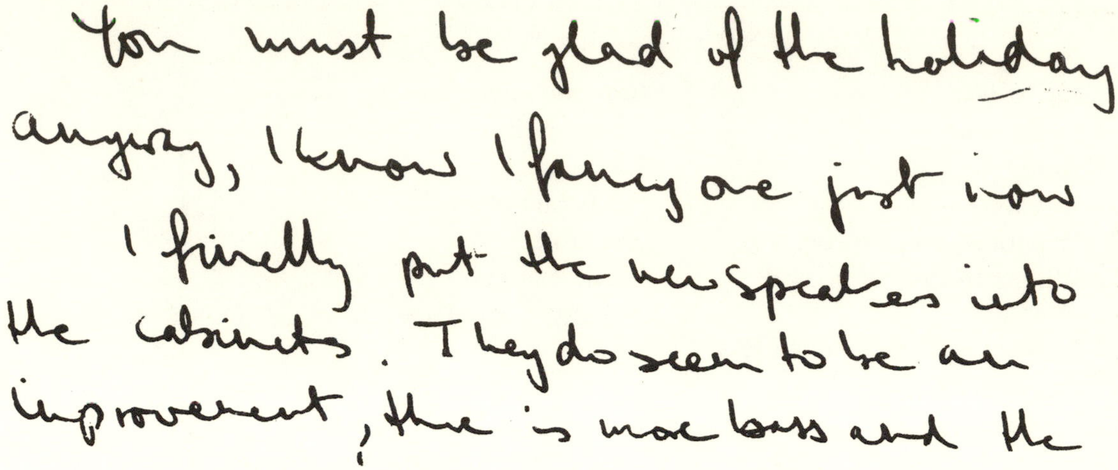

You must be glad of the holiday anyway, I know I fancy are just now I finally put the newspeakers into the cabinets. They do seem to be an improvement, there is more bass and the

Fig 50
Falling lines (see also fig 49)

Fig 51
Extreme falling lines

Fig 52
False rise (or fall) in line direction

False rise or fall (fig 52)
If lines are rising or falling but very regularly spaced and written in a straight line – albeit up or down – then the writer may well have turned the paper just to feel more comfortable when writing.

Undulating lines (*often with thread connection – fig 53*)
Wavering indecision
Unstable habits
Nervousness
Moody (variable slant)
Lack of self-control
Open to influence
Versatile
Restless mind seeking new outlet

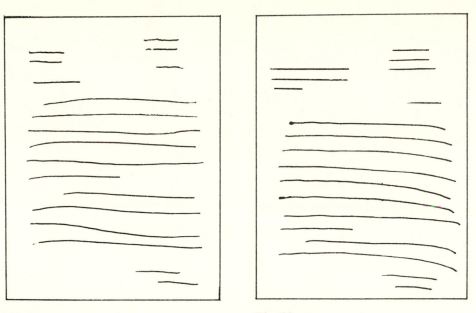

Fig 53
Undulating lines

Fig 54
Line of writing turning down at the
end of the line

Falling at the end of the line (fig 54)
Lack of forethought and planning

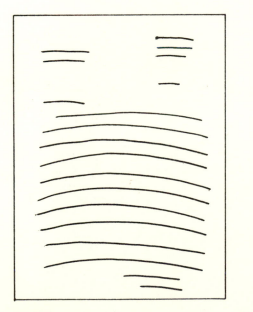

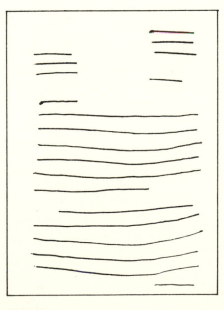

Fig 55
Convex line

Fig 56
Concave line

Convex line ⌢ (fig 55)

The initial eagerness and enthusiasm lacks perseverance and quickly loses its force

> Gives up too easily
>
> Quickly becomes bored
>
> Easily disappointed
>
> Good at making a new start
>
> Lacks persistence

Concave line ⌣ (fig 56)

After a cautious approach, self-confidence increases and spurs on these writers to take positive action

> Weariness
>
> Self-doubt
>
> Slackness
>
> Depression
>
> Usually overcomes these weaknesses
>
> Fighters
>
> Good finishers
>
> Hard workers
>
> Strong desire to reach a goal

TILING

In tiling the individual words rise or fall continuously along the line of writing, often towards the end of a page.

Fig 57
Rising tile

Fig 58
Falling tile

Rising tile / / / / (fig 57)

This writer's initial enthusiastic response is continually brought back to reality, so maintaining a straight base line. These people are putting a brake on their emotions with each return to base line, yet these emotions reassert themselves within each word.

Conflict between ideals and reality between emotions and reason

Falling tile \ \ \ \ (fig 58)

This writer is continually battling with discouragement and having to begin each word above the ending of the previous one.

Fighting discouragement, depression and fatigue

4 Word spacing

Having already considered the general layout, the margins, the line spacing and the direction of the lines, you must now look at the spacing of the words.

GOOD SPACING (fig 59)

Fluent writers will leave the normal amount of space between words, neither too crowded nor too far apart and balancing the size of their script and the space between the lines.

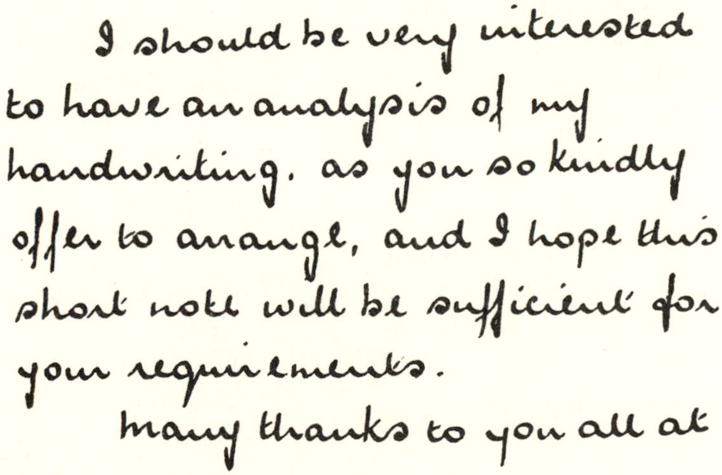

I should be very interested to have an analysis of my handwriting. as you so kindly offer to arrange, and I hope this short note will be sufficient for your requirements.

many thanks to you all at

Fig 59
Good spacing of words and lines

POOR SPACING

Poor spacing – close and irregular (fig 60)

Word spacing can be related to the way we speak. Close and irregular

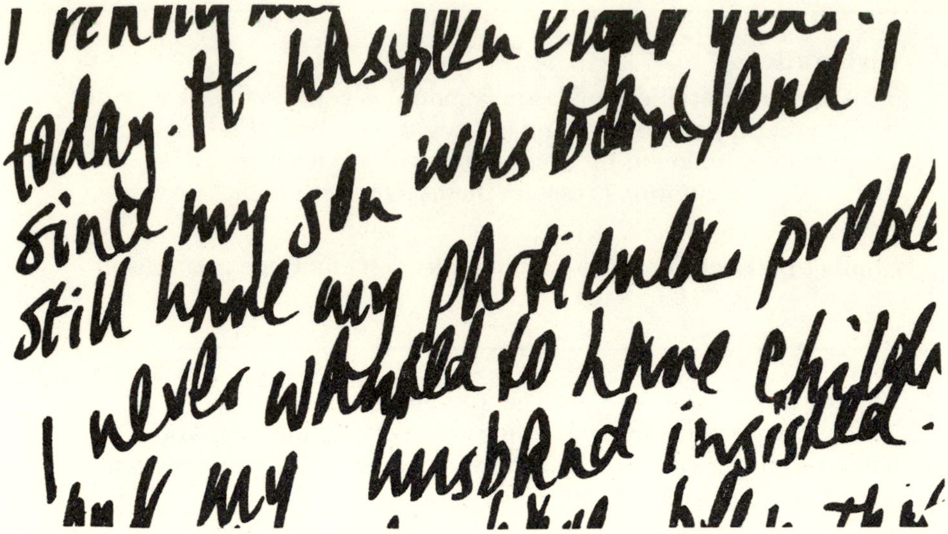

Fig 60
Poor spacing

spacing would suggest a person who gabbles, non-stop. It would indicate a lack of intelligence and organisation. This would be a person with little or no respect for privacy, who craves contact with people because of a fear of loneliness.

Close, even spacing	**Close, uneven spacing**
(usually good Form Level)	*(usually poor Form Level)*
Good self-confidence	Very talkative
Thrifty	Poor musical sense
Good balance of expression	Indecisive
Actively organised	Inharmonious personality
Clear judgement	Poor self-reliance
Integrated personality	
Good powers of observation	

Words crowded together	
Medium Form Level	*Poor Form Level*
Warm and sympathetic	Tactless
Craves company	Obtrusive
Outgoing personality	Active but unproductive
Socially active	Poor discrimination
	Temperamental
	Careless
	Impulsive

Very tight spacing with rigid script
>   Over control, but lack of intelligence
>   Compulsive, neurotic behaviour
>   Insecure feelings and anxiety

Words not separated clearly, poor Form Level
>   A lack of logical order
>   Bewildered by confused thinking processes
>   Compulsive talker without intelligent topics

Close and irregular with narrow letters
This reflects anxiety and feelings of inferiority.

WIDE SPACING (fig 61)
This writer is isolated, putting a barrier between himself and the rest of the world – an inhibited response – excluding others and preventing them, and himself, from becoming personally involved. Although he desperately needs love and affection he is afraid to get involved in an intimate relationship, either because of past, hurtful experiences or for fear of failure in a shy, emotionally withdrawn person. Should he attempt to form a relationship with someone, his fear of failing tends to become a self-fulfilling prophecy.

The distance between the words indicates the extent of this person's solitude.

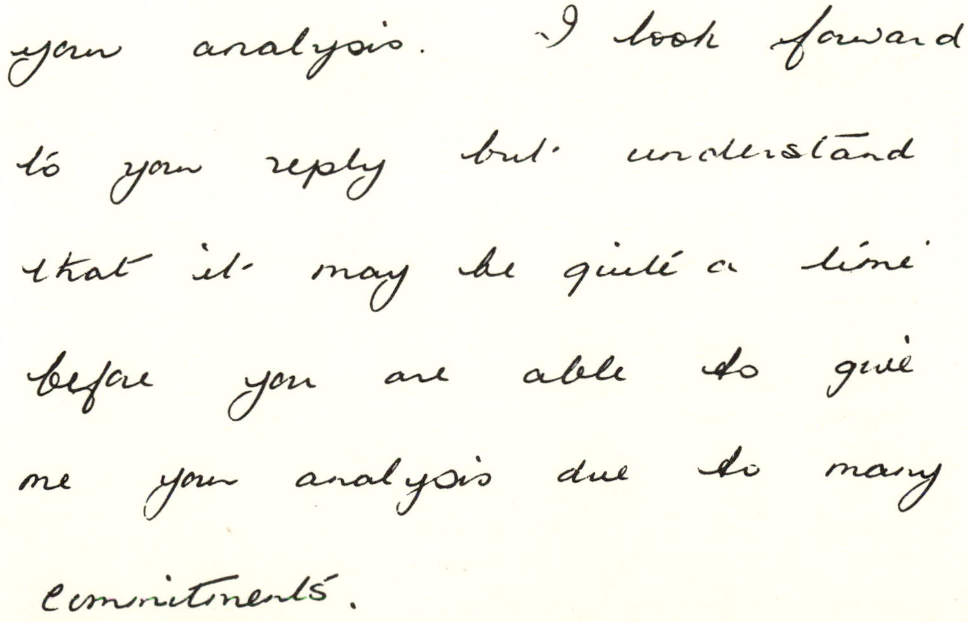

your analysis. I look forward to your reply but understand that it may be quite a time before you are able to give me your analysis due to many commitments.

Fig 61
Wide spacing

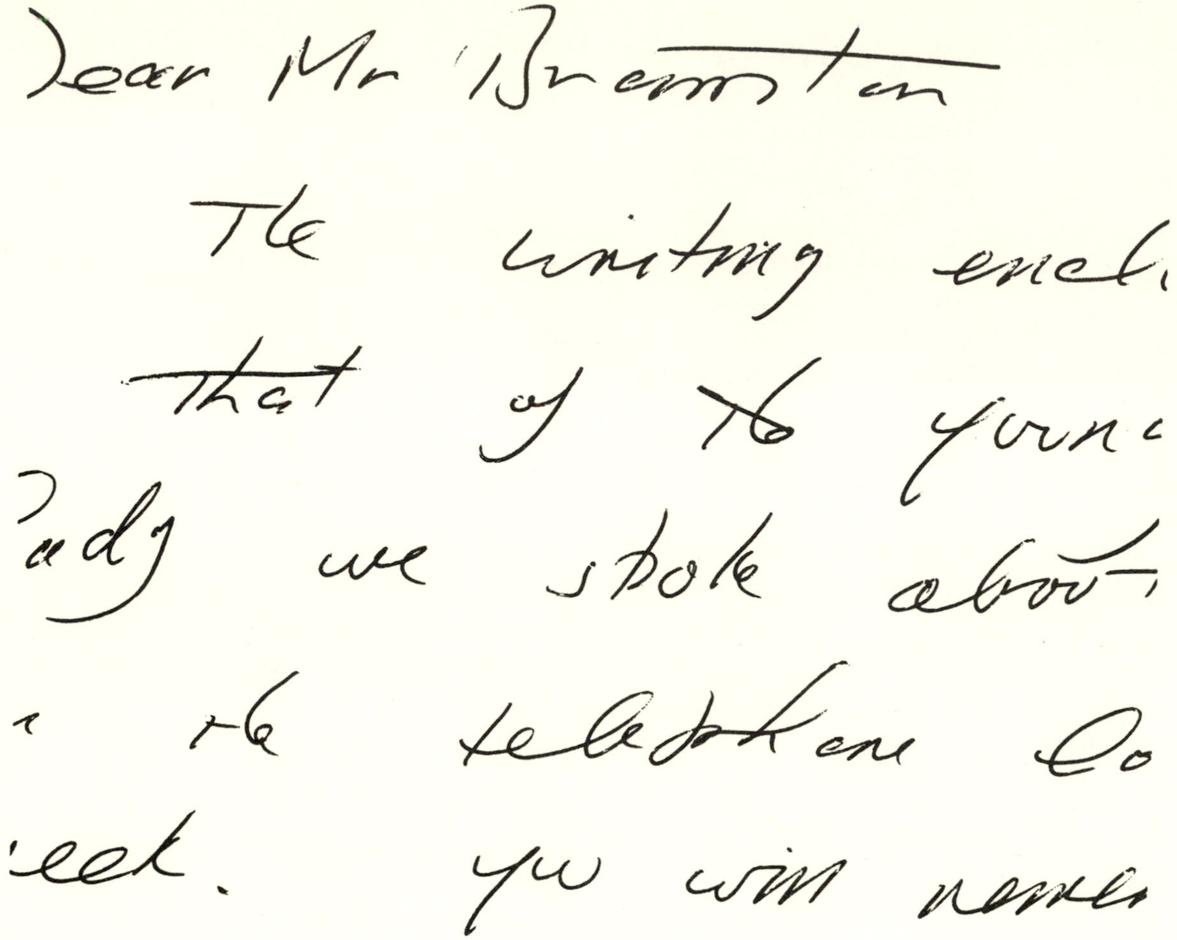

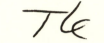

Fig 62
Large writing and spacing

Wide spacing – large writing (fig 62)
Extravagant
Affectation
Lack of objectivity
Excessive self-importance
Tendency to show-off

**Excessively wide spacing –
leftward to upright slant and avoidance of right-hand margin**
Neurotic avoidance of others
Social complexes
Total inhibition
Problems in communication

Wide spacing – small script, good Form Level
- Isolation of an intellectual nature
- Snobbish
- Proud
- No desire to become involved socially
- No wish for intimate contact, or to initiate contact
- Not willing to communicate on any level

Spacing narrowing at line endings
- Lack of forward planning
- Indecision

MIXED GOOD AND POOR SPACING (fig 63)

In our example – fig 63 – there is good letter and word spacing but tangled, overlapping lines. This would be interpreted as an ability to arrange immediate, everyday life but an inability to plan too far ahead.

As you will have realised by now, there is an almost infinite number of combinations of the variables – size, rhythm, spacing, speed, connections, slant, Form Level, pressure and so on, and you may begin to despair.

Please don't! Obviously if I included every possible combination the book would be far too heavy for you to lift off the shelf, but as you fill in the worksheets, certain characteristics will recur and be confirmed and these will form the basis of your analysis.

The examples I give of certain combinations (e.g. wide spacing, large writing) should help to show you how to link together the different characteristics when you finally come to writing an analysis.

However, that is still some way off and there is still one more source of clues to be included in the spacing section – the envelope.

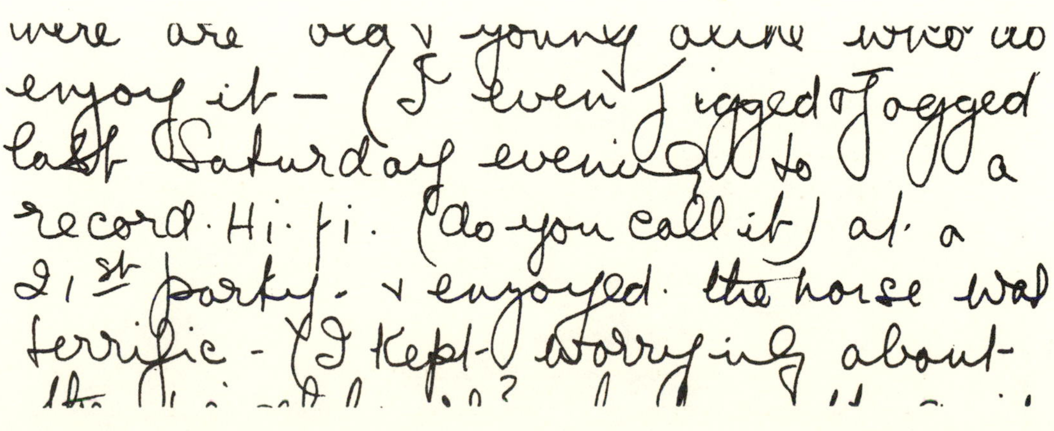
enjoy it – (I even Jigged Jogged
last Saturday evening to a
record Hi fi (do you call it) at a
21st party – & enjoyed the noise was
terrific – (I kept worrying about

Fig 63
Combination of good and poor spacing but with overlapping lines

5 The envelope

When available, the envelope should always be considered too, as it can confirm your findings in the script.

LEGIBILITY
Most people realise that if the letter is to arrive at all, the writing should be legible for the sorters and postmen. An illegible address, therefore, indicates carelessness at the least.

OVER-STYLED LETTERING (fig 64)
What better chance has this vain, affected writer to show off his pretentious false image?

UNDERLINING, URGENT etc (fig 65)
Many underlined words and phrases such as 'Confidential', 'Private', 'Do not bend', 'First Class Mail', 'For the eyes of the recipient only', 'Urgent' etc. or such words written in red ink are symptomatic of a pedantic, compulsive worrier, who cannot differentiate between what is, and what is not, essential. Also these writers like to go over the lettering once or twice again to make it clearer – usually producing the opposite effect as in our example.

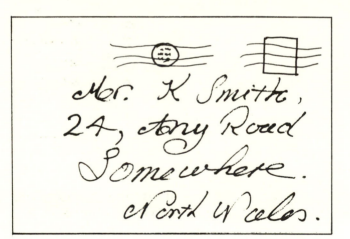

Fig 64
Pretentious, over-styled lettering

Fig 65
Example of a compulsive worrier, unable to differentiate between what is, and what is not essential

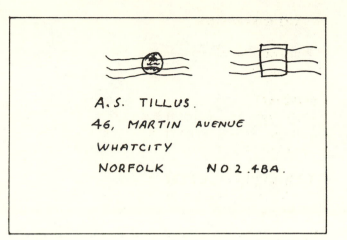

Fig 66
Central placement of
script on envelope

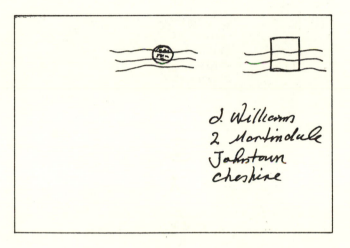

Fig 67
Address written on
extreme right, with
heavy pressure

SPACING

The area of the envelope is related to the zones and left to right significance, the space being divided into four parts – upper, lower, right and left.

If the address is placed in the centre, clear thinking, the ability to organise, balance, orderliness, care and consideration are all indicated (fig 66).

If the address is written on the extreme right, with heavy pressure, this indicates impulsiveness and aggressive tendencies and a need to be involved socially and emotionally (fig 67).

With the address highly placed and with a rightward slant, enterprise, progression and a need to express opinions together with an avoidance of isolation are shown (fig 68).

Where only the upper half of the envelope is used, such writers are usually immature and prone to daydreaming (fig 69). A very young person will often address an envelope in this way, forgetting that the stamp area needs to be left free.

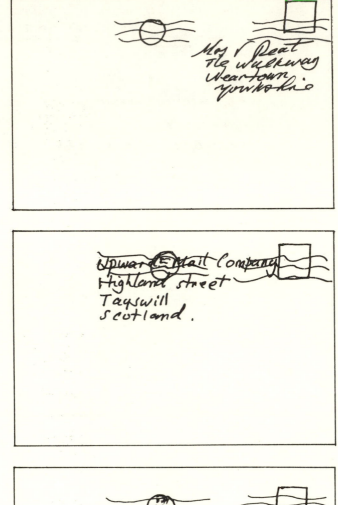

Fig 68
Address placed high on
envelope with
rightward slant

Fig 69
Example showing only
upper half of envelope

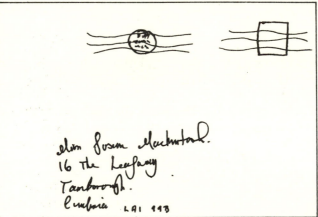

Fig 70
Very low, central,
slightly leftward
placement

A very low, central or leftward placement indicates an anxious and pessi-
mistic outlook and also a materialistic frame of mind (fig 70).

If all the space is taken up from left to right there is a need to participate fully
in all spheres of life, a showmanship, larger-than-life attitude (fig 71).

If the placing of the script is leftward and central, the writer tends to adopt a fearful attitude to life and is generally reserved – interested in things rather than people (fig. 72).

Using only the bottom left-hand corner. The author knows personally a woman periodically on anti-depressant drugs, who will write the address on the envelope normally, but when she is not taking this medicine she will use

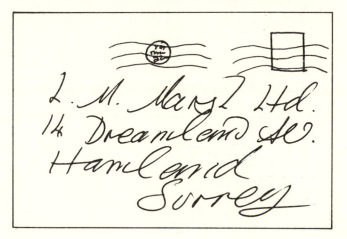

Fig 71
All space taken up from left to right of envelope

Fig 72
Leftward and central placement of writing

Fig 73
Bottom left-hand corner placement, indicating an inner need for security

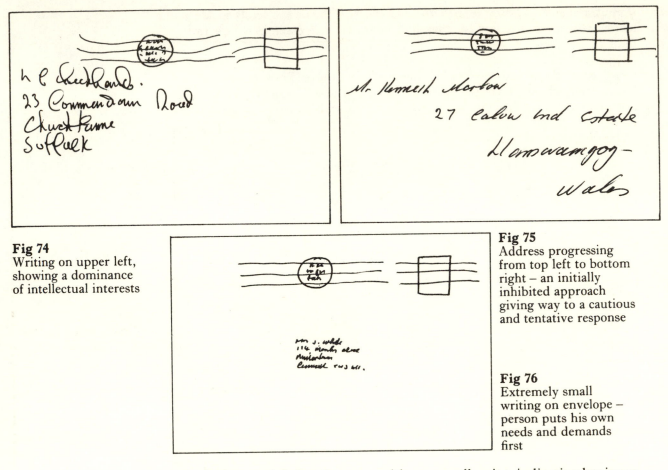

Fig 74
Writing on upper left, showing a dominance of intellectual interests

Fig 75
Address progressing from top left to bottom right – an initially inhibited approach giving way to a cautious and tentative response

Fig 76
Extremely small writing on envelope – person puts his own needs and demands first

only the bottom left-hand corner, with very small script, indicating her inner need for security (fig 73).

If the writing is on the upper left, there is a dominance of intellectual interests but such a person is a 'loner' – (an inhibited response) (fig. 74).

Where the address progresses from the top left to the bottom right an initially inhibited approach gives way to a cautious and tentative response (fig 75).

When the writing on the envelope is so small that it is not easy to read within a reasonable distance, then this person puts his own needs and demands before those of others (fig 76).

The famous Swiss graphologist, Dr Max Pulver, made a special study of addresses and found that not only are the writing and placement of the address significant, but so is the way the figures are written for the house numbers. If these are oversized with long lower loops, the person is money-minded and competent in handling this. Even if the figures are small this writer will write them clearly.

Conversely, a sloppy, misformed number points to a person who has little interest in numerical subjects.

Now you can make worksheets for the layout.

WORKSHEET FOR LAYOUT

Layout General (good/poor)	
Margins Left Right Top Bottom Summary	
Line spacing General (good/poor, wide/narrow etc) Special points (mingling, lower zone loops etc.)	
Direction (slope) of lines (straight, rising, falling, undulating, ⌢, ⌣, tiling)	
Word spacing General (good, poor, mixed) Special features	
The envelope Spacing (4 areas) Legibility and size of writing Special features (over-styled letters etc.)	

FORM: ORIGINALITY AND CONNECTIONS

Chapter 4 | Slant

Handwriting is a means of communicating thoughts and feelings, and it is therefore an extrovert action. It can be likened to a bridge built from one person to another, reaching out to the environment and other people. The degree of slant which a writer develops in relation to the copybook pattern he or she learned at school is significant in terms of personal expression and originality. However, before beginning the analysis it is necessary to establish, if possible, the age of the writer within a few years and the national style of handwriting learned at school at that time, so that any deviation from this style will be in terms of individual progress and mental growth.

In Great Britain, for instance, the Vere Foster method (fig 77) – a simplified version of copperplate taught from 1898 until about 1935 – is set at approximately 80° rightward slant. From this the Marion Richardson style (fig 78) took over and children were taught an upright handwriting with a more rounded form. This is still being used as a basic style by schools today. Some schools, particularly private ones, taught an Italic style of script (fig 79) which is still encouraged in some establishments. Any change from these scripts is the result of individual development of introvert or extrovert tendencies.

The extrovert puts stress and importance on an external object and relates to other people continually. This person forms many relationships: some shallow acquaintances only, some close. He needs, and functions best, with people.

The introvert values the inward side of experience more than the outward. He will feel awkward and uncomfortable in a group and can be difficult to get to know well, but any close relationship will have deep roots. It will take him a long time to make friends, but once made, he will often keep them.

UPRIGHT WRITING
An upright writing will have a slight variation of 2–3° each side of the vertical; 88° to 92° is normal (fig 80).

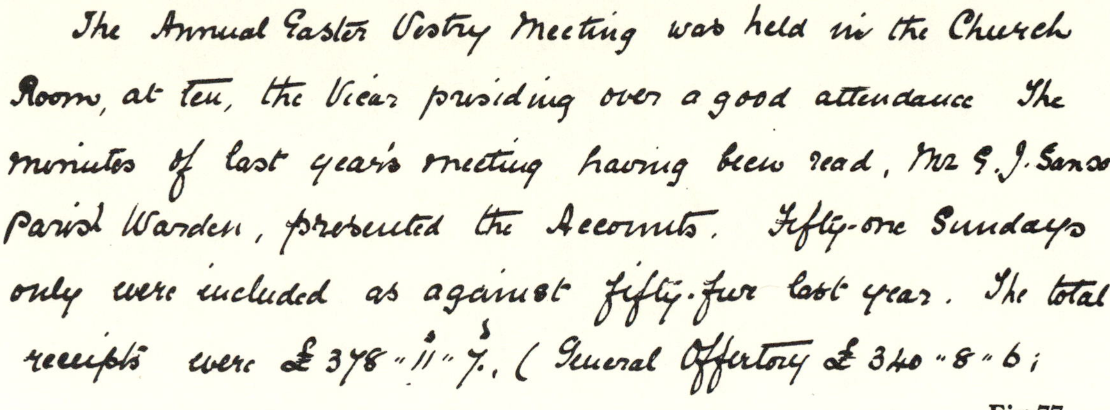

The Annual Easter Vestry Meeting was held in the Church Room, at ten, the Vicar presiding over a good attendance The minutes of last year's meeting having been read, Mr G.J. Sansome, parish Warden, presented the Accounts. Fifty-one Sundays only were included as against fifty-five last year. The total receipts were £ 378 " 11 " 7. (General Offertory £ 340 " 8 " 6 ;

Fig 77
A 1910 handwriting

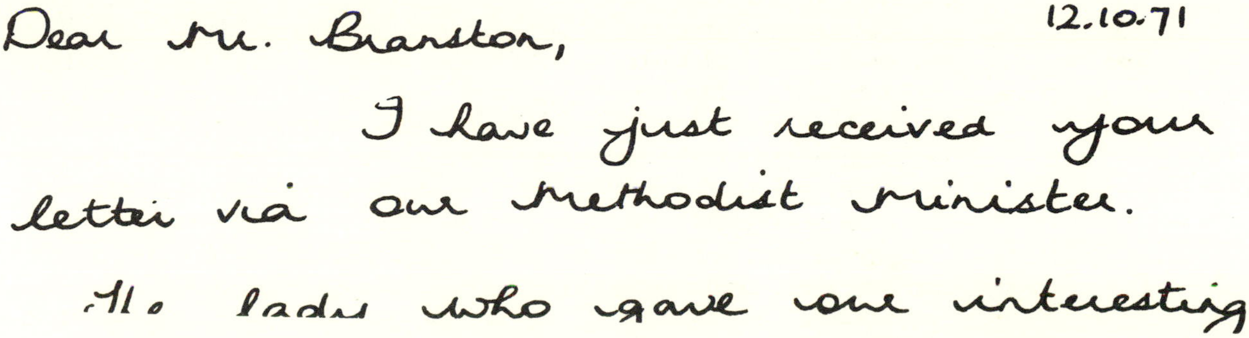

Dear Mr. Branston,   12.10.71

        I have just received your letter via our Methodist minister.

    No lady who gave one interesting

Fig 78
A Marion Richardson style handwriting

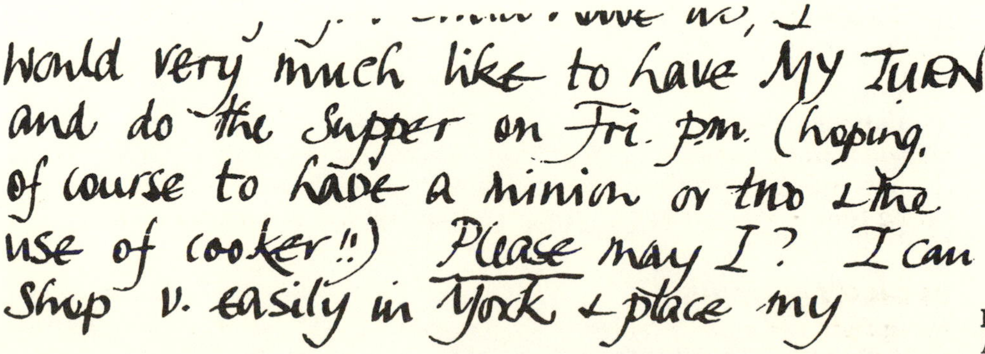

...would very much like to have MY TURN and do the Supper on Fri. p.m. (hoping, of course to have a minion or two + the use of cooker!!) Please may I? I can Shop v. easily in York, + place my

Fig 79
An Italic style script

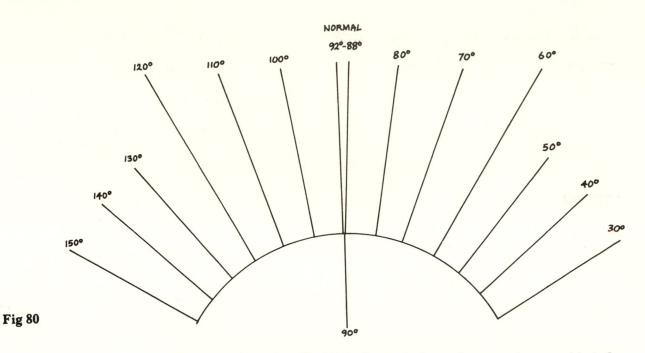

Fig 80

The upright script (fig 81) indicates independence against outside influence – a mind that wishes neither to meet the outside world nor to shrink away from it. This person will have a self-sufficient attitude, with an informal response to friends and a formal approach to strangers.

The upright writer is dominated by reason rather than emotion (i.e. the head rules the heart). Because of this he seldom fluctuates and will usually cope in emergency conditions by remaining fully in control of himself. Upright writers are able to see both sides of an argument and will take the middle-of-the-road point of view.

Normal upright slant

Positive traits	*Negative traits*
Good self-control	Lack of emotional response
Prudence	Indifference
Reserve	Self-centredness
Caution	Rigid-minded
Pride (large capitals)	Aloofness
Ability to concentrate	Critical observation
Objectivity	Inactivity
Impartiality	Frugality
Judiciousness	Pessimism
Maturity	
Reliability	
Independence	
Restraint	
Diplomacy	

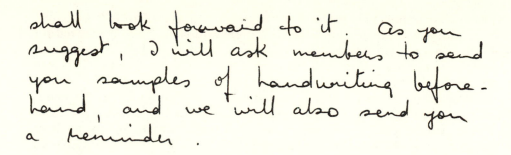

shall look forward to it. As you suggest, I will ask members to send you samples of handwriting beforehand, and we will also send you a reminder.

Fig 81
An upright script,
88–92°

LEFTWARD SLANT

No copybook styles have a leftward slant and it is, therefore, a purely personal trait. The leftward slant writer normally has an introverted nature (fig 82) and relates to past experiences rather than future expectations. Thus, spontaneity is curbed.

Any leftward slant, depending upon the degree of incline, relates to a 'mother tie' attachment. The writer's mother has usually played a greater role in shaping his life than the father, who is seen as a weak character.

Such writers find comfort in behaving in an unconventional way or, alternatively, they will register their protest against society by increasing the leftward movements, thus projecting their lack of sociability. The compulsive extreme leftward slant writer (fig 83) finds his greatest threat in change of any kind, and is usually inflexible.

A leftward slant is found more often in women's handwriting; men are normally more upright and rightward-tending towards the father figure.

Male leftward slant handwriting reveals a sensitive, tender home-loving type with a sentimental approach to life combined with a devotion to his partner – who incidentally, for compatibility, should not be a rightward slant writer unless she is very understanding and willing to lead. The male leftward writer who also uses narrow letters and words can be very jealous of his wife's social life and will watch every move she makes towards others – not a good foundation for marriage!

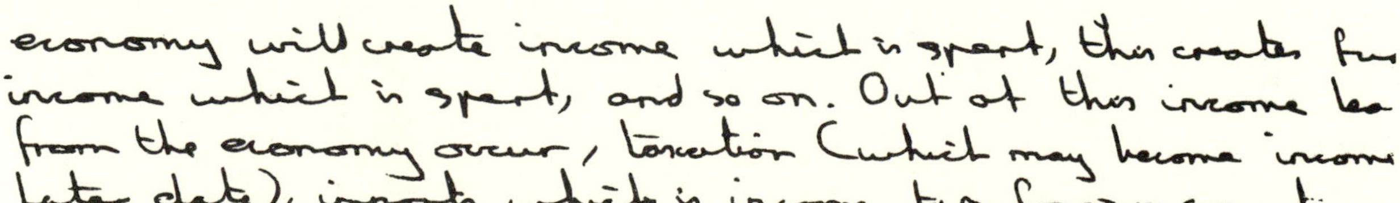

Fig 82
A leftward slant

economy will create income which is spent, thus creates few income which is spent, and so on. Out of this income lea from the economy occur, taxation (which may become income later date), imports which is income to a foreign country.

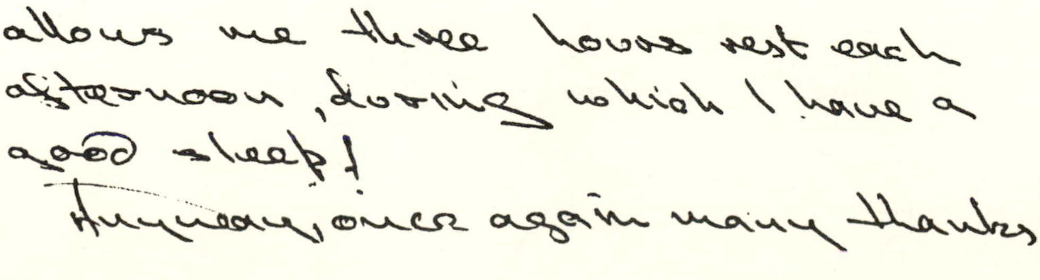

allows me three hours rest each afternoon, during which I have a good sleep!

Anyway, once again many thanks

Fig 83
A pronounced leftward slant

The writer in his early teens with a leftward slant is probably striving for a more independent and adult lifestyle. A leftward slant is often adopted for originality and, within a year or two, will be abandoned for a more natural upright or rightward slant, commensurate with maturity. Such a writer will often find the leftward slant easier to manipulate, but should he wish to become one of the crowd he will subconsciously attempt to make his handwriting appear upright by turning the paper leftwards. This is not easy to detect, especially on a lined paper, which is not really suitable for analysis anyway because of the restricted space of the lines. If you do detect it, make a mental note of introversion. The slant should be considered as it appears – i.e. upright or rightward – because this is how the writer is thinking socially.

Extreme leftward slant

An extreme leftward slant with heavy pressure (fig 84) indicates opposition to almost everything where communication and social contact is concerned. The writer would have a strong degree of emotional insincerity, and could even be in need of psychological assistance. He would be known as awkward and anti-social and therefore have no friends – an outcast from society.

Normal leftward slant	*Excessive leftward slant*
Over-control	Fear of commitment
Over-cautious	Forced behaviour
Traditional	In conflict with reality
Fear of the future	Withdrawn
Curbed spontaneity	Obstinacy
Persistent	Maliciousness
Adherence to strong principles	Arrogance
On the defensive at all times, particularly in a male writer	Insecure
	Dissatisfied
Sentimental	Insincere
Tenderness	Pettiness over details
Domestic type, eager to please	Pedantic attitudes
Devoted	Fussy
	Selfish

Fig 84
Extreme leftward slant, with heavy pressure

Where the slant is leftward with very narrow letters and words, the writer is not very active sexually and has little interest in normal sexual outlets. He compensates with the belief that he is guarding public interest, and makes subjective protests over what he would consider to be in poor taste – shows, reading matter, television, etc. He can also be jealous of his partner's social ease (see page 63).

RIGHTWARD SLANT

As explained in the first section, the bridge of communication is from 'me' (leftward) to 'you' (rightward). The rightwardness of the script is an extroverted action towards people rather than away from them.

A rightward slant is therefore a willingness to share experiences and thoughts, depending upon the degree of rightwardness – the average today being 80°, 70° to the right of upright. In the early copybooks before 1910, it was 60°, but there are of course variations throughout history.

During one piece of writing (fig 85), a slant can intensify from upright to very rightward in the course of a few minutes. This can happen once the writer has awakened his self-control or become more actively involved in what he is writing, having first 'broken the ice' by introducing himself and explaining his motive.

On the other hand a writer may begin to write with a strong rightward slant and then, towards the end of the line or paragraph, this may decrease and become more upright. In this case he needs time to develop emotional control, and caution (fig 86). His interest diminishes and his scepticism

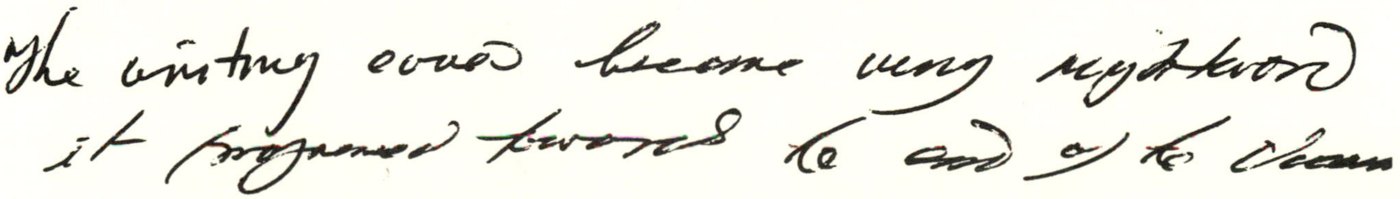

Fig 85
Progressive rightward slant

Fig 86
Decreasing rightward slant

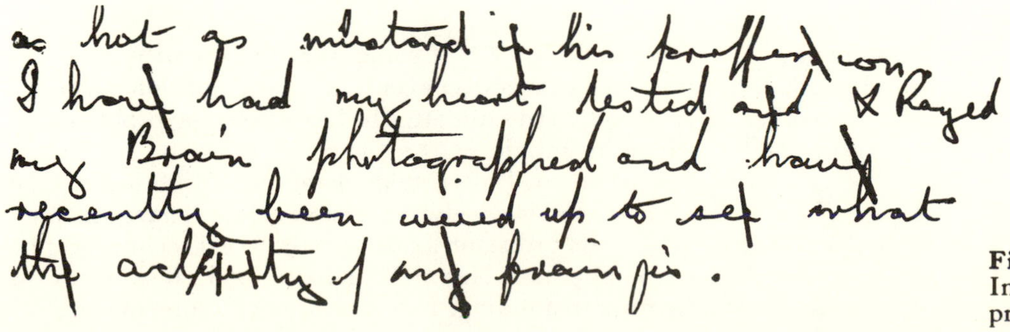

Fig 87
Inconsistent slant and pressure

becomes stronger than his confidence. He will often back out of an agreement and want better terms for his own security, distrusting agreements already made.

With an erratic personality this could happen in every other word (fig 87) – in which case there would be a lack of constancy also in the rhythm and regularity, with uneven pressure throughout. This shows a neurotic response, in which the writer would be a nervy, anxious and highly strung individual.

Extreme rightward slant
An extreme rightward slant of approximately 30–20° in poor quality writing would point to an uncontrollable excitement threshold amounting to hysteria (see fig 88, Hitler's signature). Since this is coupled with irresponsible behaviour and little resistance to stressful conditions, there would be other indications in the script to look for, such as haphazard line direction, extreme irregularity and poor rhythm, thread connection and inconsistent pressure, from light to very heavy.

Fig 88
Extreme rightward slant (Hitler's signature)

In general terms a very rightward slant denotes a person who must always keep in touch with happenings around him to alleviate loneliness, usually a wish for love. These writers are frequently found to be exhausted physically due to over-activity (fig 89).

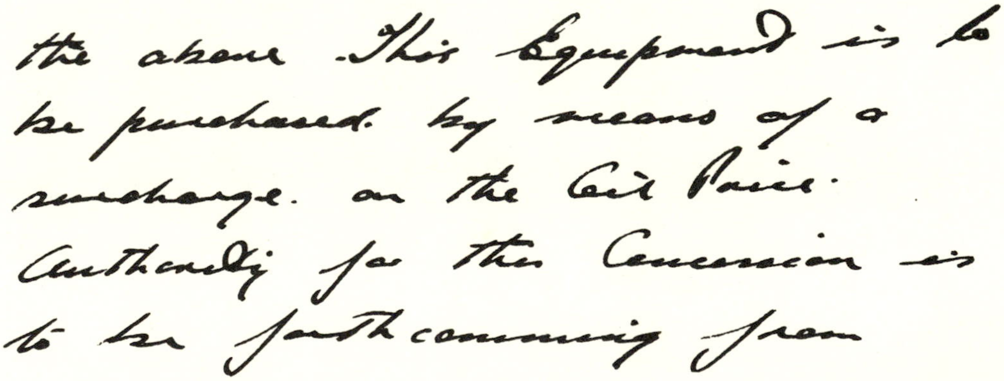

Fig 89
Consistent very rightward slant

Interestingly, a rightward writer will sometimes temporarily adopt an upright hand in order to keep calm and concentrate on the solution to a problem. He will return to a rightward slant after he has solved the problem and feels more comfortable in his mind.

The rightward slant writer will often take chances, will be inclined to change jobs more frequently and is not always reliable. He will have sex more often than the upward or leftward slant writer, using varied techniques; he will learn faster, but remember less. He will be more influenced by the mood of the moment and by his surroundings and immediate circumstances.

Normal rightward slant	Excessive rightward slant
Sociable	Lack of restraint
Emotional	Haste
Affectionate	Restlessness
Active	Lack of discipline
Trust in the future	Excitable
Impressionable	Easily distracted
Sympathetic	Hysterical
Adaptable	Impatient
Uses initiative	Uninhibited
Progressive	Lack of contemplation
Enterprising	Exaggerated opinions
Shows curiosity	Gullible
	Wasteful
	Accident-prone
	Forgetful
	Gregarious
	Very demonstrative

VARYING SLANT (fig 90)

Where a writer is torn between introvert needs and extrovert urges (unresolved conflict), he shows a varied writing slant in accordance with his current emotional mood or ambivalence (fig 91). In the case of an adolescent, this is part of the growing-up process. A teenager often takes on a contra-

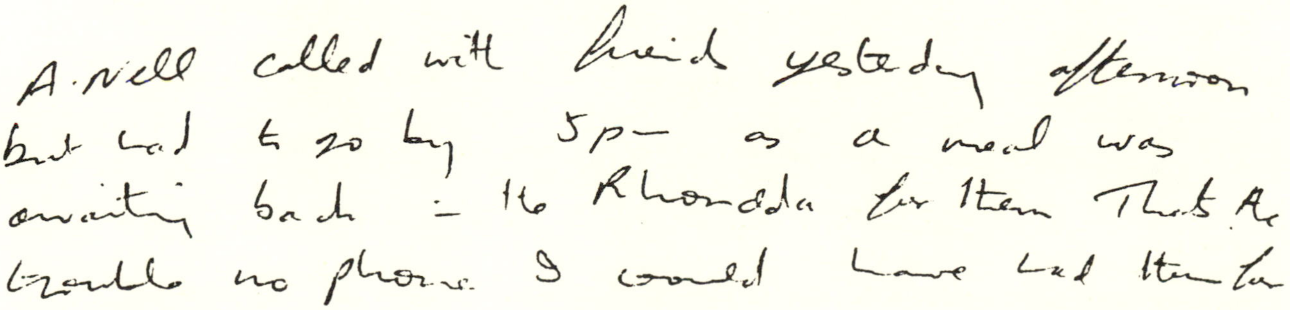

Fig 90
Extreme varying slant

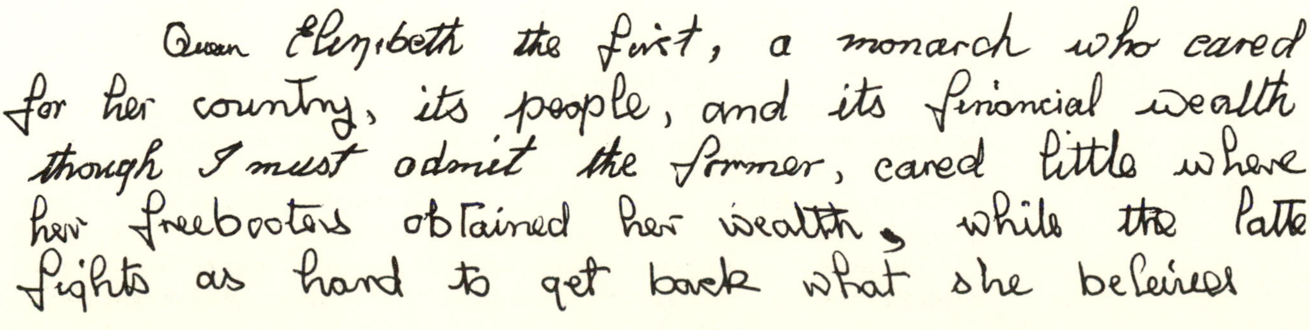

Fig 91
A mixed slant

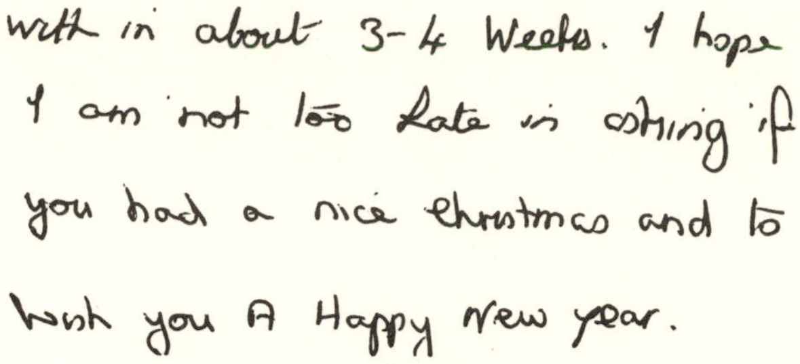

with in about 3-4 Weeks. I hope
I am not too late is asking if
you had a nice christmas and to

Fig 92
Adolescent mixed slant

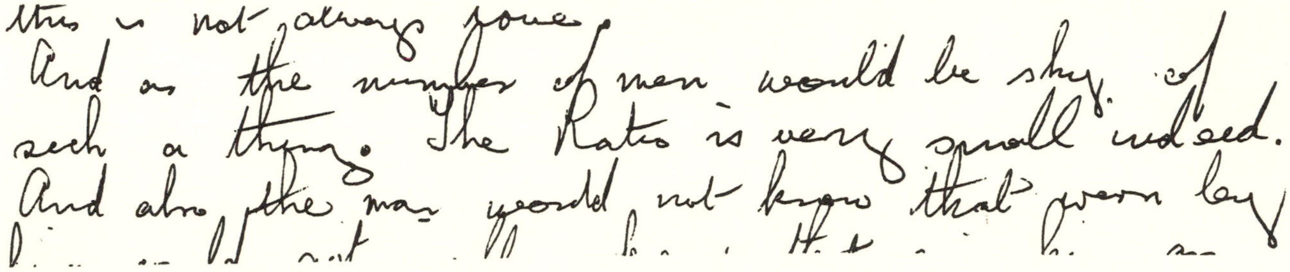

wish you A Happy New year.

Fig 93
Leftward slant, in
lower zone

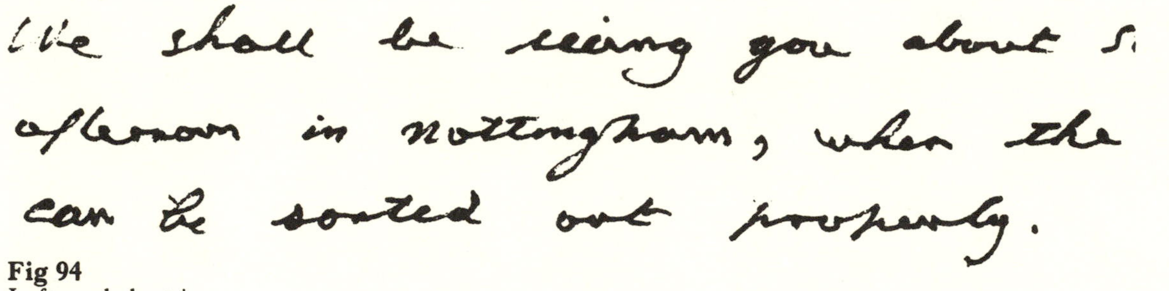

Fig 94
Leftward slant in
middle zone

dictory, fluctuating frame of mind and is frequently of a belligerent disposition! This is normally outgrown, as a result of which the slant stabilises and maturity emerges (see fig 92).

A person can be extrovert in some areas of his personality while being introvert in others, as shown in the three zones (chapter 2). For instance, a sexually withdrawn writer (fig 93) can show this by being leftward in the lower zone but rightward or upright in the others.

Leftward strokes in the middle zone of a dominantly rightward slant handwriting (fig 94) indicate a reluctance to communicate in everyday social situations. However, because of the dominant rightward slant, the writer would be able to relate formally – as a public servant would need to do, for example – but not freely in his social (non-work) life.

This writer is pulled in all directions. His emotional response is unpredictable: sometimes outgoing and sociable, at other times withdrawn and inhibited, often neurotic and unstable. This will also show in varying pressure, irregular writing, poor spacing, disconnected writing and other varying factors (fig 95). It ultimately depends on the quality of the hand-writing (Form Level) on which all the positive and negative interpretations are based.

Varying slant
(Depends on Form Level)
> Unpredictable
> Unstable
> Neurotic
> Ambivalent
> Conflict

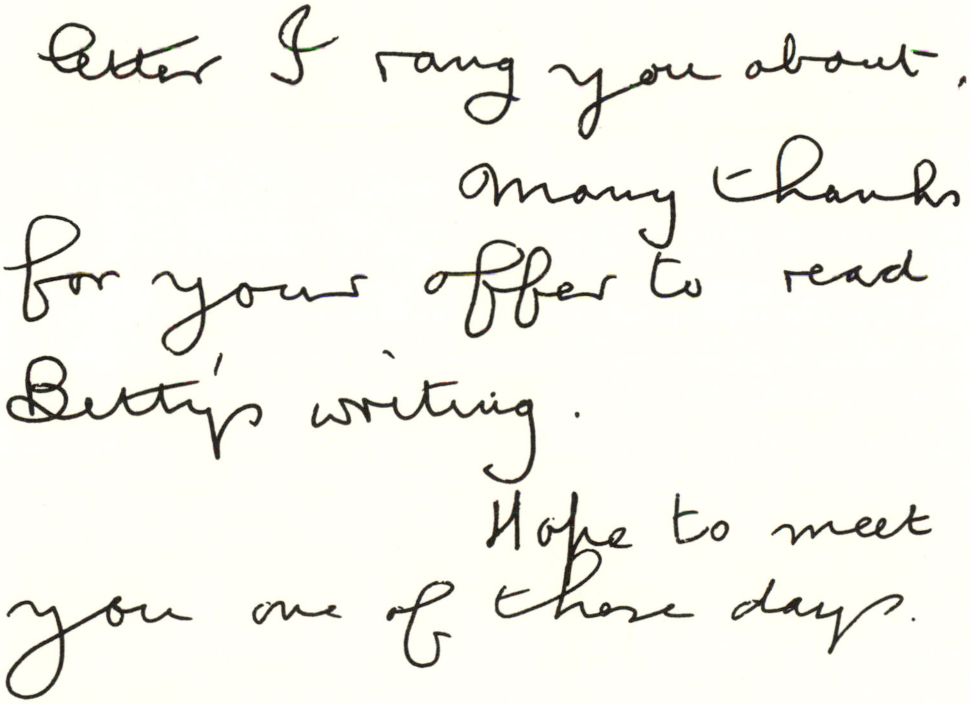

---

letter I rang you about,

many thanks

for your offer to read

Betty's writing.

Hope to meet

you one of these days.

Fig 95
Varying slant, with wide letters

WORKSHEET FOR SLANT

Slant	Interpretation
Upright, rightward, leftward or varying	
Excessive slant	

FORM: ORIGINALITY AND CONNECTIONS

Chapter 5 Connections

The way we connect, or fail to connect, the letters can reveal our thought processes, our attitudes towards others and whether we rely more on logical or intuitive faculties when finding solutions to problems. There are two main factors to look at here, the degree of connection and the form.

1 Degree of Connection

There are two basic degrees of connection; one is where most letters are connected together to form a continuous movement, to promote fluency and a lively tempo, and the other is where they are varying amounts (figs 96 and 97).

CONNECTED SCRIPT

A connected script is developed through maturity from infant to secondary school where note-taking is essential and the joining of the letters becomes a

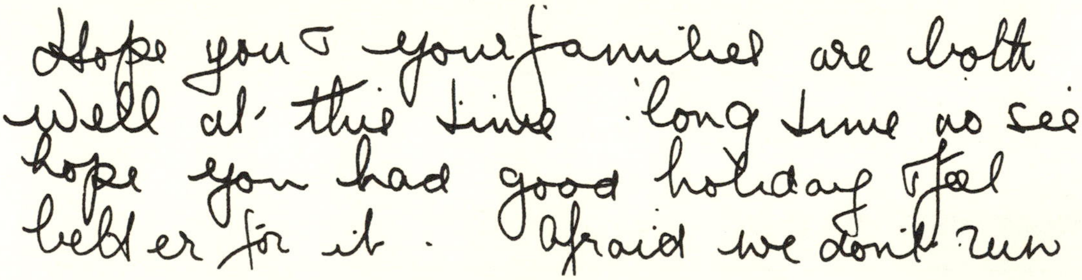
Hope you & your families are both
well at this time long time no see
hope you had good holiday & feel
better for it. Afraid we don't run

Fig 96
Most letters connected

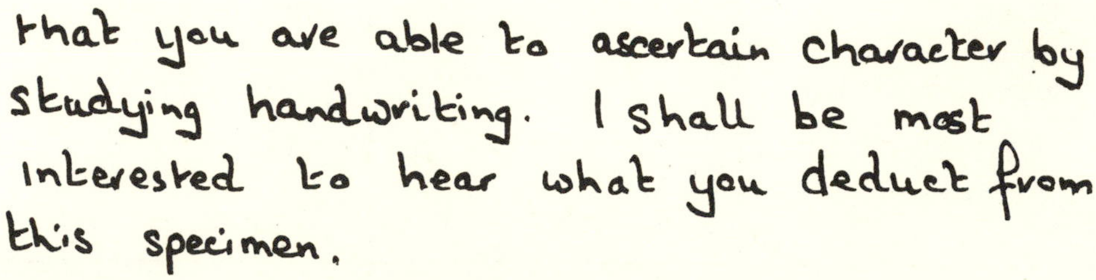
that you are able to ascertain character by
studying handwriting. I shall be most
interested to hear what you deduct from
this specimen.

Fig 97
Letters disconnected

arrival in London.

Fig 98
Break for 'i-dot'

natural process in developing a spontaneous, speedy script. It is worth noting that speech tempo is related to the handwriting pattern, because as we write we literally 'hear' the words. Thus, some writers disconnect the syllables as in phonetic presentation. Breaks for 'i-dots' and 't-bars' are not considered (fig 98). Extreme connection is indicated by the writer joining not only the letters but also some, or all, of the words. Those writers do not want to lose the continuity of their thoughts by lifting the pen from the paper. They are often people working under pressure and they find it a mental strain to keep going, especially when the extreme connection is in the upper zone (fig 99).

Ideally a connected script should be combined with simplicity, legibility and rhythmic letter forms, indicating a clear mind whose thinking processes are logical and well organised. Thus 't-bars' and 'i-dots' that are connected to the next letter without loss of speed are also an indication of a logical mind and mental agility (fig 100).

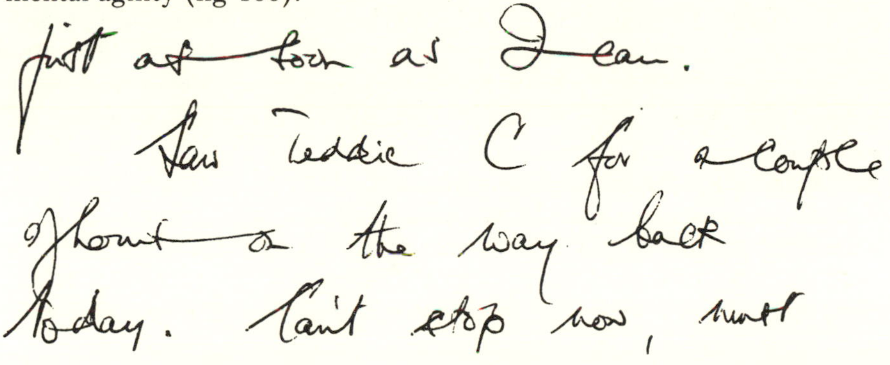

just as soon as I can.

Saw Teddie C for a couple

of hours on the way back

today. Can't stop now, must

white written

Fig 99
Extreme connection

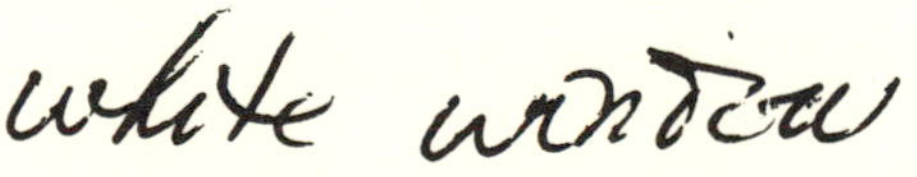

Fig 100
'i-dots' connected to the next letter

THE INVISIBLE CONNECTION

This can be considered as connected. There are those writers who mentally connect their letters but who lift the writing movement from the paper while still forming the connection; therefore the end stroke of the previous letter can be in line with the next letter, giving a fluid movement throughout the word, like a ski jump track (fig 101 but unlike fig 102).

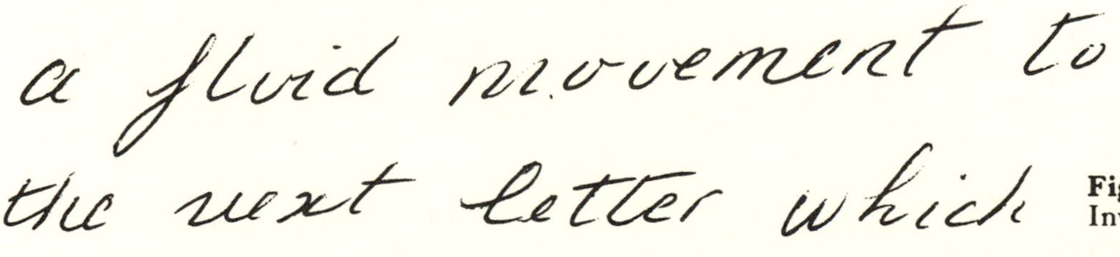

a fluid movement to

the next letter which

Fig 101
Invisible connection

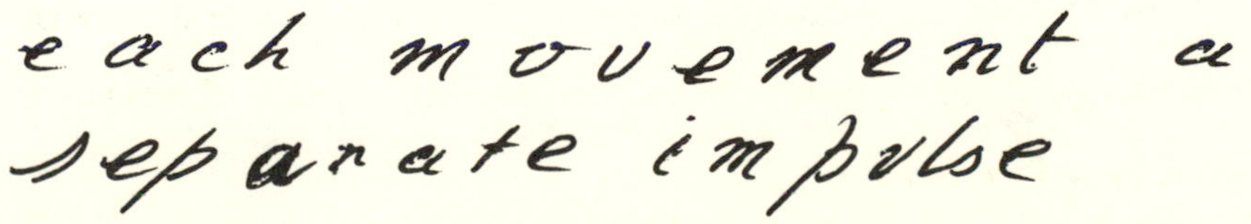

each movement a

separate impulse

Fig 102
Each letter separate

Connected script

Positive traits (Form Level)	*Negative traits (Form Level)*
Deductive thinking	Hasty in drawing conclusions
Systematic working	Superficial and flighty thinking
Logical mind	Over-anxiously dependable
Consistent	Inconsiderate
Co-operative	
Purposeful	
Realistic concepts	
Sociability	
Good memory	
Adaptable	

DISCONNECTED SCRIPT

A disconnected script is one in which not more than three letters are connected together without a clear break (fig 103). A completely disconnected script is 'print script' (fig 104). A disconnected handwriting would point to either a thought process influenced by intuition or a lack of concentration. The general Form Level should help you to decide which is the case. In any event, there is usually also a lack of adaptability.

If there are strange gaps in the words (fig 105) or extraneous marks, you should try to find out whether there were any external factors affecting the writer at that time, such as writing on a bus or knee or receiving 'help' from children.

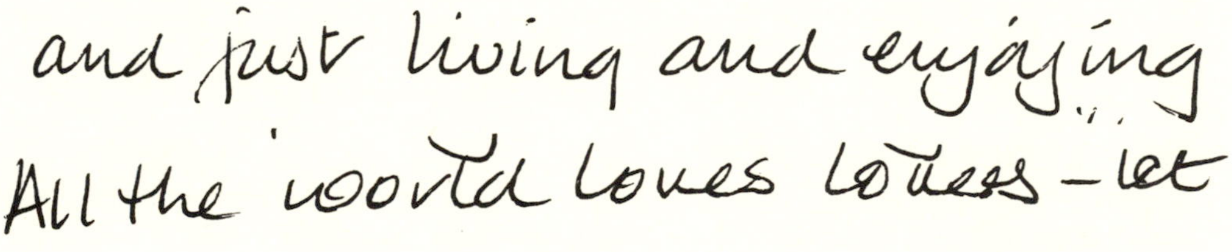

Fig 103
Not more than three letters connected

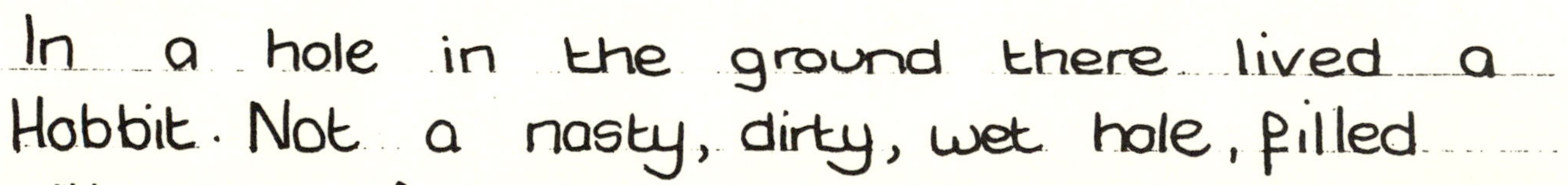

Fig 104
Printed script

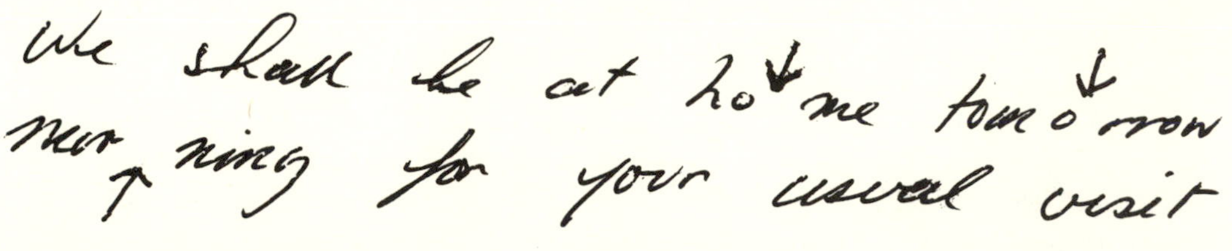

Fig 105
Wide gaps within words

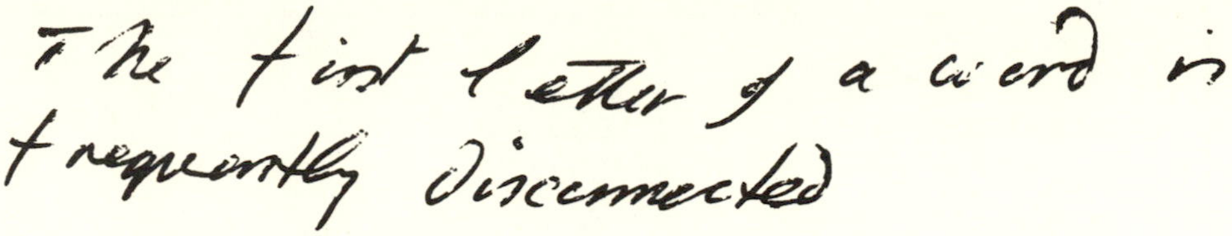

The first letter of a word is frequently disconnected

Fig 106
First letter
disconnected

most letters where the last one is broken

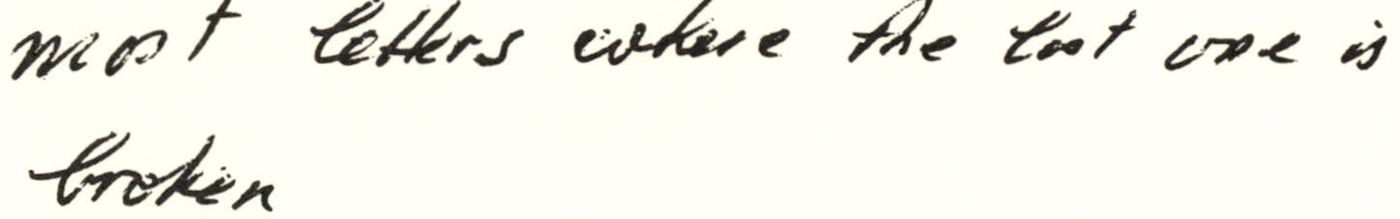

Fig 107
Last letter disconnected

Some writers leave a break between the first letter and the rest of the word (which is connected) (fig 106), or they may connect the word except for the last letter (fig 107). The former hesitates before he acts. The latter momentarily stops to check that he has achieved what he intended – to write that particular word correctly – and will not promise anything until the last moment when he is sure of his ground; he will not take chances that are not calculated.

Some nervous writers disconnect not only their words but also their letters and then join or 'solder' the joints as it were by going back over them often with a heavy stroke, making the whole word much less legible (fig 108). This points to an anxious and compulsive writer.

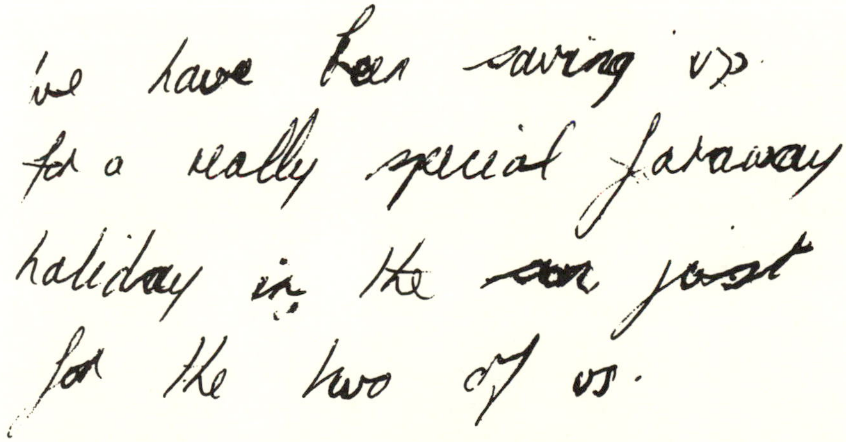

we have been saving up for a really special faraway holiday in the ~~an~~ just for the two of us.

Fig 108
Soldered joints

People who write with a disconnected script are generally more inclined to be individuals and are open to influence from their intuition, which they find very difficult to ignore. Socially they prefer to keep a distance and erect a fence around themselves to avoid close encounters. Although this is what they choose to do, they usually suffer loneliness inwardly, although they do not let it be known. The imaginative ones can, however, channel their inventiveness into, for example, an artistic outlet, whether it be for profit or just personal satisfaction.

Disconnected script

Positive traits	*Negative traits*
Intuitive thinking	Unsociable
Productive observation	Spasmodic thought processes
Individualistic	Lack of forethought
Inventive	Stubborn
Self-reliant	Lonely
Independent	Unco-operative
Imaginative	Moody
Cautious	Not adaptable
	Unreliable

Connected and disconnected scripts i.e. no dominant pattern

Positive traits	*Negative traits*
Versatile	Irritable over trifles
Adaptable	Impatient
Creative	Strong likes and dislikes
Individualistic	
Unconventional	
Emotionally sensitive	
Resourceful	

2 Form of connection

The way that a writer chooses to connect the letters can be divided into six main categories – copybook, garland, arcade, angle, wavy line and thread. These forms of connection are important in giving the writing its particular style.

COPYBOOK

This is the basic form of letter connection as taught in schools (fig 109). Since this can vary, according to the age and nationality of the writer (e.g. Vere Foster, Marion Richardson, Italic etc – see page 60), you should try to determine how the writer was taught (see chapter 32) as handwriting assessment is concerned with the degree of deviation from this primarily learned style.

The basic copybook writer has not developed a personality or way of thinking beyond that of their school days. They have no strong forces to project; just an inner desire to be conventional and to feel safe by conforming to prescribed and accepted patterns of thought and behaviour generating little or no originality.

This impersonal form of connection is sometimes used deliberately in order to disguise. Usually the contents of the letter, always anonymous, will point to this but only the experienced graphologist can decide.

your counterpart goes out in the Radio car, he nearly made our road but **(i)**

too good. My Daughter came & fetched me so have decided to give my home up & stay with them so I thought I had better **(ii)**

(iii)

entirely yours. We would very much like you to visit us again and hope that you will consider doing so.

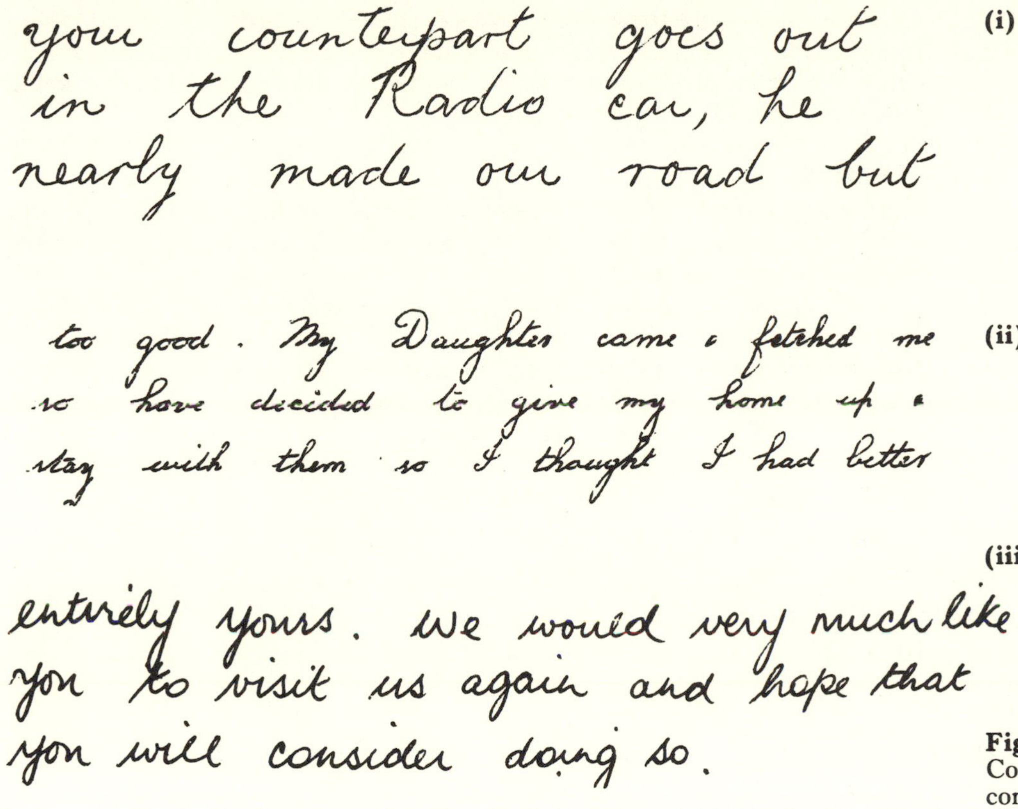

Fig 109
Copybook forms of connection

Copybook

Conventional
Orthodox habits
Uninspired imagination
Mundane personality
Need to obey authority
Lack of originality
Lack of initiative
Poor educational background
Predictable
Not easy to motivate

Positive traits
Could show genuine humility where service to the community is more important than personal desires and needs, e.g. nun, nurse, priest, devoted teacher etc.

Negative traits
Very slow and deliberate but showing no signs of illness. Could be disguised – criminal tendencies.

In contrast, where there has been a developed maturity and individuality from starting school and learning to write to spontaneous subconscious formation of words, other more mature styles of connection gradually develop quite naturally. One of these is garland.

GARLAND (fig 110)

The garland is formed when a curved downstroke is followed by an upstroke in the form of a 'u' (fig 111). The ideal garland is firm and even, neither too wide nor too narrow (fig 112).

Characteristically, garland writers are expressive, co-operative and at ease in their environment. They prefer to be with others with whom they can share active experiences and thoughts, and they normally try to avoid conflict. Some garland writers are too open to emotional influence and are therefore gullible. The normal garland writer does not wish to compete and will compromise by taking the way of least resistance in their need to be liked and admired, which most of them feel to some degree.

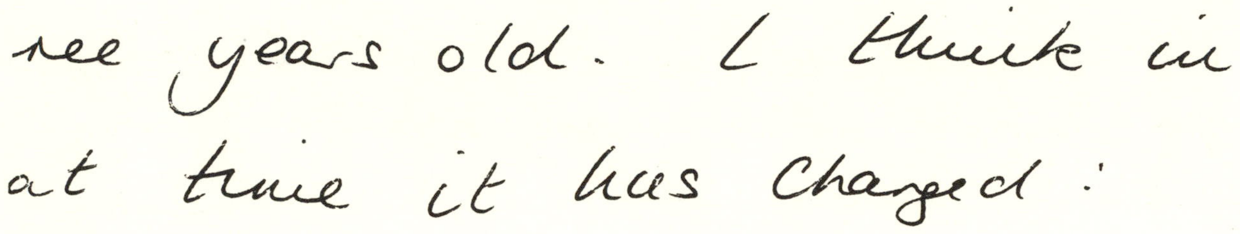

Fig 110
Garland form of connection

Fig 111
Garland connection –
upstroke in the form of
a 'u'

Fig 112
Firm and even garland
but out of proportion

Garland	
Positive traits	*Negative traits*
Sincere	Easily influenced
Tolerant	Easily distracted
Adaptable	Over-confident
Warm nature	Lack of discipline
Socially minded	Changeable attitudes
Ready to help	Weak willpower
Open and receptive	Dependent upon others
Responsive	Lazy
Sympathetic	Immature attitude

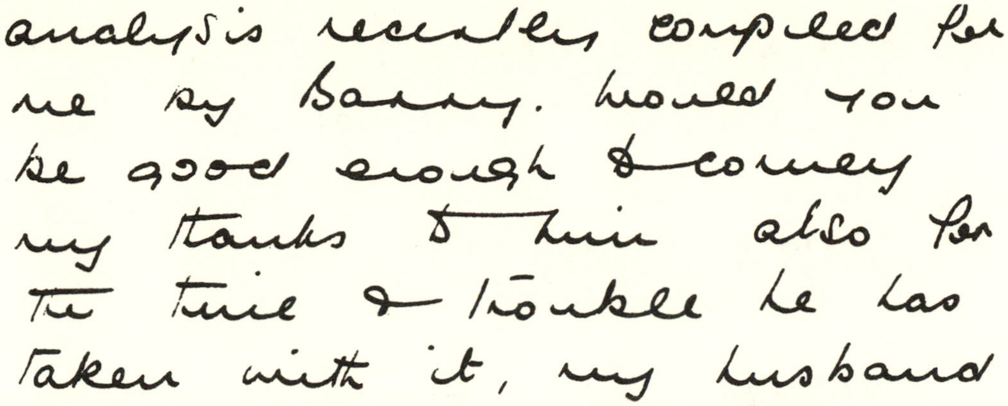

[handwritten text] analysis recently compiled for me by Barry. Would you be good enough to convey my thanks to him also for the time & trouble he has taken with it, my husband

Fig 113
Shallow garlands

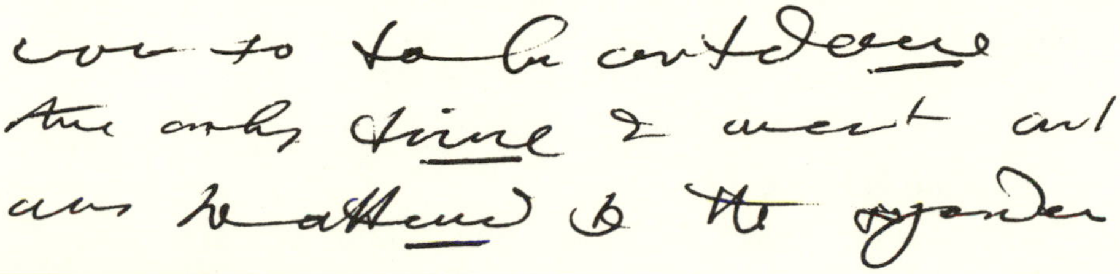

[handwritten text] ... to be confidence the only time I went out was he attend to the garden

Fig 114
The shallow garlands are underlined

Shallow garland (figs 113, 114)
These writers will be very kind and sympathetic.

Shallow garland

Positive traits
Will try anything new
Open to suggestion
Keeps in touch with progress
Obliging manner
Optimistic outlook

Negative traits

Hasty	Complacent attitude
Unstable	Cuts corners
Elusive	Lack of deep feelings

Gullible
Inconsiderate
Tactless
Thoughtless
Talkative
Careless
Indifferent

Deep garland (figs 115, 116)

Deep garland
Depressed, resentful feelings sometimes, but can also be sympathetic towards people needing help.
Usually quiet and contemplative.

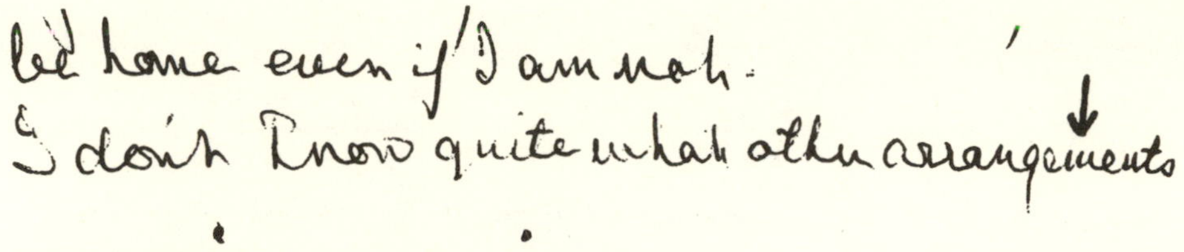

Fig 115
Deep garlands

Fig 116
Deep garlands

Supported garland (figs 117, 118)
These writers need sympathy and encouragement to free them from their emotional inhibitions. They can be calculatingly kind and scheming in their approach to friendship. They can also win their way through life without being temperamental, but they will lie if necessary.

> **Supported garland**
> Repressed and inhibited personality who will put on a façade of genuine social co-operation but who is, in fact, shy and retiring.
> A calculated friendliness meant to deceive.

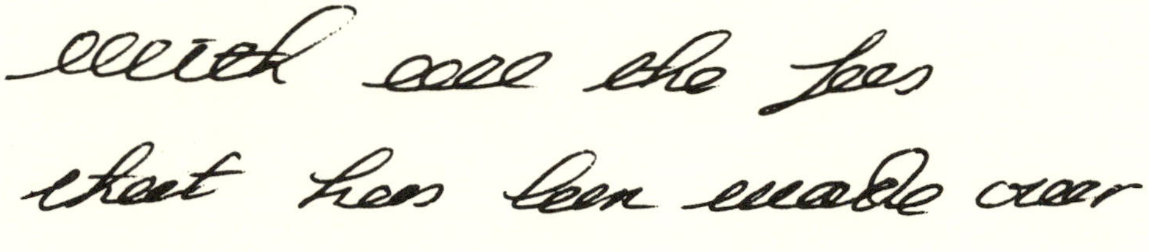

Fig 117
Supported garlands

Fig 118
Supported garlands

Square garland (fig 119)
These writers are very conventional and have a closed mind to anything new or not understood. They often reject their instinctual drives, and are narrow-minded.

Fig 119
Square garlands

ARCADE (fig 120)
Where the garland writer is open to the world, the arcade writer is the reverse. As the name implies, the arcade is in the form of an arch which is closed at the top and this writer is closed to the demands of the world.

Arcade writers find their security by dominating the environment where and when they are allowed to do so. In this way they can get a feeling of control over their lives.

Emotionally they are not so open as garland writers and are therefore not easily influenced. They maintain a reserved friendliness, preferring to remain strictly formal and keeping their inner thoughts and feelings to themselves. Although arcade writers can be emotionally activated, they will be very reluctant to allow their emotions free expression and will control them to the point where they may seem to be cold-hearted. They try to be seen as formal and conventional authoritarian figures, and it takes some time to get to know them intimately.

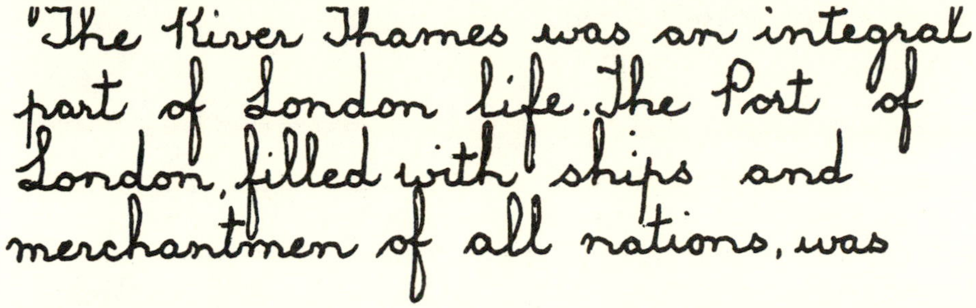

"The River Thames was an integral part of London life. The Port of London, filled with ships and merchantmen of all nations, was

Fig 120
Arcade connection

Arcade

Positive traits	*Negative traits*
Reserved personality	Insincere
Observes tradition	Critical
Cautious	Anti-social
Self-protective	Distrustful
Confidential	Suspicious
Formal manners	Closed mind
Likes to meditate	Rigid attitude
Rather sensitive	Unreliable statements
Retentive memory	Hypocritical
Constructive	Inflexible

as if it's not running centrally. Please do this

Fig 121
Flat arcades (practical writer)

Flat arcade (particularly in leftward slant) (fig 121)

Positive traits	*Negative traits*
(rightward slant, good Form Level)	Hypocritical
Practical	Dishonest
	Scheming
	Narrow-minded

High arcades (fig 122)

Positive traits

Self-sufficient

Pride of achievement

Very reserved

Arcades very narrow in middle zone (fig 123)

Very inhibited

Anxious

Very secretive, to neurotic levels

Fig 122
High arcades

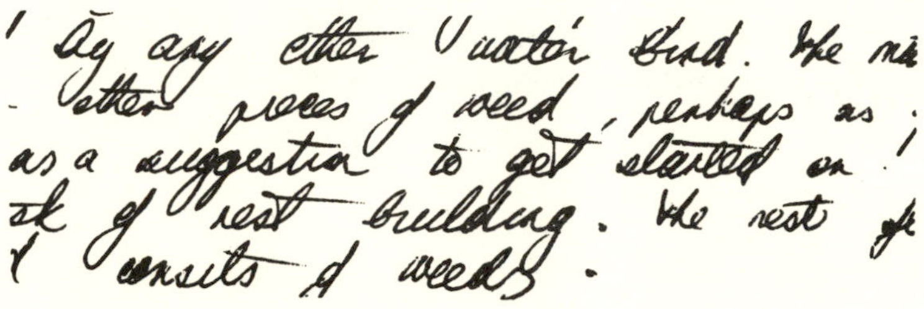

achieve greatness employ this secret of getting things

Fig 123
Narrow arcades

[handwritten sample]

ANGLE (fig 124)

The people whose connections are dominantly angular, or pointed, like a constant challenge and find their security by opposing and fighting difficulties in the environment. They are persistent and will undertake the less easy tasks in life with a keen interest and commitment. They have an intellectual approach, and being self-disciplined they possess strong willpower, along with a willingness to work, especially in jobs which demand constant attention to detail.

Should angle writers be placed in the wrong job, with little to occupy their minds, they will quickly become restless and irritable, and could make trouble just for the sake of it.

They are not people to compromise and need to say either 'yes' or 'no', unlike the indecisive garland writer. Angle writers are rather rigid in their approach to life, with very little flexibility. This can produce, in time, an anxious, inhibited mind trying to maintain an emotionally frustration-free path, and this can turn to aggressiveness.

They are not really concerned by what other people think of them; as a consequence their friends may be few. Unlike the garland writer they shun social life unless it is in the way of duty. Then they will take an active, business-like role, to produce results in their own way and on their own terms. A challenge acts as a spur to enterprise, in which they will drive relentlessly towards their goal and enjoy fighting any opposition.

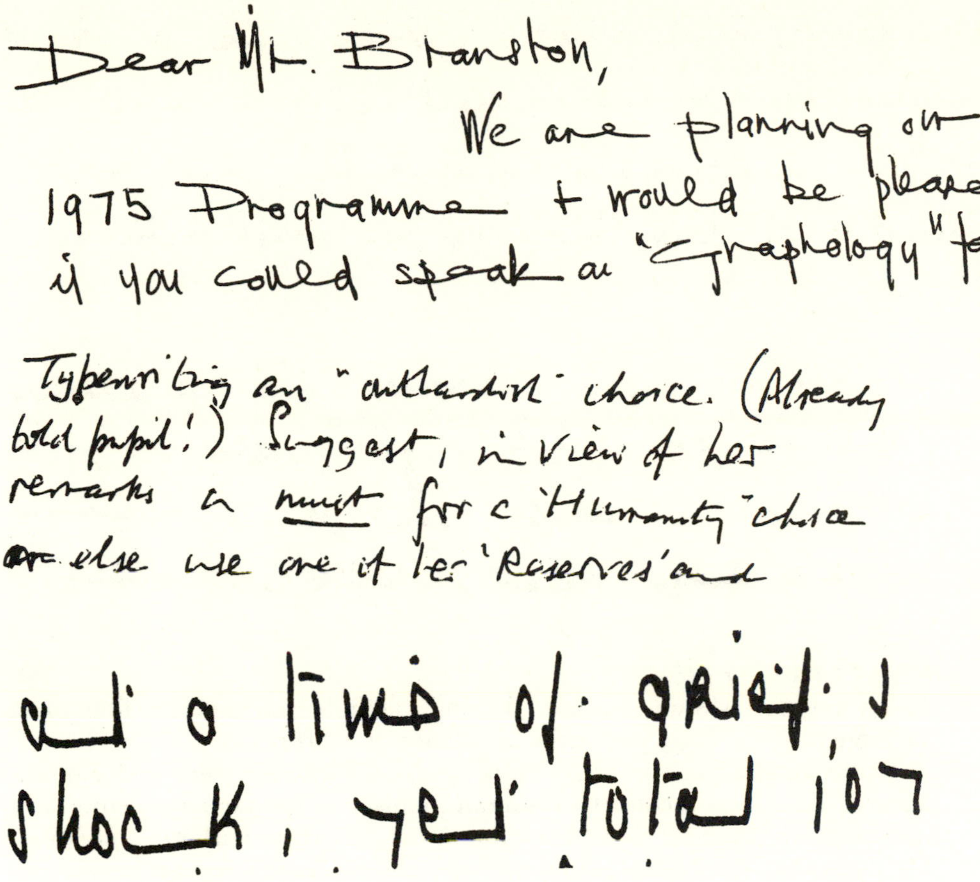

(handwritten letter)

(i)

Dear Mr. Branston,
          We are planning our
1975 Programme + would be pleased
if you could speak on "Graphology" for

(ii)

Typewriting an "antisocial" choice. (Already
told pupil!) Suggest, in view of her
remarks a must for a 'Humanity' choice
or else we are it her 'Reserves' and

(iii)

and o limits of grief; J
shock, yet total 10.

Fig 124
Angle connections

Angle	
Positive traits	*Negative traits*
Purposeful	Rigid
Stable	Obstinate
Strong motivation	Unyielding
Determined	Inflexible
Sincere	Indifferent
Responsible attitude	Argumentative
Critically minded	Aggressive
Creative thinking	Irritable
Strictly ethical	Unsympathetic
Decisive	Compulsive
Logical reasoning	Pedantic
Can work alone with ease	

Angular garland (fig 125)
An angle writer often has a secondary garland connection. This suggests an
'iron fist in a velvet glove' approach – the angle resists, the garland yields.

(i) *Counsellor, and since I shall have to spend ummm of six and a half hours a week on ork, in addition to doing a full time job, I must cut down most of my other activities.*

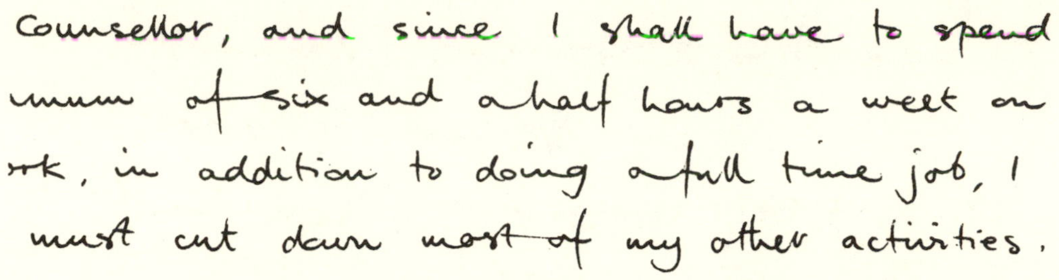

(ii) *d that's it in a nutshell. Low temperature inverts the grain into a form which the yeast on to produce alcohol, but doesn't necessarily a sufficiently clear solution to ensure*

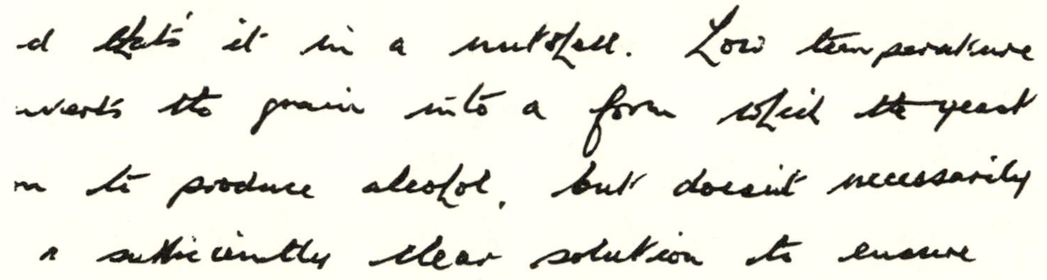

Fig 125
Angular garland forms

WAVY LINE (fig 126)
The wavy line shows a loose, flowing, flexible movement. The basic movement of the wavy line is the avoidance of sharpness.

These writers need freedom to adapt to the environment and circumstances. They have no desire to commit themselves fully to any event. They only want to preserve their individuality at all costs, without obligation. They possess a strong degree of diplomacy and will easily change front as and when it suits them. Their thinking is subjective and is usually flighty – without a definite pattern or goal in life, except to 'flow with the tide'. This is particularly true in cases where the pressure is weak, in which case they are related more to the next form 'thread'.

Wavy line
Needs freedom
Don't like to commit themselves
Diplomatic
Two-faced
Goes with the flow

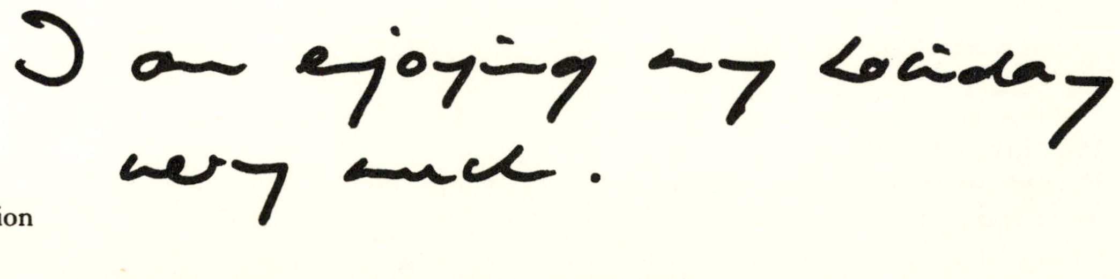

I am enjoying my holiday very much.

Fig 126
Wavy line connection

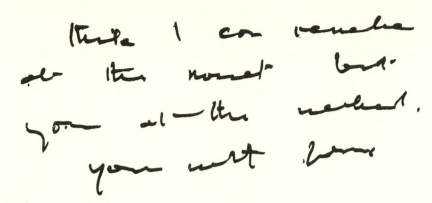

Fig 127
Thread connection

THREAD (fig 127)

The thread connection can be likened to a piece of cotton laid out between the letters, instead of the letters – therefore there is no definition: the word can be read by context, often found at a word ending, i.e. 'ing', which would be written on a line with a downward final movement in both primary and secondary thread.

There are two types of thread connection to consider – *Primary* (fig 128) and *Secondary* (fig 129), each formed by an inconsistent wavy line with little or no vertical extensions either within the word or at the end (e.g. '-ing'). The chief distinction between the two forms is that the primary shows more pressure and a clearer formation of the letters.

Primary thread

Primary thread writers use the environment according to their own, very strong, instincts for self-preservation. They will adapt to any situation if it is to their advantage and does not involve any loss of their individuality. They must be free to follow the dictates of any creative talent, and must not be confined by convention. They will quickly change their attitude, and like to follow an easy trouble-free path and avoid restrictions.

They have an instinctive, spontaneous understanding of others and they are always ready to manipulate the other person into following their ideas and commands, without appearing to be overbearing – such is their likeable personality. They make good workers in the field of psychology where their strong powers of observation and intelligence allow them to view both sides of the situation and to advise, without becoming involved themselves. On the

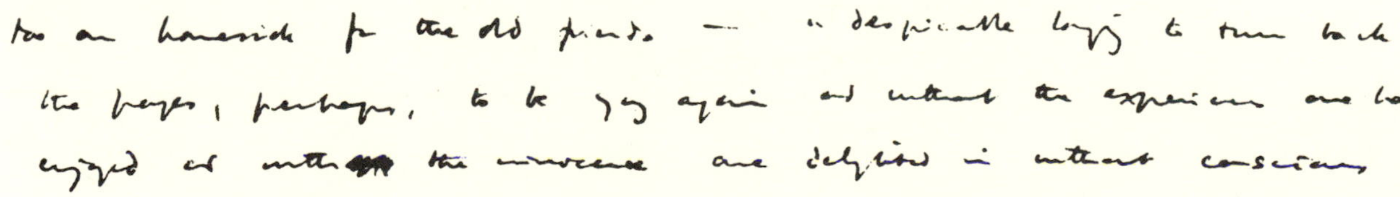

Fig 128
Primary thread

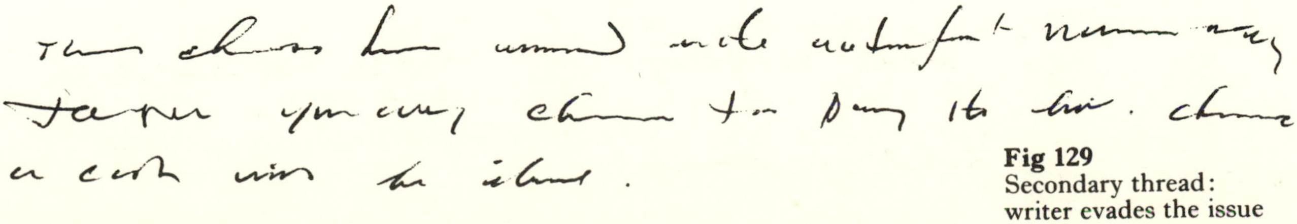

Fig 129
Secondary thread:
writer evades the issue

negative side, they can lack a sense of obligation and will act without their conscience intervening. While not being demonstrative, they can be ruthless in protecting their own rights and freedom from authority. This they will do unethically if necessary, because they lack the stamina to put up a fight. Their ways may be unconventional, but they usually succeed in getting their own way.

Secondary thread
Secondary thread writers are usually defined by the thread being inside the word (fig 130). The writing is pressureless with the movement formless. However, a thread can appear in any part of a word or even as a whole word, which at its most negative is just a letter followed by a line. This movement is fluid and smooth, the writer usually choosing an unresisting paper, as an ice skater would prefer a smooth surface on which to glide. We exclude the medical profession with their writing for prescriptions as this is usually a professional style of writing between the doctor and the dispenser – writing in synonyms and symbols which are meaningful only to the chemist. Secondary thread writers are unsure of themselves on all levels, indecisive and reluctant to take a stand. Because of this they are open to influence and find difficulty in coping with stressful external pressures. Similarly they have little control over their own inner demands. Their usual method of bypassing these pressures is to sway with the wind and go with the crowd, and since they are highly versatile, they have no difficulty in doing so. To avoid friction, they will change sides and evade the issue more readily than primary thread writers who will at least take a stand for their own rights.

Secondary thread writers, in order to further their own ends, will waste no time in showing sympathy in order to take advantage of others' weaknesses, by deceit if necessary. They are of course also able to manipulate, without feeling a sense of wrong. They are generally unreliable where promises are concerned and will make ambiguous statements to avoid binding commitments.

They can be creative and prefer to learn by experience rather than by formal teaching.

Thread	
Primary thread (with pressure)	*Secondary thread (without pressure)*
Relies on instinct	
Gets his own way without effort	Unstable
	Hysterical
Very self-aware	Insecure feelings
Needs scope for freedom	Impressionable
Dislike of authority	Flighty ideas
Will avoid conventions	Haphazard temperament
Agile mind	Avoids aggression
Broad-minded	Versatile
Individual ideas	Prefers to learn by experience
Attractive personality	

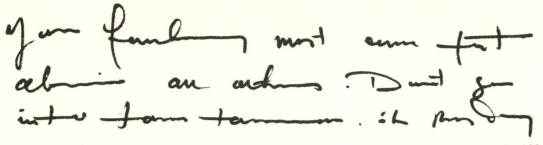

Fig 130
Thread inside a word

DOMINANT AND SECONDARY CONNECTIONS

There is often a dominant connection along with a secondary connecting form and you should note in which zone the dominant occurs – usually the middle zone of course (fig 131).

An equal mixture of angle, garland, arcade and the occasional thread, for example, would point to a writer who has no clear or firm inclination towards anything (fig 132). These people are considered capricious and are difficult to classify. There is disharmony with conflicting tendencies. In this kind of script also look for counter strokes, i.e. strokes contrary to the normal direction, such as terminal strokes turning leftwards (fig 133). Such a person will

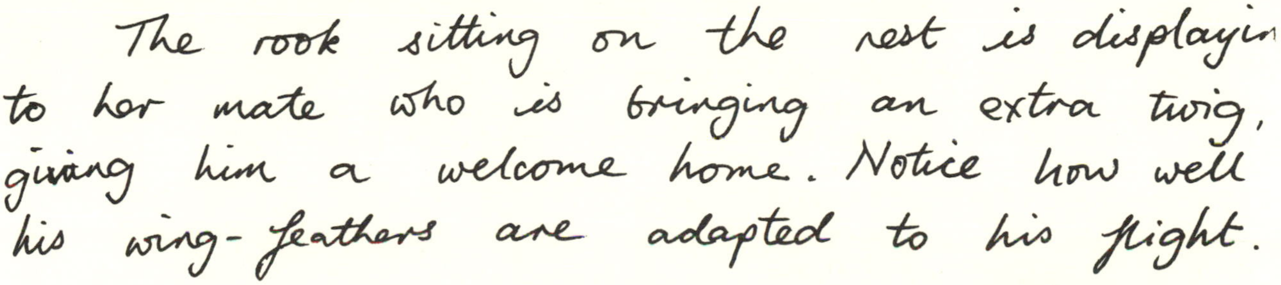

The rook sitting on the nest is displaying to her mate who is bringing an extra twig, giving him a welcome home. Notice how well his wing-feathers are adapted to his flight.

Fig 131
Arcade and angle
connection

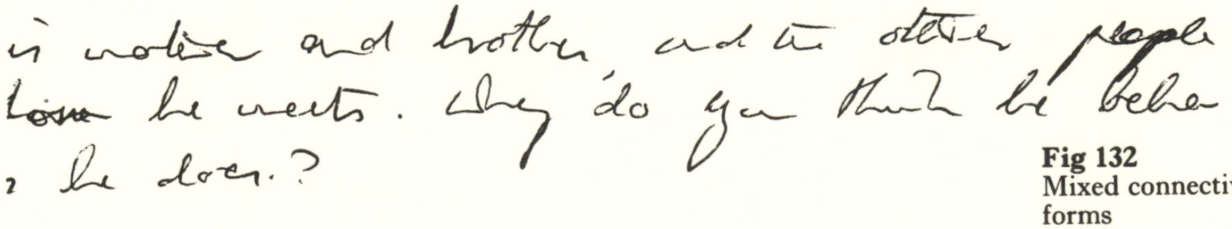

Fig 132
Mixed connective
forms

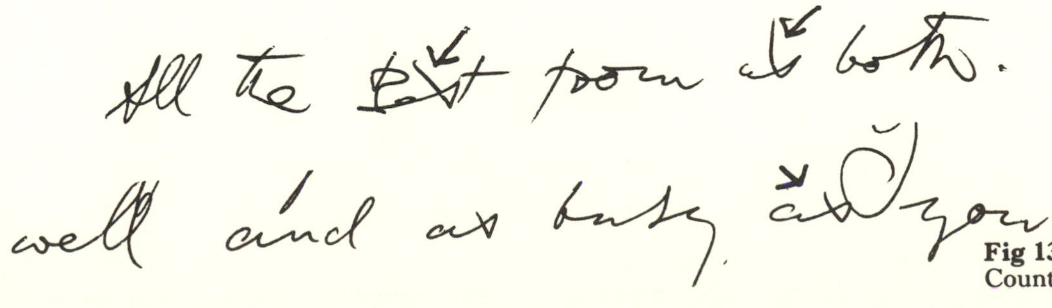

Fig 133
Counter strokes

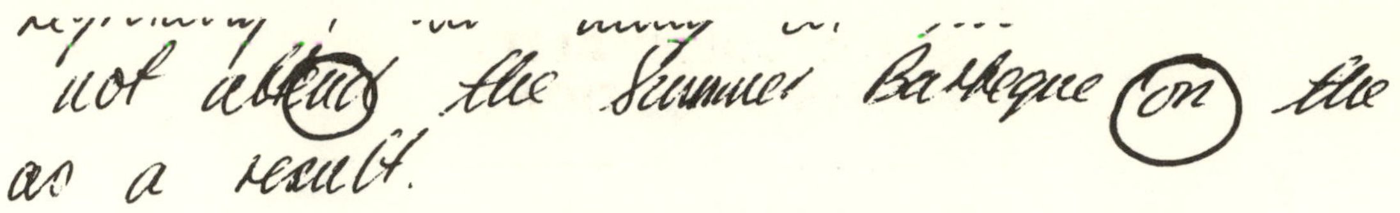

[handwritten sample] "not about" the Summer Barbeque (on) the
as a result.

Fig 134
Garland with arcade

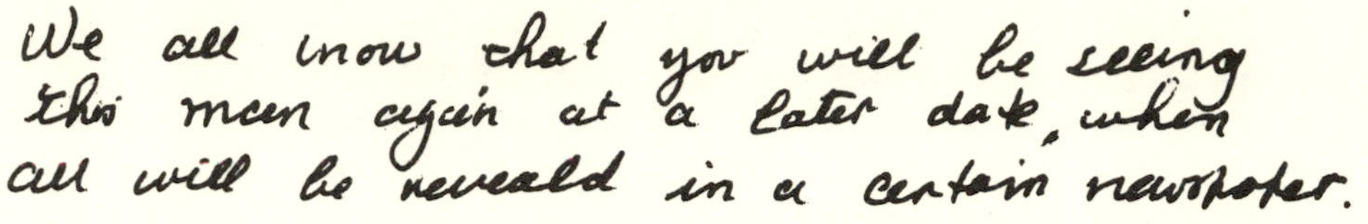

Fig 135
Slowly written arcades

[handwritten sample] We all know that you will be seeing this man again at a later date, when all will be reveald in a certain newspaper.

act contrary to conventional standards, often indicating a form of dishonesty or deceit.

A script can show a dominant arcade with a secondary garland (fig 134) – a positive combination which would indicate a balanced emotional response, neither too favourably disposed and lacking critical faculties, nor too reserved.

Very slowly written arcades (fig 135) in a graphologically mature hand, not affected by muscular trouble or any apparent incapacity, are not a good sign, since there is usually a deceptive element in the personality – if not downright dishonesty; but it must be emphasised that other factors will prove this point (see chapter 26).

WORKSHEET FOR CONNECTIONS

Connections	Interpretation
Degree of connection (connected or disconnected)	
Form of connection (copybook, garland – which? arcade – which? wavy line, thread – which?)	
dominant	
secondary	

FORM: ORIGINALITY AND CONNECTIONS

Chapter 6 Form of letters

Letter forms may be over-emphasised by flourishes and embellishments, or reduced to their basic forms to the point of neglect, with in-between variations. For a positive assessment, the script should be legible, original, natural and spontaneously written. These are the four main groupings.

1 ARTISTIC (fig 136)
Naturally intelligent, artistically talented writers could add some ornamentation to their script while still retaining a positive interpretation, because of the naturalness with which they form their letter styles.

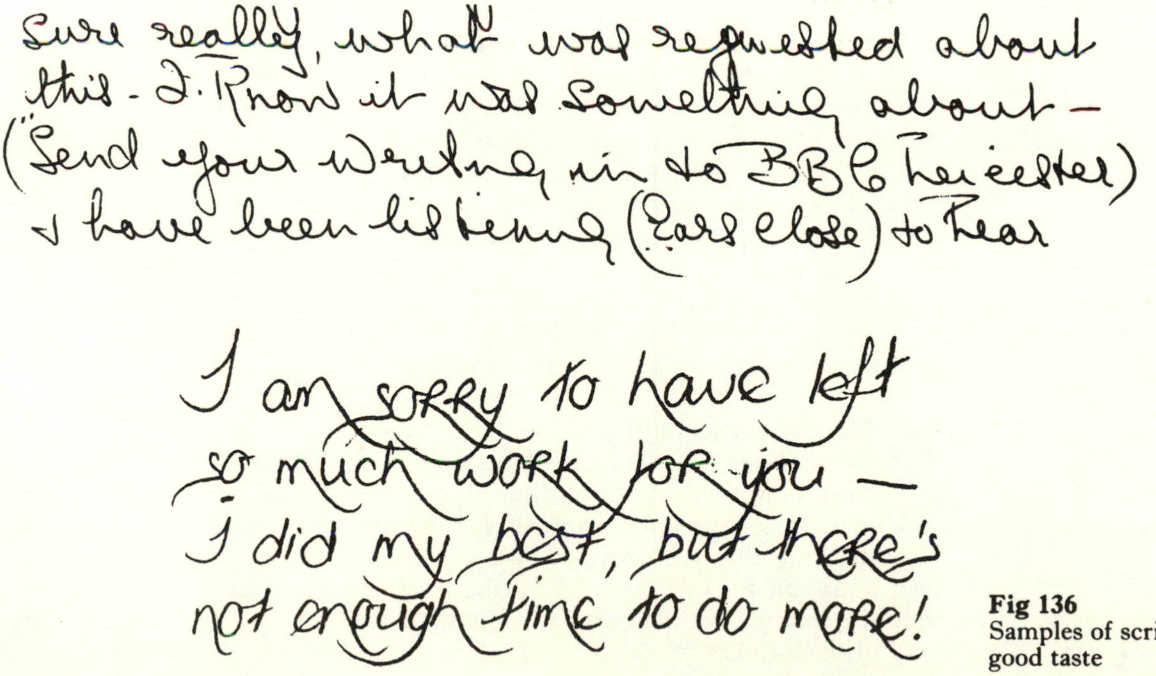
Sure really, what was requested about
this - I know it was something about -
(Send your writing in to BBC Leicester)
I have been listening (ears close) to hear
I am sorry to have left
so much work for you —
I did my best, but there's
not enough time to do more!

Fig 136
Samples of scripts of good taste

2 ARTIFICIAL (fig 137)

The vulgar, pretentious person, whose only intention is to create an artistic impression for which he has no talent, over-reacts and produces letters that offend and render the script false, looking artificial, ostentatious and illegible. Also, because the presentation is forced, the letters would be slowly written in a cumbersome fashion. This reveals to the graphologist a self-important person needing to compensate for an inferiority complex by presenting a false image which, after a time, becomes a way of life to deceive not only others, but himself.

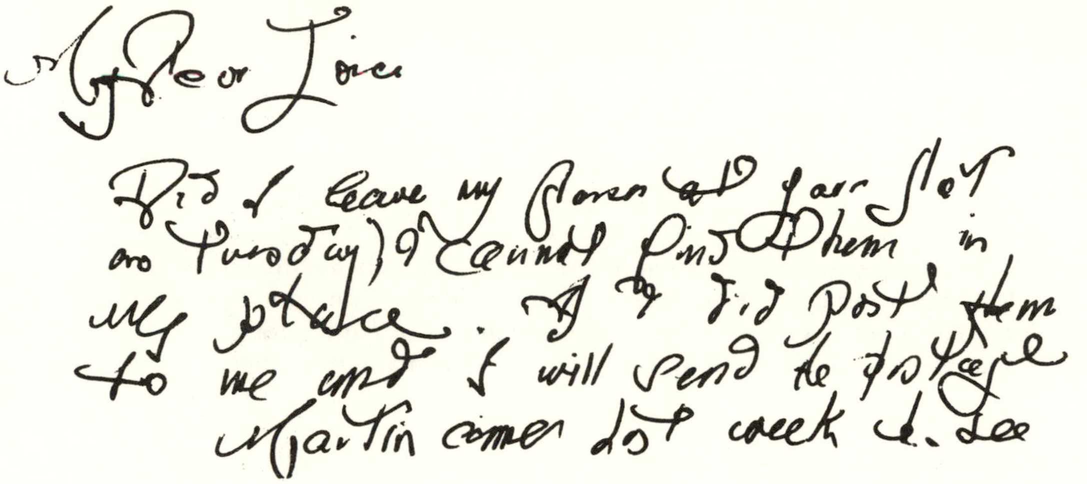

Fig 137
Script of bad or poor taste

3 SIMPLE (fig 138)

A simplified writing is defined as strokes reduced to the bare essentials whilst still retaining legibility. This form of writing is very seldom less than a high Form Level rating – a person used to writing, who has no time for fancy styles: not necessarily someone in a hurry but one with an active mind and aesthetic awareness. Their speech is also without ambiguous statements. They prefer friends who can keep up with their own intellectual pursuits and interests, and they have no time for fools.

Writers who cut out all they consider inessential from parts of letters to the point of *neglect* warrant a negative interpretation (fig 139). Such people cut corners and simplify anything they undertake to save time and effort. They would therefore be unreliable in any situation demanding concentration or minor details which they would find extremely tedious, and they would very quickly become bored and restless. These writers are, however, intelligent and mentally agile; this is combined with a lively vitality.

4 COPYBOOK (fig 140)

The average form of letters is the basic copybook. While it is correct in style, there is little individuality and therefore writers adhering to this form are lacking in imagination and originality. It is difficult to motivate such people into anything that requires out-of-the-ordinary concepts. However, these people are reliable in any situation where repetitive activity is necessary and they are content to remain within imposed restrictions, their minds requiring very little stimulus.

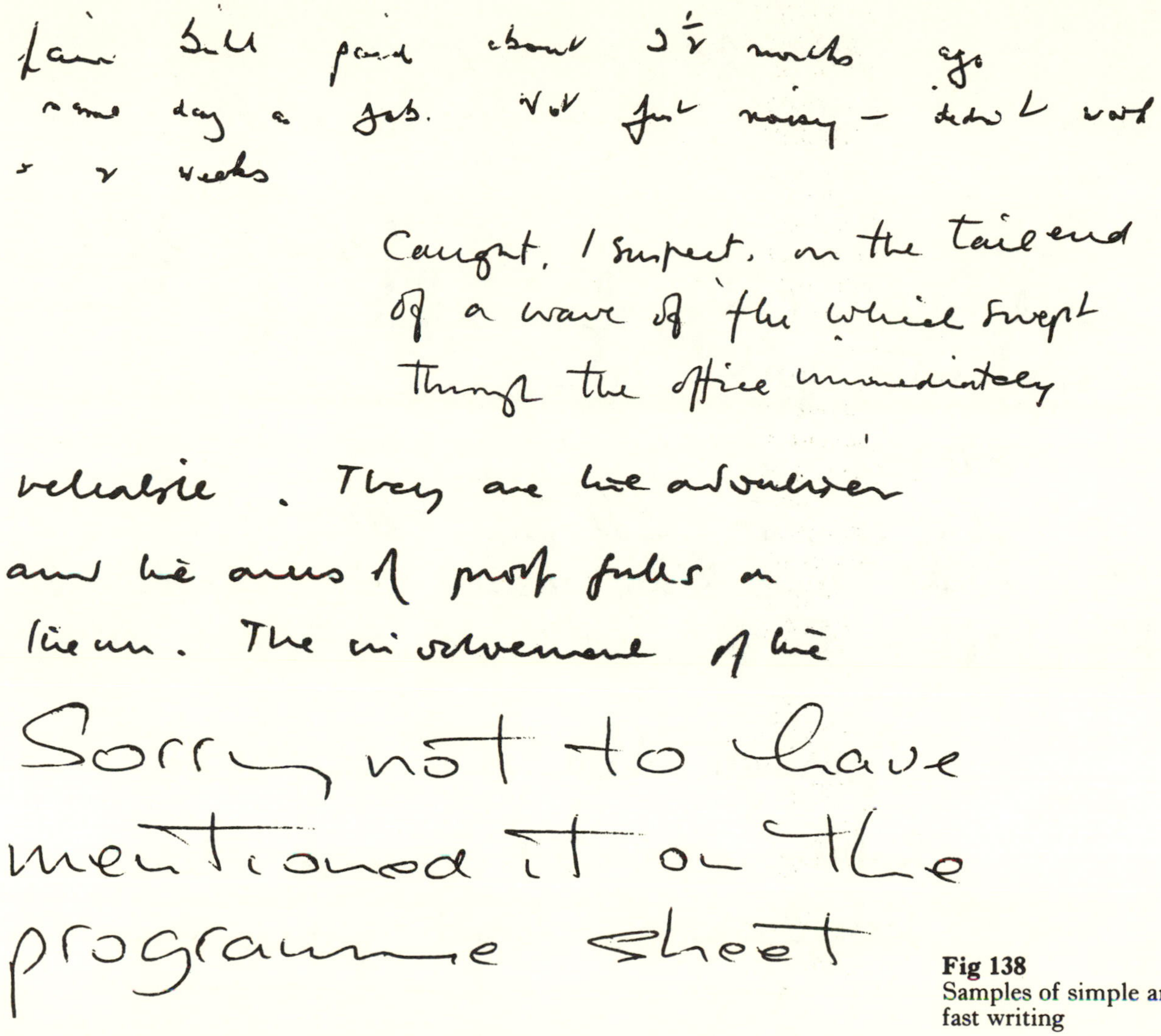

[handwritten sample, partially illegible]

Caught, I suspect, on the tail end
of a wave of flu which swept
through the office immediately

reliable. They are the advisers
and the onus of proof falls on
them. The involvement of the

Sorry not to have
mentioned it on the
programme sheet

Fig 138
Samples of simple and
fast writing

Simple form, with speed (fig 138 – see above)

Legible	*Illegible*
Clear judgement	Neglect
Mature attitude	Insincere
Intellectual faculties	Unreliable
Economical in time and effort	Inconsiderate
Ability to see the essentials	Ambiguous
Objective attitude	Tactless
Natural behaviour	Lack of principles
Mental agility	Slapdash attitude
Clear expression of opinion	Lack of precision
Good taste	
Purposeful sense of order	

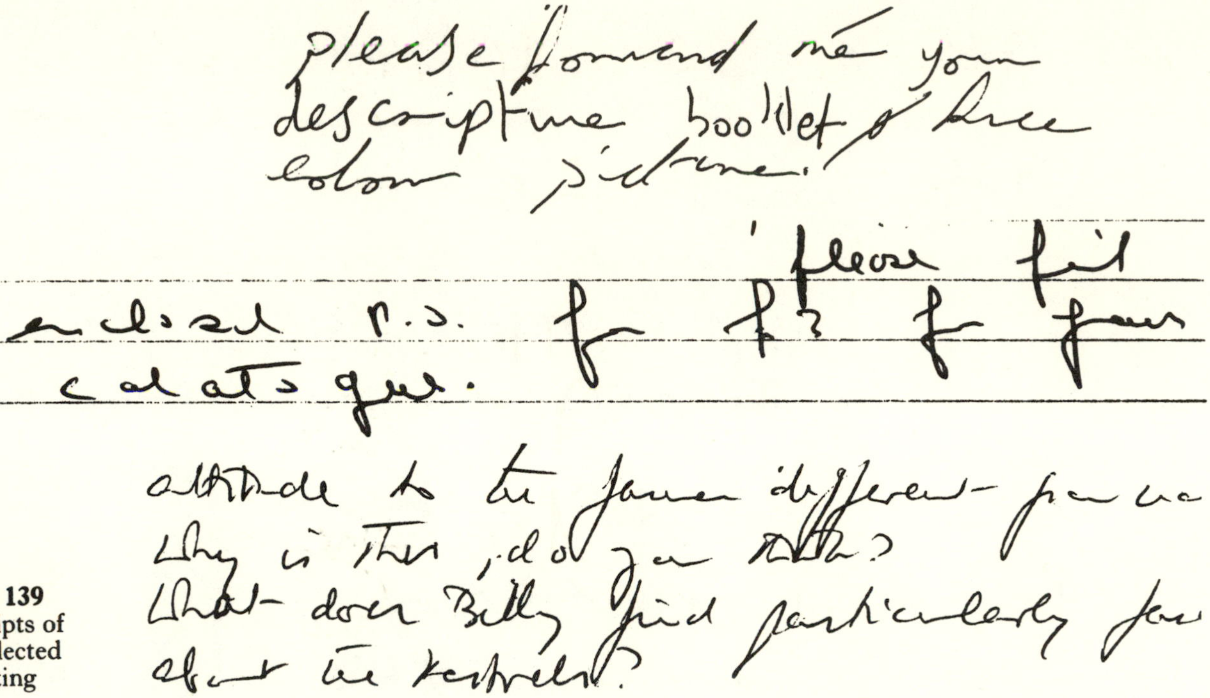

*please forward me your
description booklet of three
colour picture.*

*enclosed P.O. for £3 for your 'please fil
catalogue.*

Fig 139
Scripts of
neglected
writing

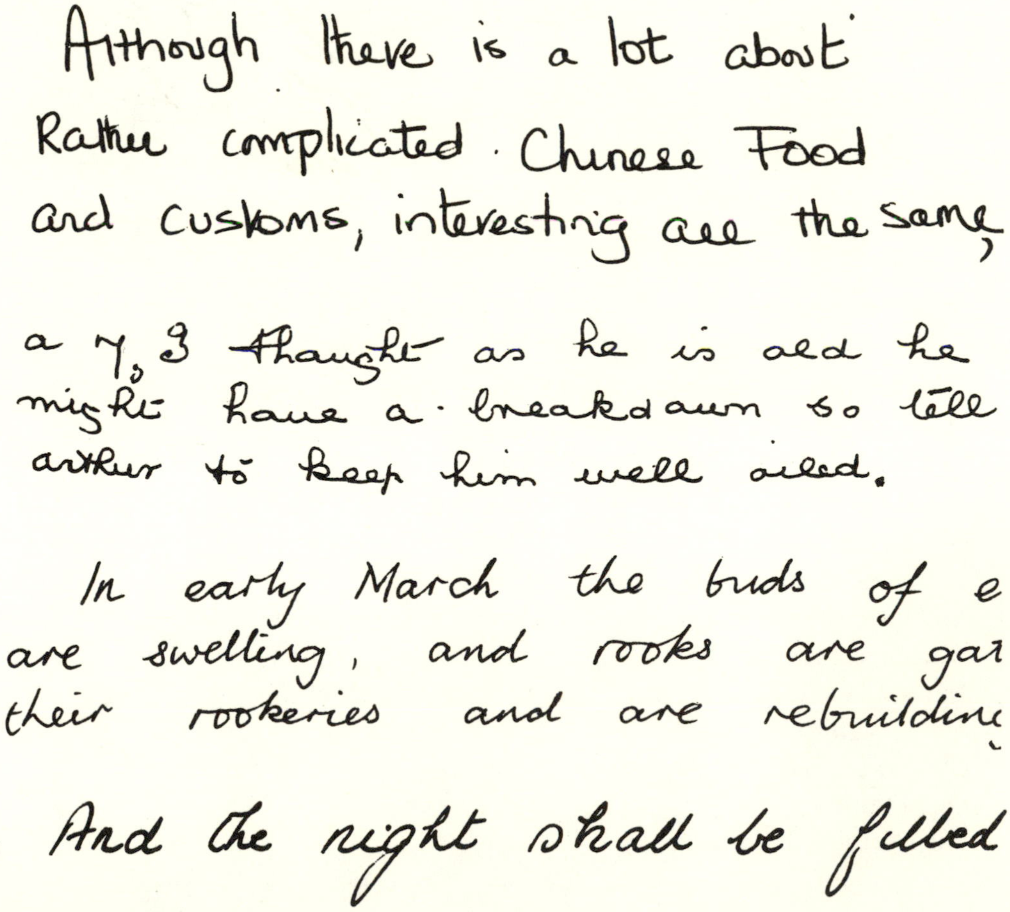

*attitude to the James different for me
Why is this, do you think?
What does Billy find particularly fun
about the festivals?*

*Although there is a lot about
Rather complicated. Chinese Food
and customs, interesting all the same,*

*a y, 3 thought as he is old he
might have a breakdown so tell
arthur to keep him well oiled.*

*In early March the buds of e
are swelling, and rooks are gar
their rookeries and are rebuilding*

Fig 140
Samples of copybook
style

And the night shall be filled

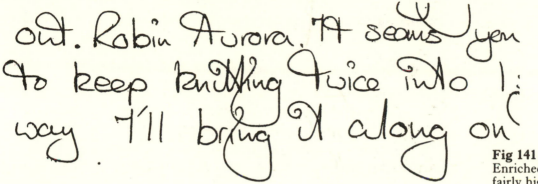

Fig 141
Enriched scripts, of
fairly high form level

Fig 142(i)
Script showing
negative ornamentation

Enriched, in a fairly high Form Level (fig 141)

    Clear and legible – good rhythm
    Creative
    Original ideas
    Artistic talent
    Flexibility to develop ideas
    Good sense of presentation
    Verbal expressiveness

Enriched in a low Form Level, poor rhythm (fig 142)

    Ceremonious attitude
    Pedantic views
    Loquacious and boring
    Lack of objective ideas
    Poor taste artistically

Fig 142(ii)
Script showing negative
ornamentation

**Ornamentation, with average speed, Form Level
and rhythm** (fig 143)

Vanity

Pompous and boastful

Conceited

Need to be accepted by others

Pretentious display of personality

Over-compensating for an inferiority complex
by using insincere methods to impress others.

Fig 143
Ostentatious script

WORKSHEET FOR FORM OF LETTERS

Form of letters	Interpretation
(Simple, copybook, artistic, artificial?)	
Other features	
(speed, rhythm etc)	
(You can fill these in later)	

FORM: ORIGINALITY AND CONNECTIONS

Chapter 7 | # Fullness and leanness

Fullness and leanness are concerned with the amount of inflation and exaggeration used to form the letter parts, or the absence of any open loops. We are therefore looking for the sideward movement rather than the vertical, as associated with size. Fullness and leanness are quite separate factors from width and narrowness.

FULLNESS (fig 144)

Fullness is found in letters that are more curved or rounded than the copybook model specifies. Again, the zones are important, indicating the dominant sphere of life in which the characteristics of fullness and leanness occur.

Genuine fullness is found in the middle zone which, for a positive indication, should balance the upper and lower zones, regardless of the size of writing (fig 145). Where roundness is found in the upper and lower zones only and there is a meagre middle zone (fig 146), *artificial fullness* is shown. The imagination which the fullness indicates in this case is unrealistic and is not being fully integrated into the total personality. Schizophrenia is one condition in which this could be encountered. However, in such a case there would probably be some mingling of upper and lower loops and lines, poor rhythm, ornamentation, abnormal underlining of words and the splitting of individual letters, leading to a bizarre-looking script (fig 147).

Here are some guidelines to help you.

Upper zone fullness	Upper zone exaggerated
Realistic imagination	Daydreamer
Constructive thought	Over-enthusiastic response
Creative mind	Fantasy thinking
	Projects which are unrealistic
	Lack of self-criticism
	Lack of concentration

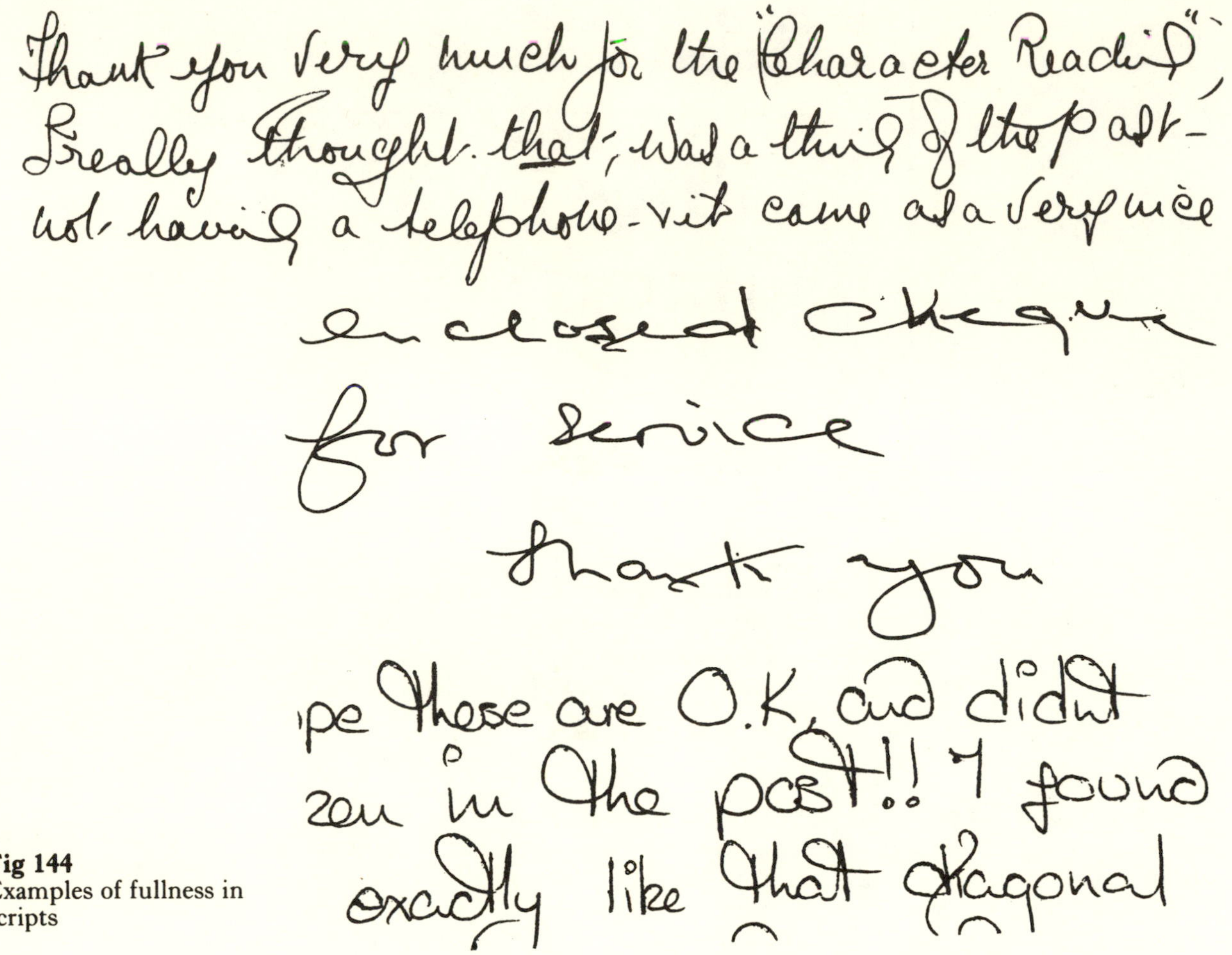

Thank you very much for the "Character Reading", I really thought that was a thing of the past — not having a telephone — it came as a very nice

enclosed cheque

for service

thank you

pe these are O.K, and didn't zen in the post!! I found exactly like that diagonal

Fig 144
Examples of fullness in scripts

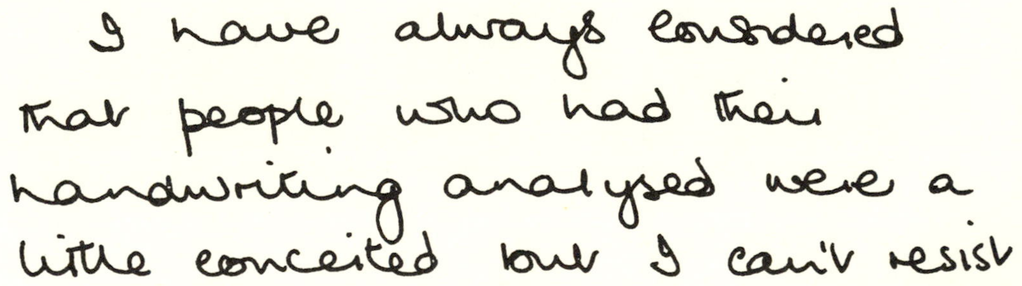

I have always considered that people who had their handwriting analysed were a little conceited but I can't resist

Fig 145
Middle zone fullness

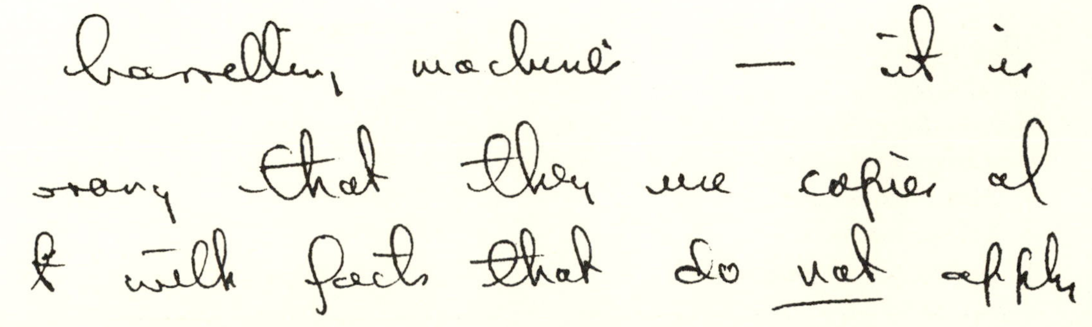

barely machine — it is many that they are copied at

Fig 146
Upper zone fullness

& with facts that do not apply

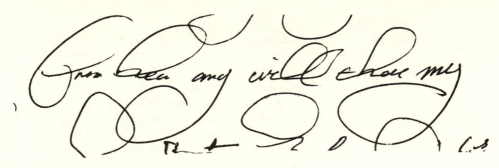

Fig 147
Examples of scripts showing artificial fullness, full upper and lower zones with meagre middle zones

Middle zone fullness	**Middle zone exaggerated**
Strong emotional response	Needs special attention
Individualist	Lacks clear reasoning
Genial temperament (if regular)	Turns everyday life into daydreams
Warm-hearted	Emotional cravings
Full participation in life	
Realistic routine behaviour	
Lower zone fullness	**Lower zone exaggerated**
Sensual qualities (pastose strokes)	Erotic fantasy
Sexually active (if heavy/medium pressure)	Unrealistic desires
Money-conscious	Unrealistic materialistic desires
Strong instincts	
Strong sexual imagination	

LEANNESS (fig 148)

Leanness is indicated by the letters being less rounded than the copybook model. The lean writer is a rational thinker, clear-sighted, with a strong critical sense. Such people distrust imagination and need facts to be clear-cut and objective. Where a full writer and a lean writer are sharing their lives together, there can be conflicting tendencies in the area of love and affection: the full writer is usually overt in romantic situations, but the lean writer is concerned with showing a realistic attitude and is therefore often reluctant to share his feelings. They are often described as 'cold and lacking in humour'.

Lower zone leanness

Positive traits
Realistic instincts
Financial acumen
Business-minded attitude, which overrides sexual feelings (this need not be a negative trait if man and wife, and of the same mind over which is the more important, i.e. business)

Negative traits with weak pressure
Sexually indifferent
Devoid of sensuality
Lack of sexual imagination
Low physical drive
Anxiety and guilt feelings

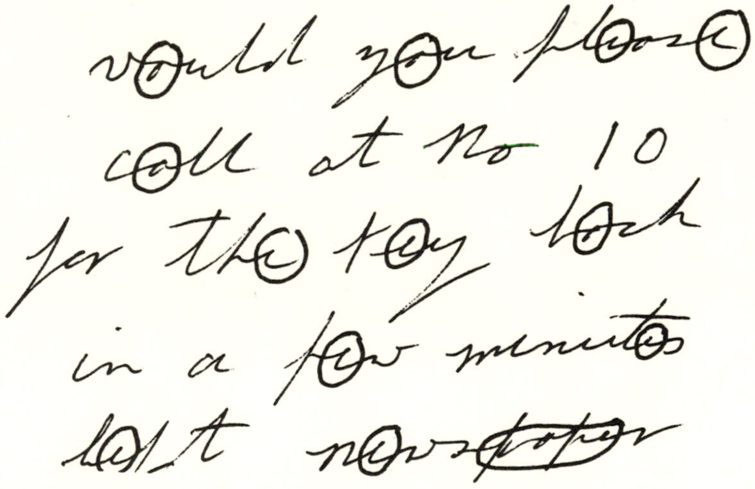

Fig 148
Leanness

WORKSHEET FOR FULLNESS AND LEANNESS

Fullness/leanness	Interpretation
Upper zone	
Middle zone	
Lower zone	

FORM: ORIGINALITY AND CONNECTIONS

Chapter 8 Width and narrowness in small letters

The width indicates the writer's degree of imagination in relation to his introvert or extrovert nature – as revealed by the slant. Therefore slant and width are interrelated. To measure the width of the small letters we measure the width in relation to the downstrokes. A letter is normal when it is as wide as it is high (fig 149), the middle zone being the part to measure for the dominant – wide, narrow or mixed – restriction, freedom, or the two combined.

WIDE SCRIPTS

A wide script in a leftward slant points to a socially inhibited person (leftward slant) who inwardly desires to express his freedom-seeking personality (wide script) – see fig 150. A socially motivated writer (rightward slant) with a narrow script (fig 151) is basically extroverted but also very cautious and wary (narrow script).

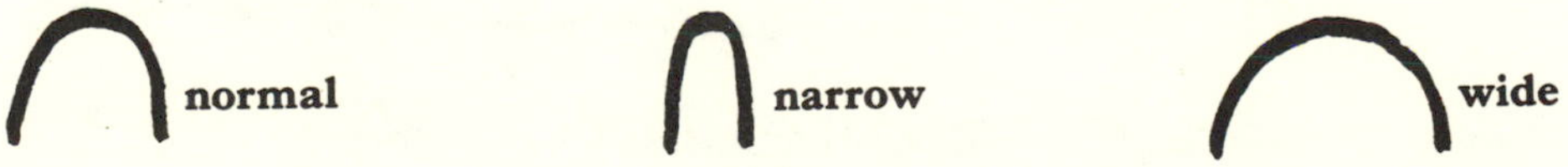
normal
narrow
wide

Fig 149
Normal width, small letters as wide as they are high

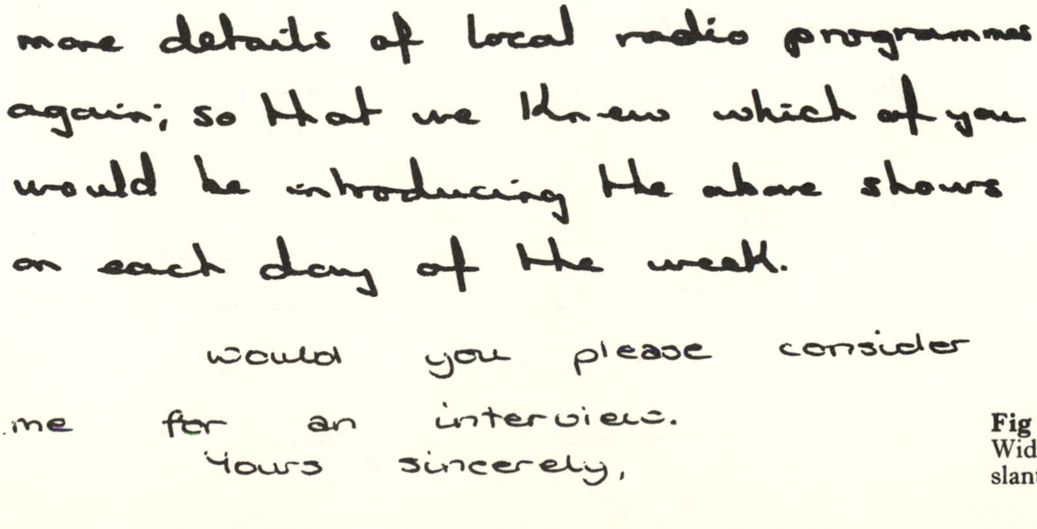
more details of local radio programmes
again, so that we knew which of you
would be introducing the above shows
on each day of the week.
would you please consider
me for an interview.
Yours sincerely,

Fig 150
Wide scripts – leftward slant

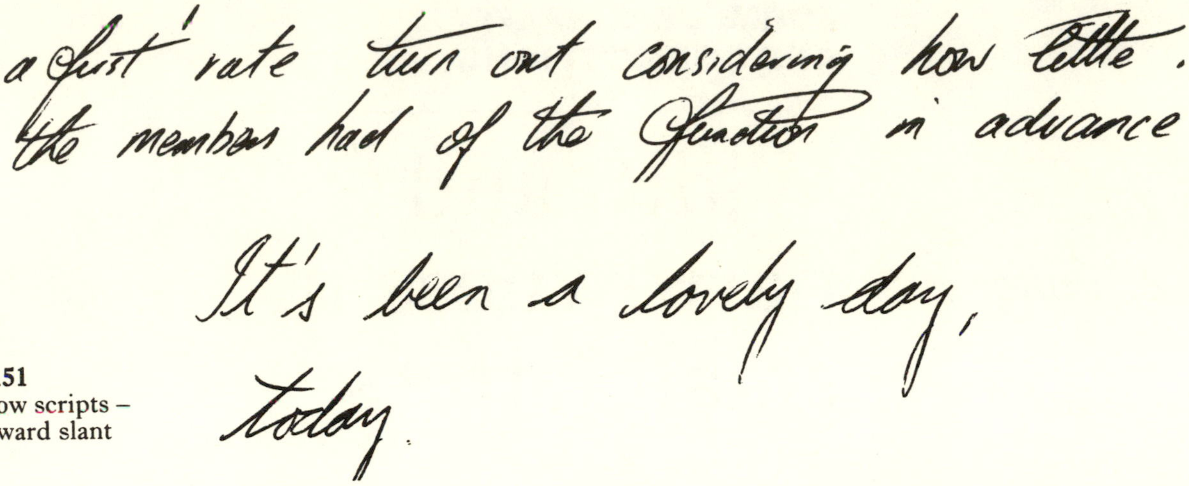

a first rate turn out considering how little.
the members had of the function in advance

It's been a lovely day,

today.

Fig 151
Narrow scripts –
rightward slant

Wide script with good pressure and rightward slant (fig 152)

Positive traits	*Negative traits*
Active ambition	Lack of control
Drive	Lack of reserve
Frankness	Lack of discipline
Sociable	Tactless
Spontaneous	Reckless
Generous	Impulsive
Persistent	Inconsiderate

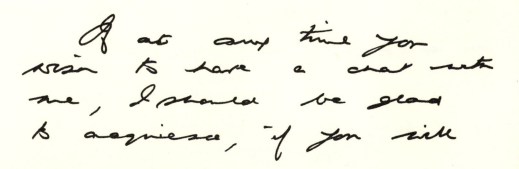

Fig 152
Wide scripts with good
pressure and rightward
slant

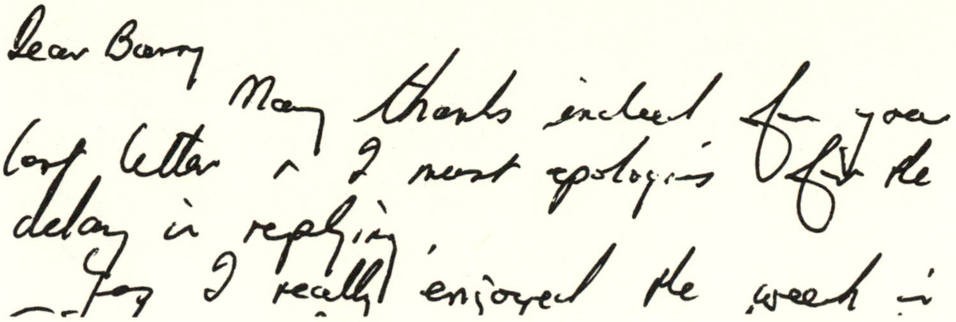

Fig 153
Script with heavy lower loops and rightward slant

With heavy lower loops and rightward slant (fig 153)
        Sensual and athletic

With light lower loops and rightward slant (fig 154)
        Realistic
        Business-minded
        Materialistic

Without pressure (fig 155)

Positive traits	*Negative traits*
Sympathetic	Careless
Imaginative	Impatient
Warm-hearted	Superficial
Aesthetic awareness	Hasty
Obliging	Insincere
Amenable	Lack of affection

Extreme width

Positive traits (fig 156)	*Negative traits*
Expansive, expressive imagination	Unable to control feelings
Friendly disposition	Weak discipline
Purposeful drive	Hysteria
Generous	Self-interest
	Vain
	Could take advantage of others' weaknesses
	Lacks concentration
	Little resistance – easily led
	Extravagant

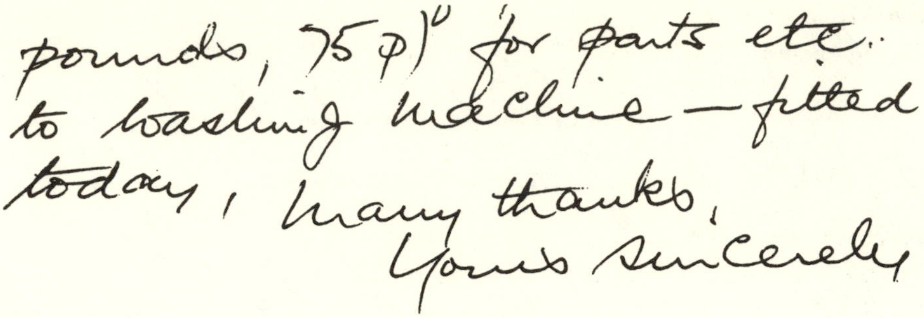

*pounds, 75p)" for parts etc.
to washing machine — fitted
today, many thanks,
Yours sincerely*

Fig 154
With light lower loops
and rightward slant

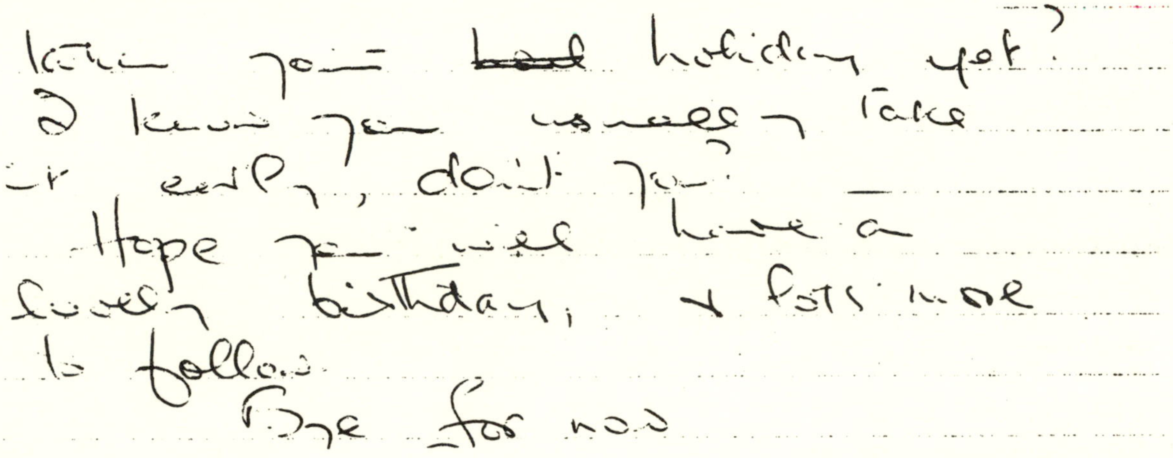

*Have you had holiday yet?
I know you usually take
it early, don't you? —
Hope you will have a
lovely birthday, + lots more
to follow.
Bye for now*

Fig 155
Without pressure and
wide middle zone

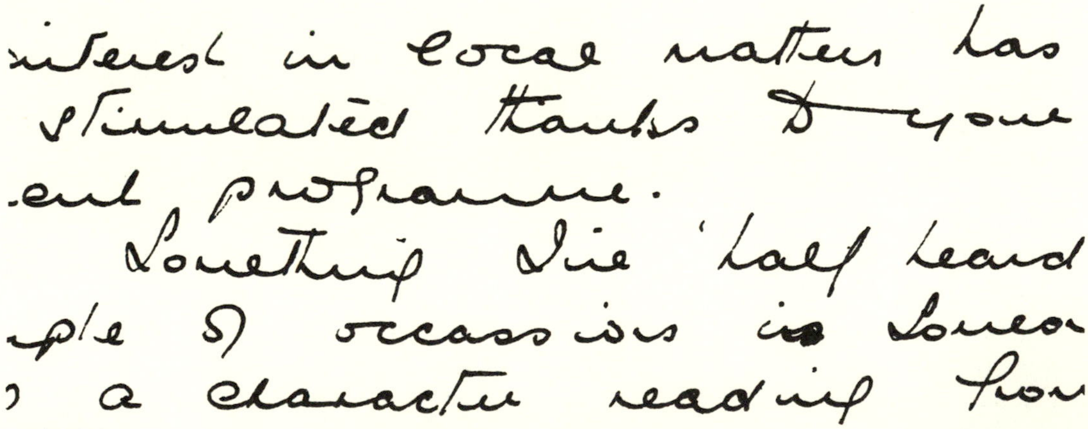

*interest in local matters has
stimulated thanks to your
evl programme.
Something like 'half heard
ple of occassions is lower
, a character reading from*

Fig 156
Script showing extreme
width – with positive
traits

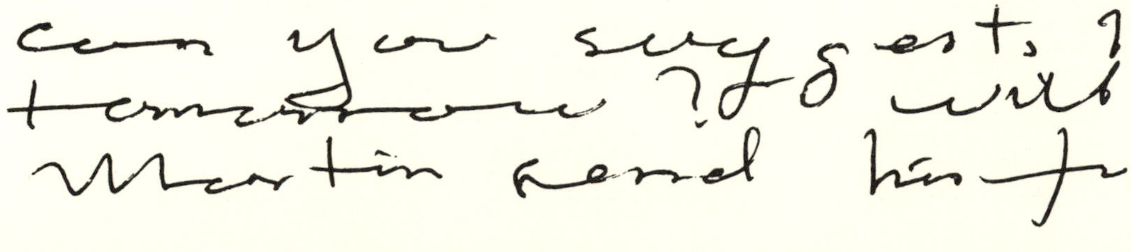

*can you suggest, ?
tomorrow ?? I will
Martin send his f*

Fig 157
Extreme width –
negative traits

NARROW SCRIPTS

Narrowness inhibits the flow of movement. It can therefore be an impediment to clear expression, causing illegibility. The narrower the script, the more the introversion, particularly in a leftward slant writing.

Narrowness

Positive traits	*Negative traits*
Dependable	Distrust
Realistic	Repressed feelings
Practical	Greed
Reserved	Argumentative
Tactful	Spiteful

WORKSHEET FOR WIDTH/NARROWNESS – SMALL LETTERS

Width/narrowness in middle zone	Interpretation
Wide or narrow	
Other features	

FORM: ORIGINALITY AND CONNECTIONS

Chapter 9 Horizontal tension

Closely linked to connection is horizontal tension – the degree to which there is a continuous rightward progressive movement towards the right-hand margin unbroken by disconnected letters and leftward strokes (fig 158 shows two samples). This movement can be achieved with weak pressure; indeed heavy pressure, even in a rightward slant, can impede the natural flow. With a leftwards slant, if is not too pronounced the continuity can still be maintained adequately.

The horizontal tension shows us how strongly a writer pursues his goals; how determined he is to achieve his ambitions in life. A good movement is associated with a logical thought procedure: there will be no unnecessary breaks in the continuity, each stroke ending rightwards to form the next letter or word. Even the words can be connected together. See fig 159 for two samples of extreme connection – probably ambitious career people, although in these particular cases there could be strain and tension also present.

(i)

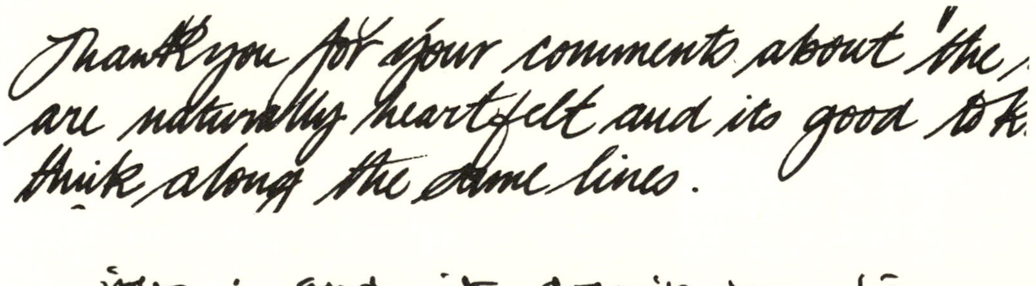

(ii)

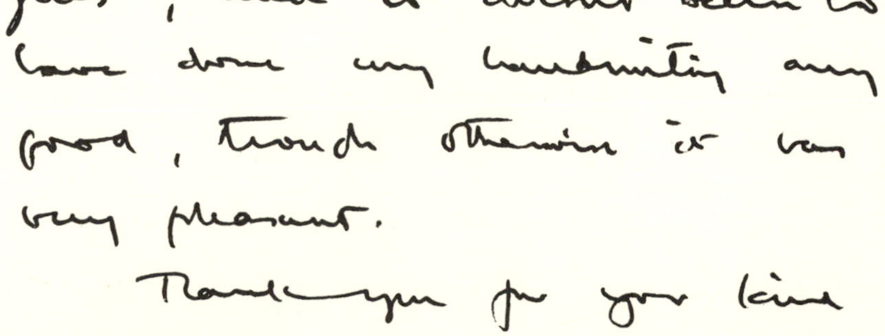

Fig 158
Strong horizontal tension in **(i)** rightward slant and **(ii)** leftward slant

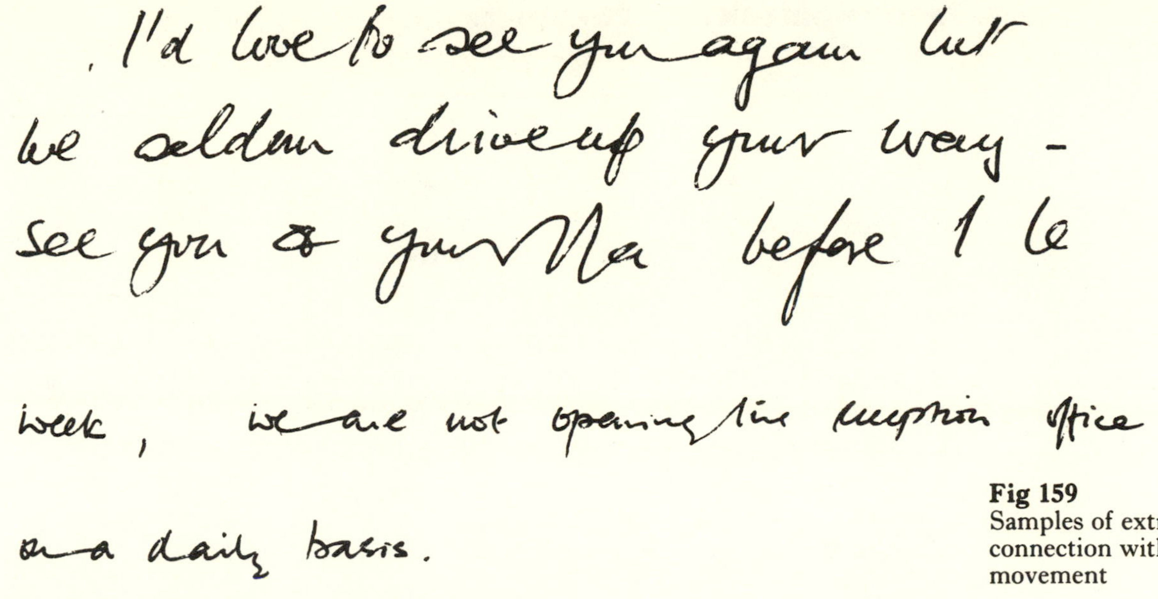

I'd love to see you again but we seldom drive up your way – see you or your Ma before I be week, we are not opening the reception office on a daily basis.

Fig 159
Samples of extreme
connection with strong
movement

GOOD HORIZONTAL TENSION (fig 160)
(Lively rhythm, simplified letter forms and an evenly distributed pressure throughout the script)

Adaptability and perseverance
Deals efficiently with obstacles
Logical
Tends to achieve goals

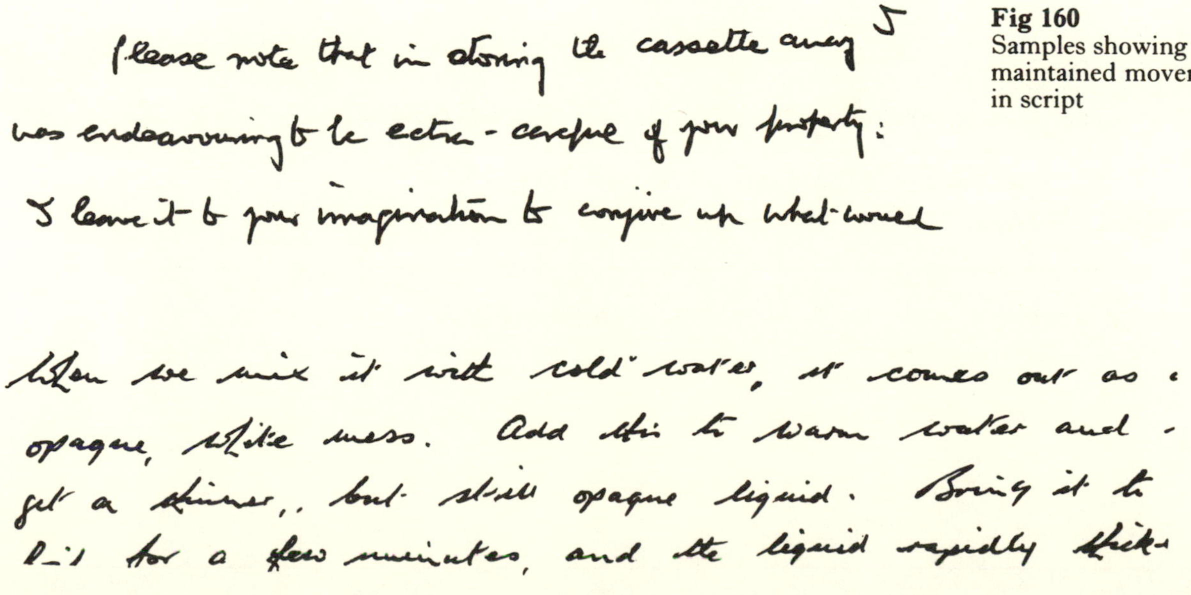

Please note that in storing the cassette away was endeavouring to be extra-careful of your property: I leave it to your imagination to conjure up what would

Fig 160
Samples showing well
maintained movement
in script

When we mix it with cold water, it comes out as a opaque, white mess. Add this to warm water and get a thinner, but still opaque liquid. Bring it to b-1 for a few minutes, and the liquid rapidly thick-

POOR HORIZONTAL TENSION (fig 161)
(Heavy pressure, complex letter forms, leftward tendencies)

> Uses unnecessary energy and
> effort in trying to reach goals
> Shortage of stamina
> Has to rest between projects (burnout)

Any reader wishing to delve further into horizontal tension should read 'Guiding Image' in Eric Singer's book, *Personality in Handwriting* – also 'The Mobile Axis' in *Personality in Handwriting* by Alfred Mendel. (See bibliography.)

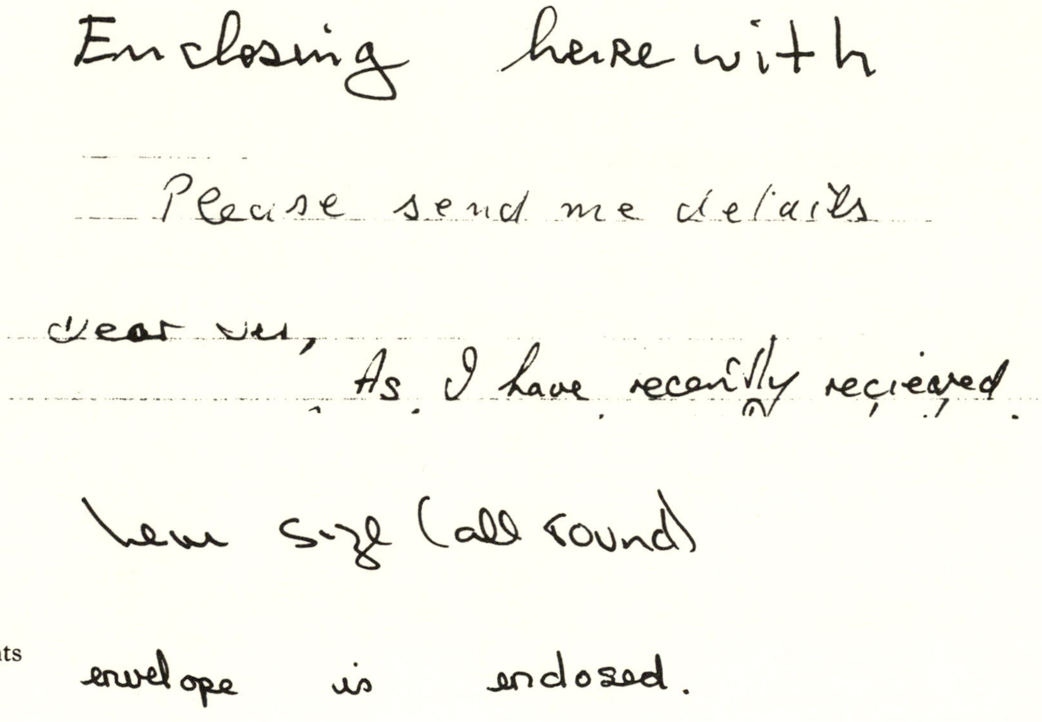

Enclosing herewith

Please send me details

dear sir,

As I have recently recieved

hem size (all round)

Fig 161
Samples of poorly maintained movements in various scripts

envelope is enclosed.

WORKSHEET FOR HORIZONTAL TENSION

Horizontal tension	Interpretation
Good/Poor	

Chapter 10 | Pressure

Pressure in handwriting is a natural expression of the writer's vital impulse of energy.

Pressure is produced by the fingers pressing the point of the writing instrument into the surface of the paper, using an interplay of muscular contraction and release – the flexor muscles moving the pen downwards and the extensor muscles producing the upstroke. Normally more pressure is exerted on the downstroke, resulting in a handwriting with heavier downstrokes (fig 162). This 'shading', as it is called, is achieved by good control over the nervous impulses along with a vital energy potential and executive drive.

The tendency to write with heavy pressure (fig 163) is not an indicator of sheer muscular power. Often people who are not accustomed to writing produce a forceful pressure through deliberation in forming the letters.

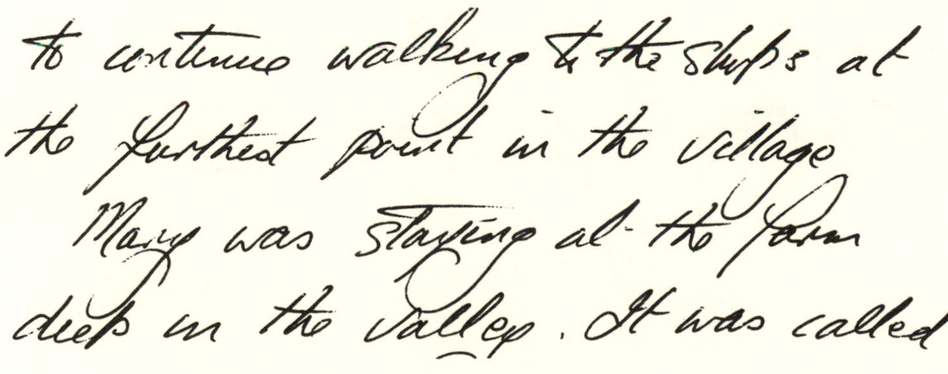

Fig 162
Shaded pressure, the upstrokes being the lighter

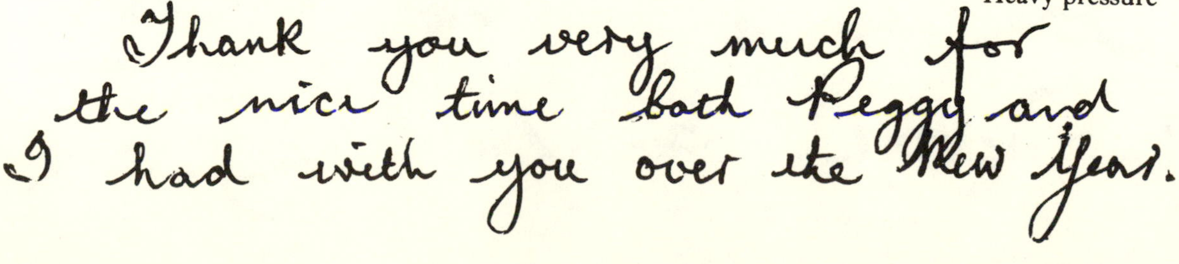

Fig 163
Heavy pressure

*you weren't interested, you can learn, even when you
And you can have a night off if you're sure
- not for me!' I've lost patience with flower as
for instance.*

*and your very kind invitation to join 'M
which regrettably I shall have to decline,
in desperation; but I do hope you have a
successful time.*

Fig 164
Samples of light
pressure

Dear Sir,

please forward your colour cai

There are those sensitive writers who produce a very light pressure, and, to do so, prefer a fine point or nib (fig 164). These writers are usually found among the highly intellectual and less physically intense people.

The heavy pressure writer often prefers a wider nib, thicker ballpoint or even a felt tip pen which gives a dense line (fig 165). However, this should not be taken for granted. A light pressure will also produce a thick line with a

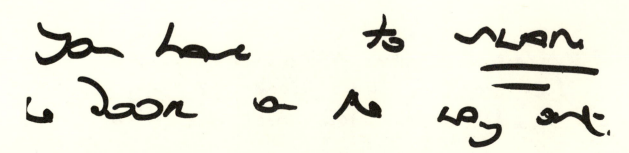

Fig 165
Samples of scripts
using a felt tip pen –
not necessarily heavy
pressure

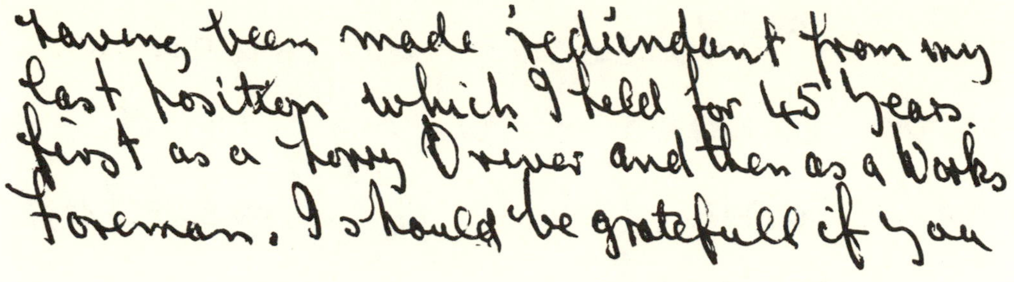

Having been made redundant from my last position which I held for 45 years, first as a lorry Driver and then as a Works foreman. I should be gratefull if you

Fig 166
Cumbersome, heavy pressure strokes

felt tip pen. Most adult writers will opt for the pen which will give them the type of stroke they consider fits their personality and will therefore always use this personal pen for important letters or signature. A pencil will also show varying shades of pressure dependent upon the grade used from very hard through to very soft, used by artists to give a thick, black line.

We are all subject to the pressures of living. We therefore produce not only a physical pressure but also a psychological one. A man with 'a heavy heart', as the saying goes, will write with a slow tempo which in time causes inhibition and an increase in finger pressure resulting in solid, cumbersome strokes (fig 166). Until an experienced eye is developed to detect a pressure rating, an effective method for the graphology student is to turn the paper over and run a finger over the indentations. Obviously this will not work with a photocopy or printed page.

After determining the grade of pressure – whether heavy, medium, or light – examine other factors of the script such as initial and end strokes which can show a varying pressure (fig 167), and note in which zone the dominant occurs.

The experienced graphologist is also watchful for uneven and wavering pressure (fig 168) – not a good sign as it indicates an emotional imbalance. The writer is unsure of himself and has an indecisive nature resulting from a possible inferiority complex; or it can show trapped sexual energy, which, being denied an outlet, results in irregularity in lower zone pressure (frustration). These writers can be hostile and aggressive.

LIGHT PRESSURE
Many cultured people of an introvert nature find their talents point to scientific work. They have very light, small, carefully written handwriting which is regular and well spaced.

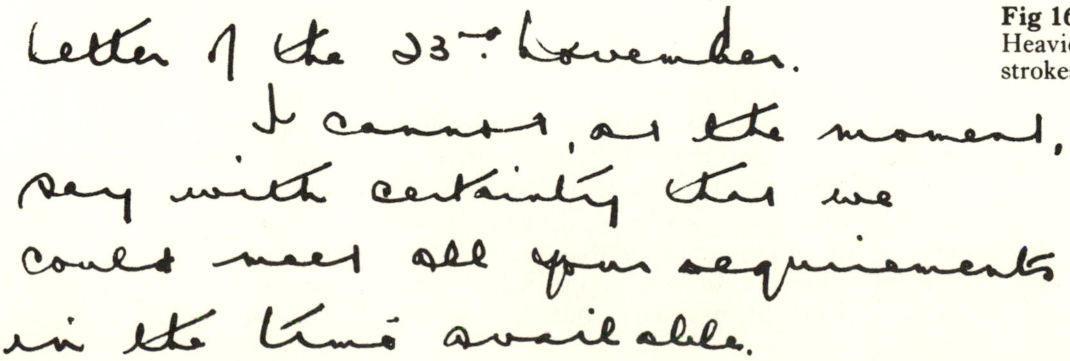

Letter of the 23rd November.
I cannot, at the moment, say with certainty that we could meet all your requirements in the time available.

Fig 167
Heavier pressure end strokes

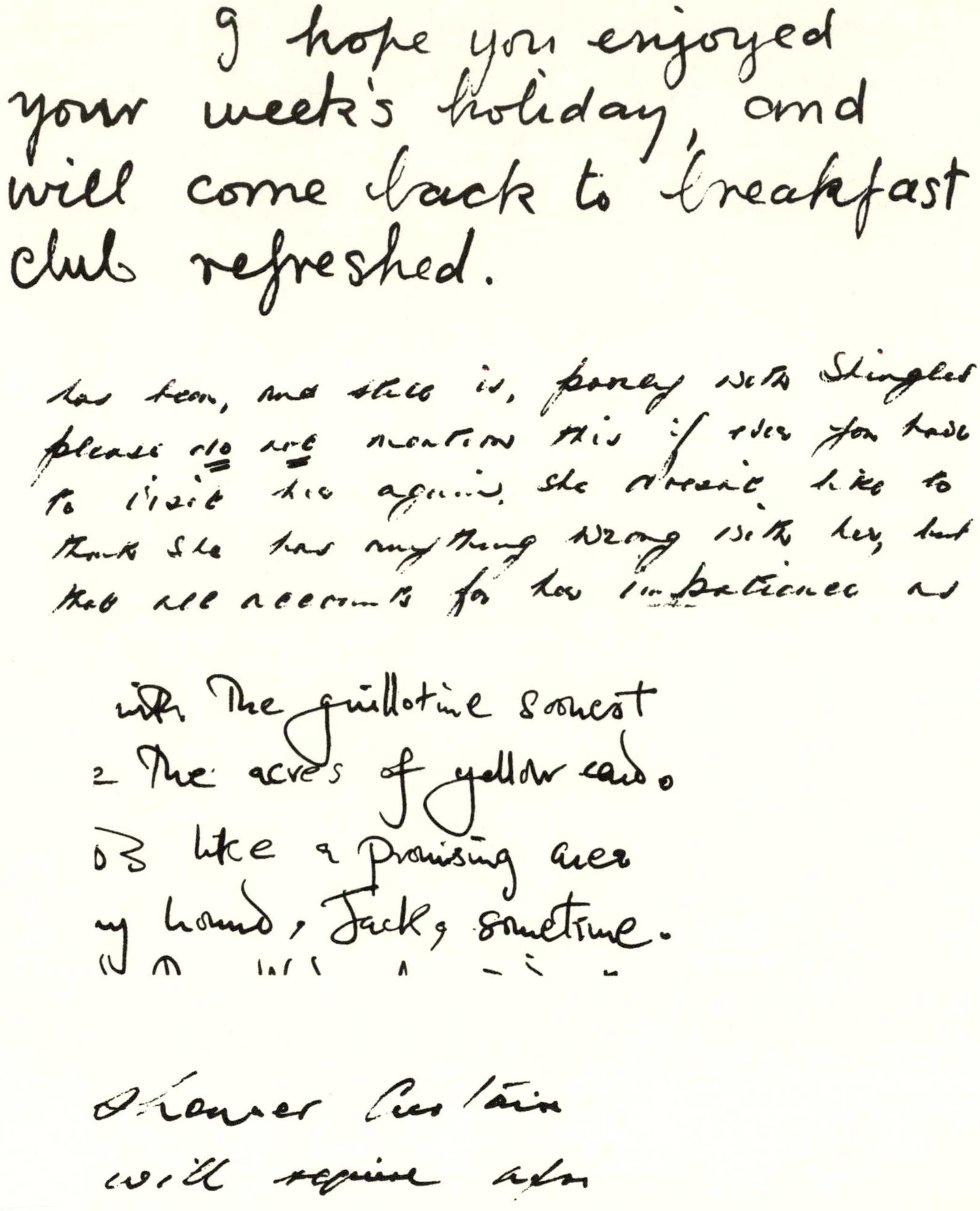

I hope you enjoyed your week's holiday, and will come back to breakfast club refreshed.

has been, and still is, poorly with Shingles please do not mention this if ever you have to visit her again, she doesn't like to think she has anything wrong with her, but that all accounts for her impatience as

with the guillotine soonest
2 The acres of yellow card.
03 like a promising area
my hound, Jack, sometime.

Fig 168
Scripts showing an uneven pressure pattern

This is a very positive indication that their psychic energy is fully dispersed into their work. There will probably be original forms of letter connection, indicating these writers' sensitive individuality with no desire for outward show or self-advertising (fig 169). Light pressure is associated with a feminine nature regardless of the actual sex of the writer, whose response is centred upon intellectual rather than physical activity. Such people show mental endurance, determination, self-control and reliability in the course of their work and life in general, but are easily hurt emotionally and for a longer time.

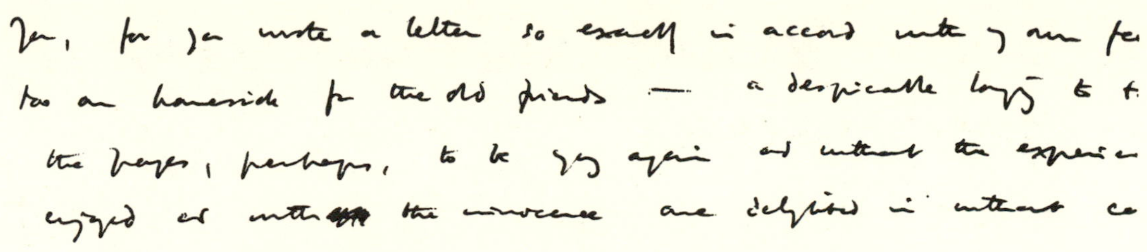

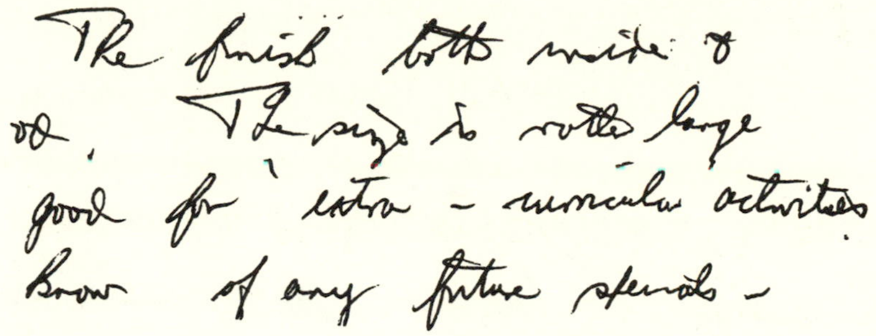

[handwritten text sample]

[handwritten text sample]

Fig 169
Light pressure and originality

Light pressure

Positive traits	*Negative traits*
Alert	Timid
Non-violent	Weak personality
Tender	Low energy level
Adaptable	Lack of enthusiasm
Modest	Lack of resistance to pressure
Idealistic aspirations	Lack of initiative
Attention to detail	Pettiness
	Capable of sarcasm

MEDIUM PRESSURE

Medium pressure is the average force that will apply to most scripts showing a reasonable amount of emotional control. It will not have the revealing features of either heavy or weak pressure.

Medium pressure

Even, medium to heavy pressure in a regular script (fig 170)

Warmth
Positively used energy and vitality
Endurance under stress
Determination to succeed without undue force
Adaptable
Strong activity level
Strong level of vitality maintained

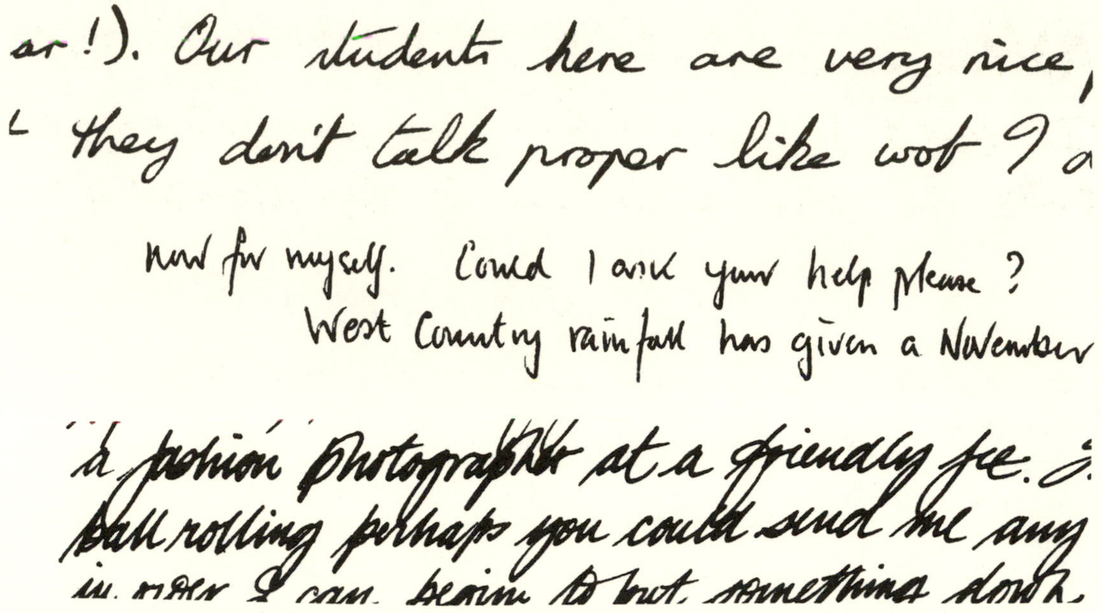

ar !). Our students here are very nice,
they don't talk proper like wot I a

now for myself. Could I ask your help please ?
West Country rainfall has given a November

'a fashion photographer at a friendly fee. i
ball rolling perhaps you could send me any
in order I can begin to but something down

Fig 170
Even, medium to heavy
pressure pattern in
regular scripts

HEAVY PRESSURE

What concerns the graphologist here is a general, even heavy pressure hand-writing. These writers are motivated by physical energy which needs to be spent in active pursuits and work involving energy output. It is a masculine representation whichever sex is involved. This does not imply any form of deviation sexually.

Heavy pressure

Heavy pressure	*Very heavy pressure*
Strong sexual development	Clumsy
Fighting spirit	Obstinate
High visual imagination	Temperamental
Love of strong colours	Aggressive
Strong initiative	Impulsive
Physical energy	Possessive
	Inhibited
	Frustrated
	Domineering attitude
	Not readily adaptable
	Could overstretch capacity

Very heavy pressure with filled in loops and
an overall smudgy appearance (fig 171)
Obscene imagination and sexual perversion, featuring brutality and violence – also dangerous if combined with heavy, blunt t-bars.

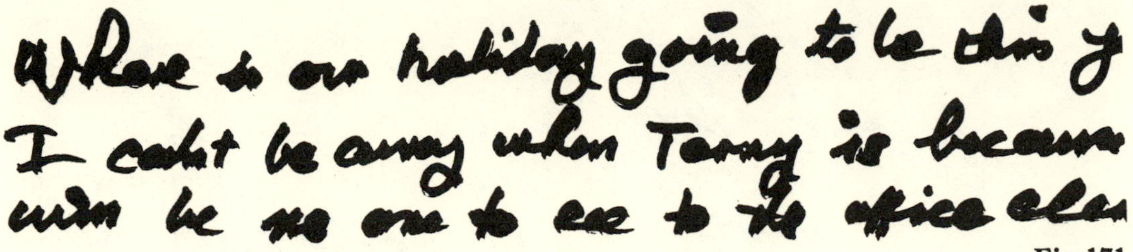

Fig 171
Heavy pressure, with
filled in loops

> *Heavy pressure with large and heavier capitals* (fig 172)
> Very possessive over possessions
> Self-controlled preoccupation
> Will get his own way by force, to prove his powerful pride of
> achievement, and will not allow obstacles to obstruct his path.

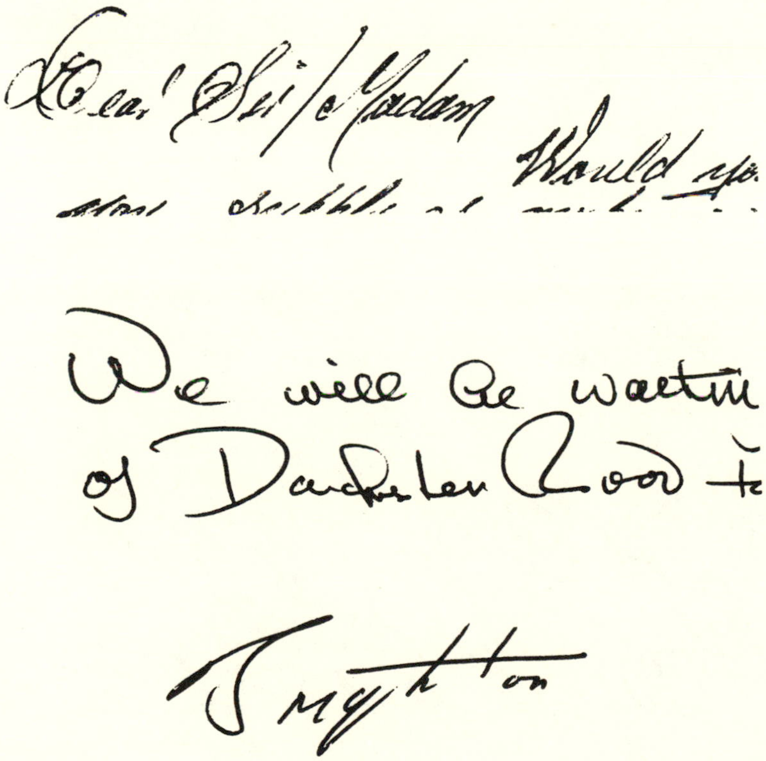

Fig 172
Samples of writing with
heavy pressure, with
dominant capitals

VARIABLE PRESSURE (fig 173)
Heavy pressure can be found at the beginning or end of a word or in capitals
only. It can also be found in spasmodic bursts throughout the script or in
only one zone.

and 17th Dec but one d
isn't. We would prefer to
early as possible. If
by booked for the period
2 would still be happy;

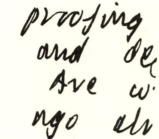

Fig 173
Scripts showing
spasmodic pressure
pattern

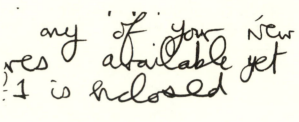

The garden center will sell
all the slats you are likely
to use in your pool.

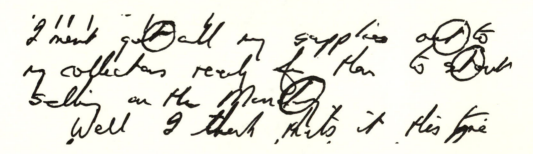

Fig 174
Samples showing
sudden pressure on
occasional strokes

Variable pressure

Sudden pressure on occasional strokes (fig 174)

> Possible violent nature
>
> Little control

Sudden loss of pressure in heavy pressure script (fig 175)

> A lapse of confidence
>
> Insecure feelings

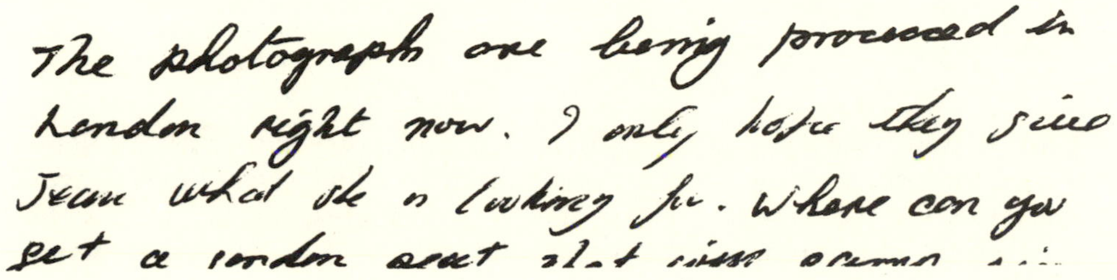

Fig 175
Sudden loss of pressure

WORKSHEET FOR PRESSURE

Pressure	Interpretation
(Light, medium, heavy or variable?)	
(Very heavy/light)	
(If variable – details)	
(Other features)	

Chapter 11 | # Tension and release

Tension and release are affected by all kinds of everyday stress problems related to work, marriage, and any other situation which can at times or even constantly put the body into a state of anger and aggression, so affecting the personality. This is reflected in muscular interplay and co-ordination, which a trained observer in body language can interpret in terms of posture or expression. To the graphologist this is far more revealing because it is shown in the handwriting and cannot be disguised in any way. A well-adjusted person has the ability to balance the tension and release co-ordination to accommodate any circumstances encountered in life.

Contraction and release factors can be likened to the guy ropes of a tent – too loose and the tent would droop, too tight and the tent would rip. In both cases it would eventually collapse. The tension must be maintained constantly, to tighten or slacken as conditions warrant (see fig 176).

The ideal balance should be on the side of moderate tension at all times, with an outlet for release, with no muscular or mental disturbances to disrupt the interplay of this highly organised and intricate system. The main indicator of this state is the writing pressure. However, in order to assess this factor properly you should consider all the following. Where the factors are balanced and would cancel each other out, either leave each section blank or tick both.

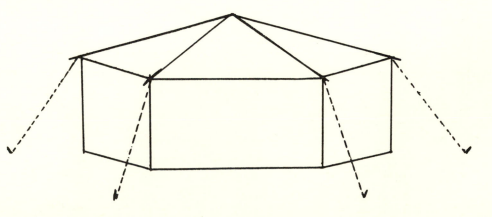

Fig 176
Tension and release

Tension (contraction)	Release
1 Regularity	Fluctuation
2 Smallness overall	Largeness overall
3 Slowness	Fast tempo
4 Heavy pressure	Lack of pressure
5 Disconnection	Connection
6 Narrowness	Width
7 Leftwardness	Rightwardness
8 Angle and arcade	Garland and thread
9 Falling lines	Rising lines
10 Narrow spacing	Wide spacing
11 Circles moving inwards	Circles moving outwards
12 Very small middle zone	Large middle zone

Here are three examples.

	Contraction	Release
1	√	√
2	√	
3		√
4	√	√
5	√	√
6		√
7	√	√
8	√	√
9		√
10		
11		
12	√	
	7	8

nicely balanced

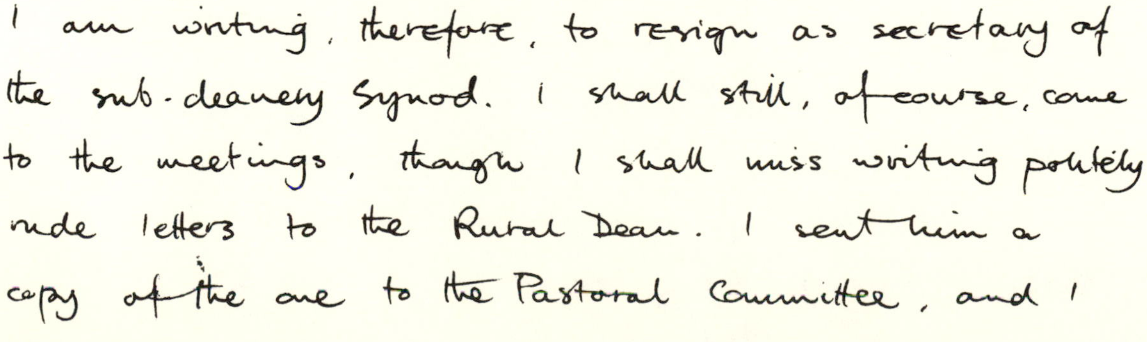

Fig 177
Balanced tension

I am writing, therefore, to resign as secretary of
the sub-deanery Synod. I shall still, of course, come
to the meetings, though I shall miss writing politely
rude letters to the Rural Dean. I sent him a
copy of the one to the Pastoral Committee, and I

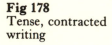

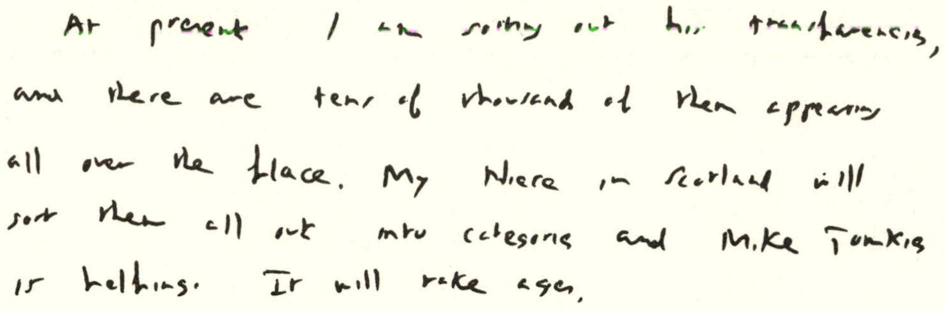

At present I am sorting out his transparencies, and there are tens of thousand of them appearing all over the place. My Niece in Scotland will sort them all out into categories and Mike Tonkin is helping. It will take ages.

Fig 178
Tense, contracted writing

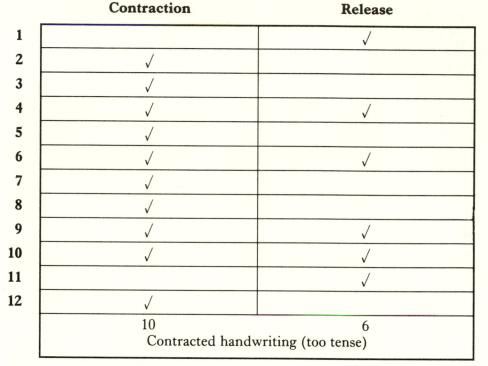

	Contraction	Release
1		√
2	√	
3	√	
4	√	√
5	√	
6	√	√
7	√	
8	√	
9	√	√
10	√	√
11		√
12	√	
	10	6

Contracted handwriting (too tense)

Fig 179
Too released

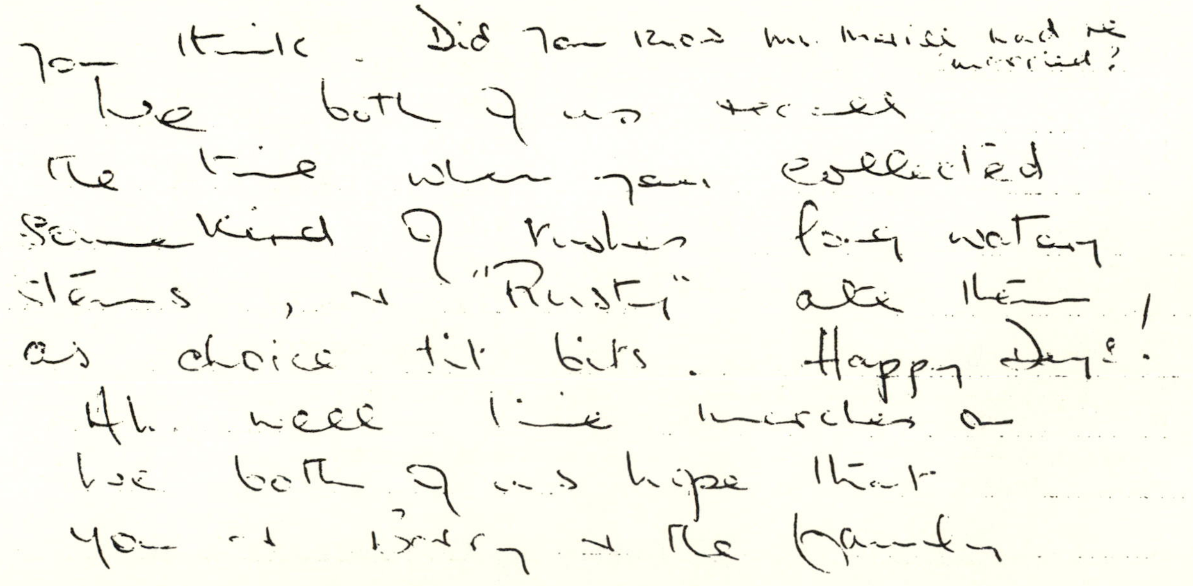

	Contraction	Release
1		√
2		
3		√
4		√
5	√	√
6		√
7	√	
8		√
9		
10		√
11		√
12		
	2	8

Very released

WORKSHEET FOR TENSION AND RELEASE

Balance release

Tension	√	×	Release	√	×
1 Regularity			**1** Fluctuation		
2 Smallness overall			**2** Largeness overall		
3 Slowness			**3** Fast tempo		
4 Heavy pressure			**4** Lack of pressure		
5 Disconnection			**5** Connection		
6 Narrowness			**6** Width		
7 Leftwardness			**7** Rightwardness		
8 Angle and arcade			**8** Garland and thread		
9 Falling lines			**9** Rising lines		
10 Narrow spacing			**10** Wide spacing		
11 Circles moving inwards			**11** Circles moving outwards		
12 Very small middle zone			**12** Large middle zone		

Balanced tension = both sides more or less equal √s

Assessment   *Interpretation*

Chapter 12 | Shading – Pastiness (or pastosity), and Sharpness

When we talk about shading we are referring to the relative thickness of the up-strokes and the down-strokes in a person's handwriting.

Shading is interrelated with pressure but must be regarded as a separate factor indicating sensuality – or the lack of it. When dip and fountain pens were in general use, users were faced with a choice of thick or thin nibs. Nowadays, people use ballpoint pens, which tend to produce a more uniform line with less shading. Rollerballs and felt tips produce more shading and some writers are aware of their stroke quality and make an effort to produce the kind of shading they feel comfortable with, so providing the graphologist with clues as to their personality.

Shading is divided into two groups – 'sharp' and 'pasty'.

SHARPNESS (fig 180)

The sharp stroke is thin, the up and down strokes being of equal width, with the actual pressure weak or medium, producing a sharp look to end strokes in all zones and in t-bars.

Fig 180(i)
Samples of sharp strokes

*would give me a call
Say around August time?
Thankyou.
This is a sample
of my handwriting*

Fig 180(ii)
Samples of sharp
strokes

Sharp writers can be critical and emotionally cold. They have penetrating acumen and an intense thought process, although many possess a refined nature. In many such writers there is a narrow-minded response. They are verbally 'cutting' with a sarcastic nature. The sharp stroke belongs to the businessman or woman who is willing to speculate but at the same time will adhere to puritan principles and strong self-discipline. They will often forego the pleasures of life in the physical sense and may become incapable of enjoyment in order to preserve a 'virtuous' existence. The sharp writer is articulate. Sharp garland writers get much satisfaction from discussion, whereas the sharp angled writer will resort to analysing the statements made for the purpose of disagreeing – with no intention of changing his opinions. These are the sarcastic ones who have a very long and pointed t-bar.

Sharpness

Positive traits	*Negative traits*
Determination	Lack of sensuality
Idealism	Coldness emotionally
Purposeful	Resentful
Discriminating	Pedantic criticism
Spiritual awareness	Quarrelsome
Analytical mind	Boring
Self-discipline	Allows little scope for experiences
Refined manners	
Strong principles	Little resistance to shock
Faculty for research	Malicious feelings
	Power conscious

PASTINESS

The *pasty* or *pastose* stroke is thick (fig 181), the up and down strokes being of equal width, having the appearance, at its maximum width, of a brush stroke. It can be made without undue pressure and can be applied by a slanting pen-hold with a ballpoint, where a sideways ink flow is maintained.

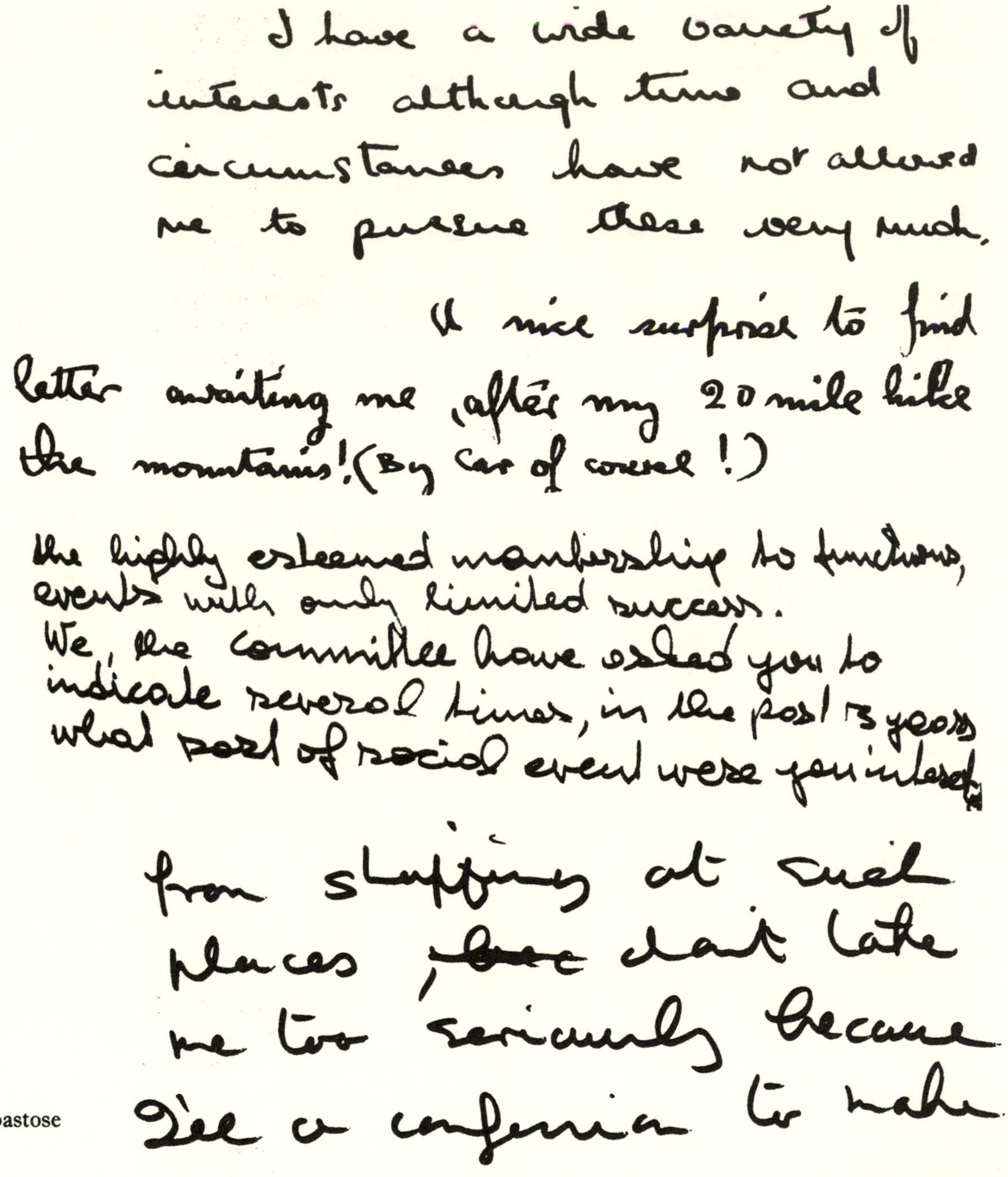

I have a wide variety of
interests although time and
circumstances have not allowed
me to pursue these very much.

A nice surprise to find
letter awaiting me ,after my 20 mile hike
the mountains! (By car of course!)

the highly esteemed membership to functions,
events with only limited success.
We, the committee have asked you to
indicate several times, in the past 3 years
what sort of social event were you interested

from stopping at such
places , but don't take
me too seriously because
I'll a confession to make

Fig 181
Samples of pastose
strokes

In a nib-type pen, freely flowing ink will also have this effect, and so will a
very wide nib. In extreme cases the ink flow will fill in the loops, producing a
dark and light smeary effect.

Pasty writers are dominated by the senses and a need for the materialistic
pleasures of life. They are sensitive to tactile stimulation, particularly in
human contact over which they may exercise little restraint, creating an

undisciplined, easygoing sensuality particularly in the sexual area, where their urges are strongly motivated by visual stimuli. The pasty writer is susceptible also to food and drink, in which they will indulge with relish. They are down-to-earth, co-operative and ready to help others, provided they are not required to assert themselves – for they can be lazy, except in their pursuit of indulgence and sensual gratification!

This stroke is often associated with 'earthy' occupations such as farming, gardening, and those in the food and drink trade; also artists who enjoy strong colours.

The writer with ink-filled loops, a smeary overall look and thick end strokes including t-bars, is capable of temper outbursts of a brutal and violent nature. This can be the result of an inadequate sexual outlet which seeks expression in some other physical way. This is especially valid where there is a disjointed rhythm with a low Form Level, pointing to inferior moral standards and crude expression of feelings.

Pasty (pastose) writing

Positive traits	*Negative traits*
Warmth	Pleasure-seeking freedom
Strong colour sense	Crude and rough
Sense of beauty	Lack of spirituality
Sense of musical appreciation	Excessive self-indulgence
Ability to enjoy intense experiences	Lack of constraint
Ability to withstand tension	Lack of moral discrimination
Sense of humour	Lazy
Love of pleasure	Sentimental
Strong imagination, especially sexual	Impressionable

AESTHETIC DISTINCT

Less common is the artistic writer who is sensitive to the aesthetic image of thick downstrokes and thin upstrokes (fig 182). This requires a play of skilful pressure necessary to produce the muscular contraction and release which results in the thick and thin strokes. This style of handwriting does not always lend itself to speed, the writer needing time to execute the desired effect. Such people are not spontaneous but have a respect for traditional methods, along with a reliable sense of duty and moral conviction.

Paul, whose book it is, has — THICK / THIN STROKE assigned me, as his secretary, to deal with the question of copyright.

Fig 182(i)
Distinct shading

I seem to recall you mentioning you have necessary photographs and if this is the case splendid. however if you wanted assistance,

I hope that you had a good Christm. with your family. & wish you all a very Happy & Peaceful New Year

Yours Sincerely

and my telephone conversation of to-day, would you please

Fig 182(ii)
Distinct shading

Hopefully I would like to explain again

Aesthetic	
Positive traits	*Negative traits*
Artistic	Not spontaneous
Sense of duty	
Moral conviction	

WORKSHEET FOR SHADING

Shading	Interpretation
(Sharp, pasty, aesthetic, distinct)	(to determine later)

PART TWO

Going deeper

Chapter 13 | Covering strokes

A covering stroke is defined as one in which the second stroke covers the first. In the letter 'e', for example, the covering stroke produces a letter which looks more like 'i'. For an example of this, look at (fig 183) below.

Covering strokes indicate severe inhibition. Because of anxiety, the writer tends to avoid future issues or needs to conceal something very personal from others, usually for self-protection. Because covering strokes are so individual the particular zone in which they appear dominantly is very important for a correct assessment.

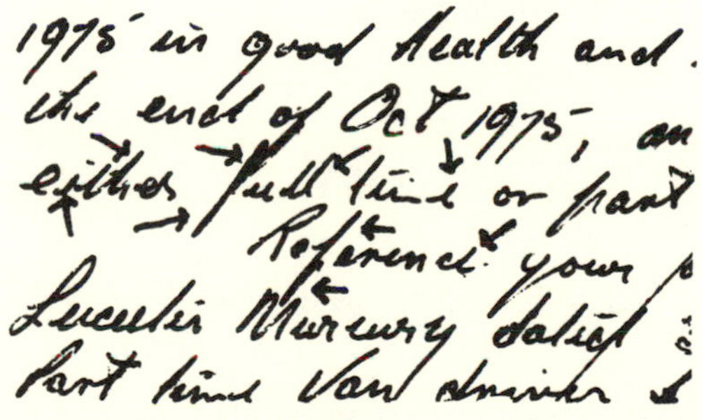

Fig 183
Covering (concealing) strokes

ZONES

Upper zone (fig 184)
          Secretive about plans and
          ideas; intellectual inhibition.

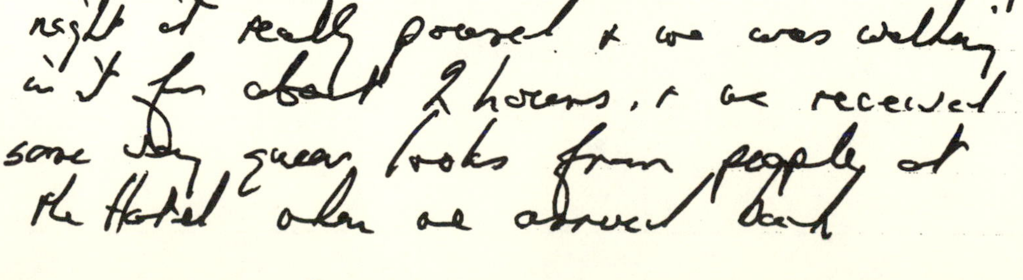

Fig 184
Upper zone covering stroke

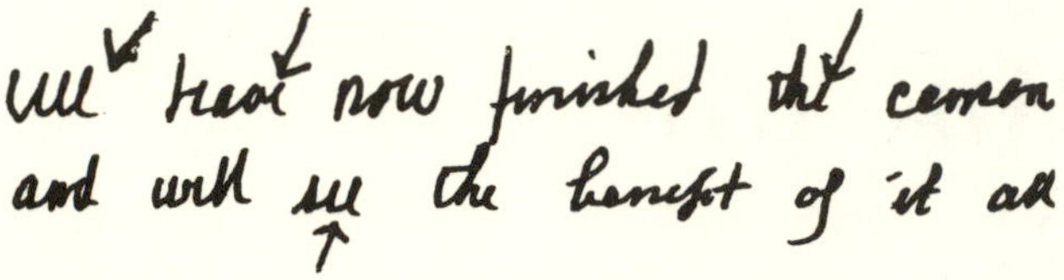

Fig 185
Middle zone covering
stroke

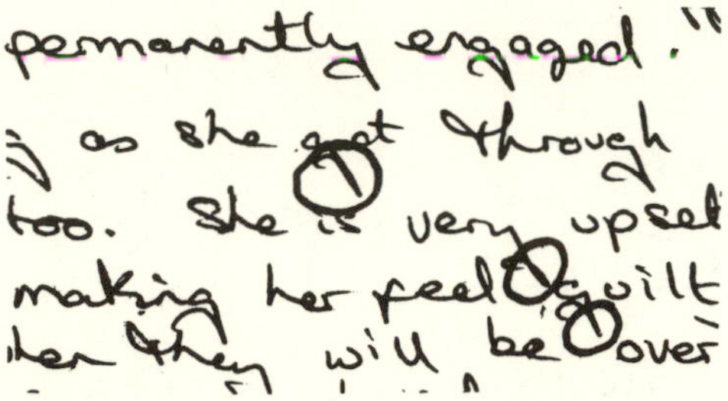

Fig 186
Lower zone covering
stroke

Middle zone (fig 185)

> Compulsive reticence and secretiveness
> over emotional feelings
> Inhibited in daily life situations
> Timid

Lower zone (fig 186)

> Secretive over sexual life, anxious, inhibited
> concealment or embarrassment

FORMS OF CONNECTION

Also important are the forms of connection in which the covering strokes are
featured.

Garland	Constraint, shyness and emotional inhibition
Arcade	Shrewdness, restraint; sly; lying and hypocritical
Angled	Insincerity, hypocrisy; shrewdness; trickery
Thread	Deceptive Will not be committed or tied in any circumstances

WORKSHEET FOR COVERING STROKES

Covering strokes (Present or not) If yes – Zone Form of connection	*Interpretation*

Chapter *14* | Punctuation and paragraphs

Education plays a very important part in punctuation, and where there is little or no punctuation, or the marks are in the wrong place, a poor education is probably the cause. There will be other indications to support this in the script. The same applies to paragraphs. There are one or two points worth noting, however.

EXCESS PUNCTUATION
In a handwriting sample containing excess punctuation the writer is trying to make an impression (often also using ornate or large capitals). Such people override any obstacle to attain recognition and praise. They can be full of enthusiasm, but this can be dissipated in time-wasting, in cramming in irrelevant activity through trying to raise the level of their mundane lifestyle. They can be difficult to live with because of their exaggerated desires and neurotic tendencies.

COMMAS MISSING
An intelligently laid out script with commas missing and a quick writing speed shows a person always in a rush. Look for other signs of neglect, such as thread connections, word endings unfinished, t-bars omitted etc. They may well speak as they write.

LONG COMMAS
Commas in their correct position but very long, '*,*' are from idealists with strong principles, also pedantic individuals who would also have powerful word endings and downstrokes in 'proving' their point.

UNNECESSARY UNDERLINING
Unnecessary underlining (particularly in scripts with heavy pressure) shows a writer convinced of and insisting on his own ideas and theories, who would not co-operate with commonsense suggestions.

WORKSHEET FOR PUNCTUATION AND PARAGRAPHS

Punctuation and paragraphs	Interpretation
(Intelligently used?)	
Irregularities	

Initial and terminal strokes

Chapter **15**

The initial and final adjustments which each writer makes as he begins and finishes a word must be taken into consideration, because they indicate how much preparation, if any, the writer needs before going into action, whether it is wasteful or constructive, and whether he finishes the task as would be expected.

INITIAL STROKES
The initial stroke is the beginning of each word, as taught in primary school for joined-up writing.

Long initial strokes
Basically the longer the initial stroke, depending upon the writing speed, the more inner preparation the writer needs before beginning a task, particularly in a slow writing revealing a slow power of comprehension and impetus (fig 187).

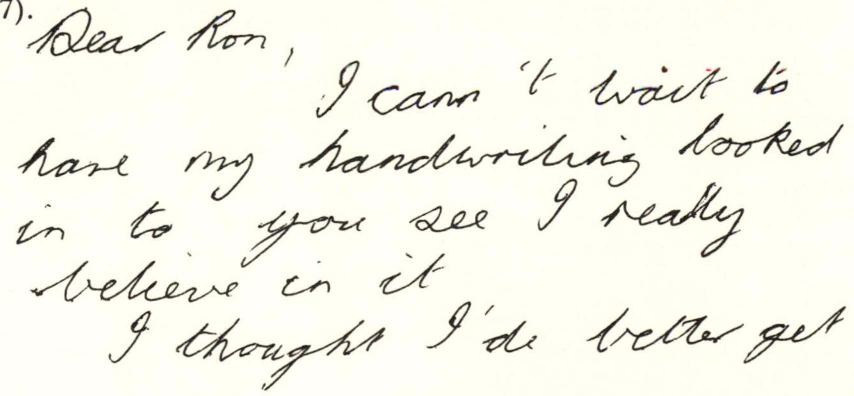

Fig 187
Long initial stroke, slow writing

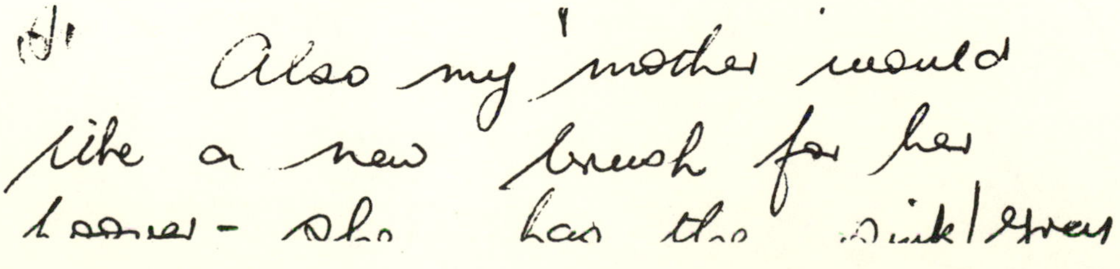

Fig 188
Long initial stroke, fairly fast speed

Where a stroke is fairly long and the speed is fast, the writer gets into the swing of things and maintains the rhythm of activity (fig 188).

A long starting stroke from below the base line can act as a springboard, but the writing must be at least moderately fast for a positive factor.

Where there is a springboard stroke and the writing is slow, the writer is strongly relating to past mother ties (leftwardness, as a starting stroke always is) and the influence of past experiences, which the fast writer does not experience too strongly to be affected by its fetters.

No initial stroke

Where there is no starting stroke, this is a constructive element in the assessment of a Form Level and a positive factor (fig 189).

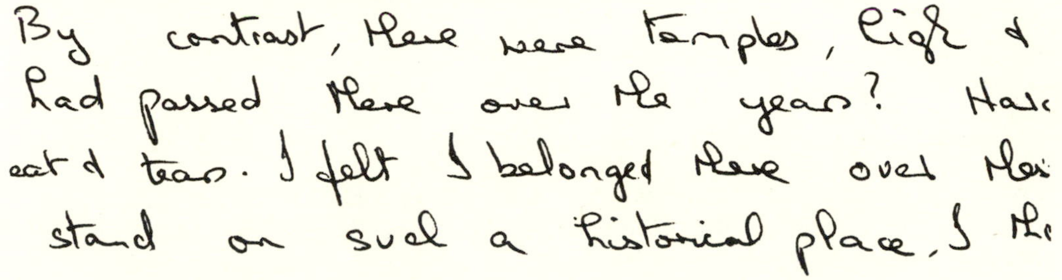

Fig 189
No initial stroke

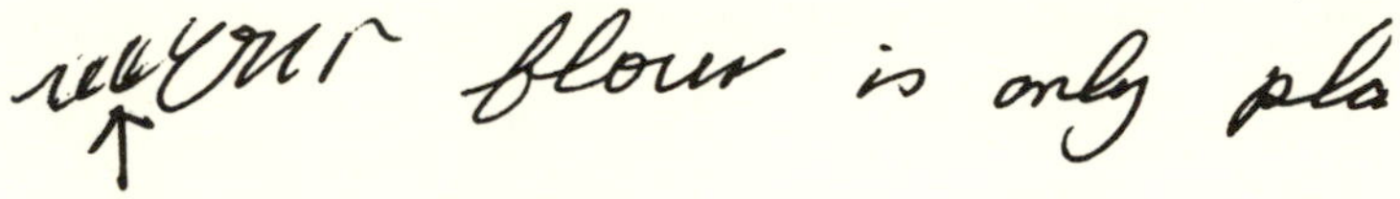

Fig 190
Initial 'feeling' strokes

Feeling strokes (fig 190)

Another form of graphic hesitation is the feeling stroke. The writer, before putting pen to paper and while making his decision to begin writing, makes a few dummy run strokes on the spot which appear as faint leading in strokes. Normally these go with a copybook style. Such writers seldom achieve any form of status because their deliberation impedes their efforts; so does their lack of self-confidence.

The feeling stroke is rare, belonging to someone who very seldom needs to write.

Hooks (fig 191)

In high Form Level writing the starting stroke can initiate constructive thinking, with a hook also at the beginning: this points to persistence, and an angry response to interruption. This 'tick-on-hook' can also be seen on a t-bar and an i-dot (fig 192).

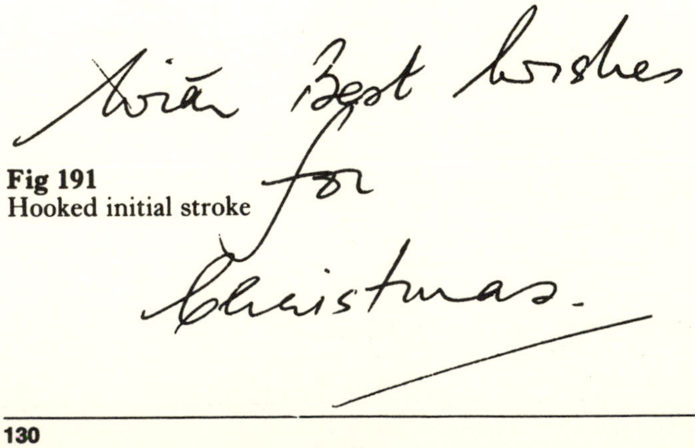

Fig 191
Hooked initial stroke

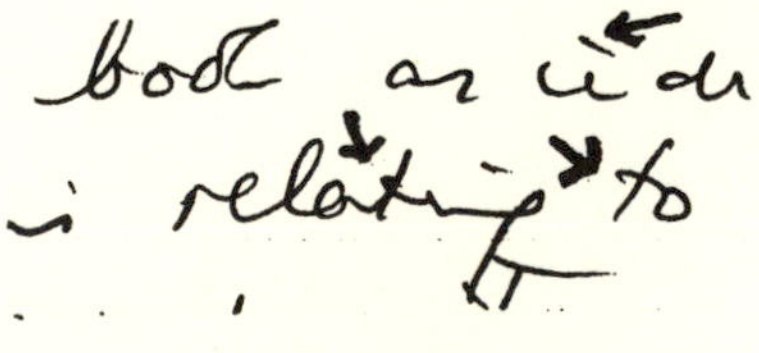

Fig 192
'Tick-on-hook' shown on t-bar and i-dot (see also fig 174)

No initial stroke

When the initial stroke is absent the writer has a positive attitude to life and cuts out inessential details; such people are less inclined to follow established patterns or methods and are able to cope with environmental issues with a self-assurance that comes through practice and experience.

Resting on the base line (fig 193)

The initial stroke that always rests on the base line, whether on lined or plain paper, in a low to medium quality writing, indicates those writers who always accept people in authority, following their regulations and advice willingly, conforming to what they consider acceptable to others. When faced with a decision, they feel inadequate and anxious: usually copybook forms of script prevail.

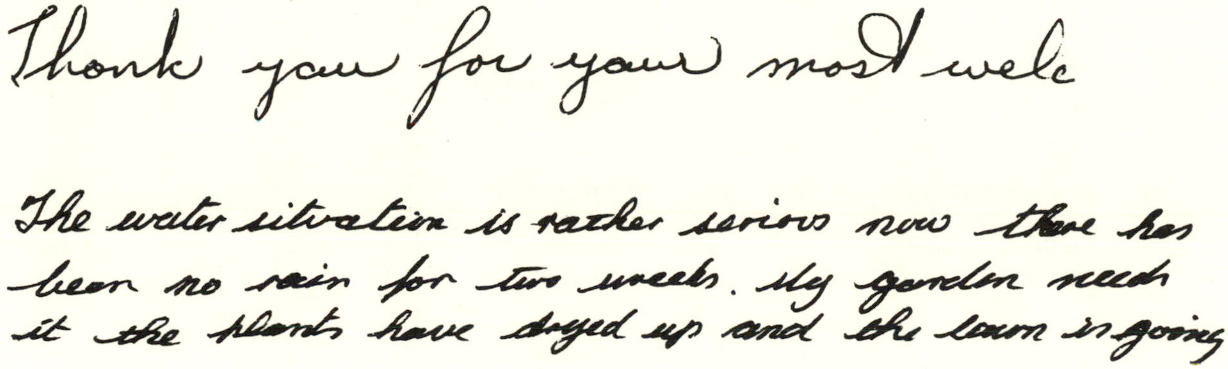

Fig 193
Two samples of script showing the initial stroke starting on the base line.

Thank you for your most welc

The water situation is rather serious now there has been no rain for two weeks. My garden needs it the plants have dryed up and the lawn is going

TERMINAL OR END STROKES

As a writer ends a word to begin the next word, a tailing off stroke is expected and these can take on many forms, from a long *e* to a curtailed *e*, (fig 194). The terminal stroke is associated with the writer's social attitude, for it is a reaching-out impulse. When the letter endings are all even, the social inclination of the writer is controlled and regular. This can show a lack of liveliness and possibly a boring personality.

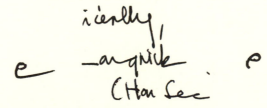

Fig 194
Terminal strokes – long 'e' to a curtailed 'e', for example

    The final stroke of the small letter 'e' is the best letter to look at, the writer being free to follow his own instincts before the next word is begun. The small letter 'd' is also useful as the writer has to change direction to produce an end stroke continuation.

    The examples that follow are representative of the variety of end strokes:

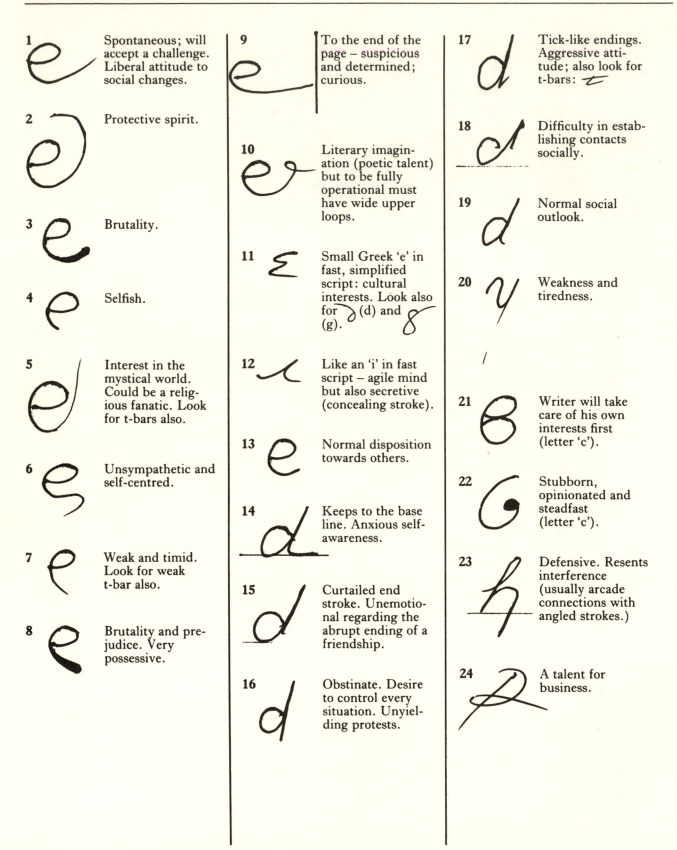

1 Spontaneous; will accept a challenge. Liberal attitude to social changes.

2 Protective spirit.

3 Brutality.

4 Selfish.

5 Interest in the mystical world. Could be a religious fanatic. Look for t-bars also.

6 Unsympathetic and self-centred.

7 Weak and timid. Look for weak t-bar also.

8 Brutality and prejudice. Very possessive.

9 To the end of the page – suspicious and determined; curious.

10 Literary imagination (poetic talent) but to be fully operational must have wide upper loops.

11 Small Greek 'e' in fast, simplified script: cultural interests. Look also for ∂ (d) and ℊ (g).

12 Like an 'i' in fast script – agile mind but also secretive (concealing stroke).

13 Normal disposition towards others.

14 Keeps to the base line. Anxious self-awareness.

15 Curtailed end stroke. Unemotional regarding the abrupt ending of a friendship.

16 Obstinate. Desire to control every situation. Unyielding protests.

17 Tick-like endings. Aggressive attitude; also look for t-bars:

18 Difficulty in establishing contacts socially.

19 Normal social outlook.

20 Weakness and tiredness.

21 Writer will take care of his own interests first (letter 'c').

22 Stubborn, opinionated and steadfast (letter 'c').

23 Defensive. Resents interference (usually arcade connections with angled strokes.)

24 A talent for business.

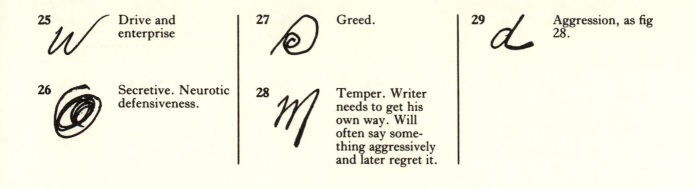

25 Drive and enterprise

26 Secretive. Neurotic defensiveness.

27 Greed.

28 Temper. Writer needs to get his own way. Will often say something aggressively and later regret it.

29 Aggression, as fig 28.

WORKSHEET FOR INITIAL AND TERMINAL STROKES

Initial and terminal strokes	Interpretation
Initial strokes	
Terminal strokes	

Chapter 16 | Regularity

Because we are human beings and not robots, natural regularity is unlikely to be as stereotyped as machine printing.

In our early years at school we were taught to keep our writing between guidelines, upper and lower, and keep to this discipline particularly in the middle zone. On leaving the confines of school we find our own degree of regularity dependent upon our control over emotional feelings. For some time younger adolescents will fluctuate from regular to irregular and back again in phases, until they reach maturity. This may be confirmed by past samples of their handwriting. The script is irregular where there is a moderate to considerable variation in the combined following factors:

The height of the middle zone letters (of prime importance and the main indicator of regularity. Are they all the same size, or do they fluctuate?)

This factor of regularity represents the writer's attitude to day-to-day routine.

The distance between the downstrokes (Are they all of equal distance depending upon the particular letter, or are they inconsistently placed?)

This factor represents the writer's reserve or friendliness, restraint or freedom in respect of progress.

The variation of the slant (Does the writing point consistently in one direction, or is it going in all directions? If so, which zone in particular?)

An indication of introversion or extroversion – a willingness to share social experience or not.

Distance between the lines (on unlined paper where no obvious guideline has been used).

Indicating a mind that is tidy or confused. (Usually the most regular of the four factors.)

REGULAR WRITING

Regular writing is a product of discipline: self-control, willpower and muscular co-ordination. The main writing movement to be assessed is the middle zone.

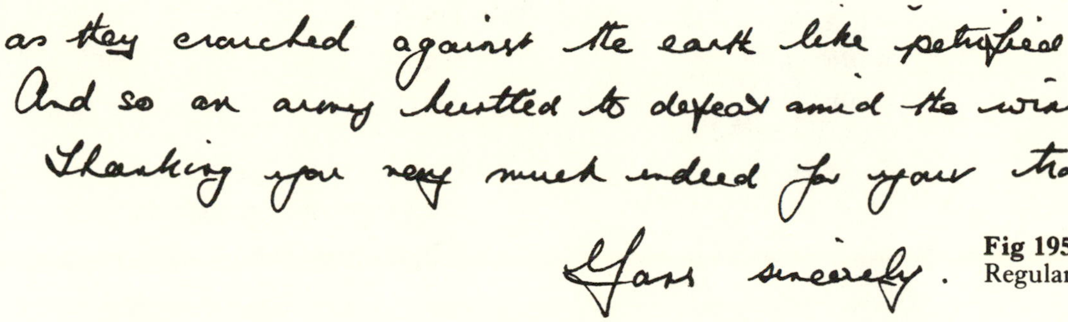

[handwritten sample]

as they crouched against the earth like petrified
And so an army hustled to defeat amid the wild
Thanking you very much indeed for your tha

Yours sincerely.

Fig 195
Regular script

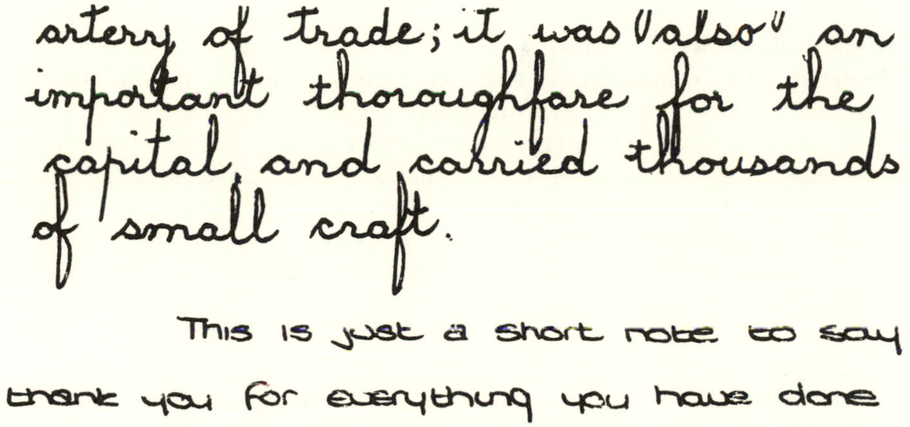

[handwritten sample]

artery of trade; it was "also" an important thoroughfare for the capital, and carried thousands of small craft.

This is just a short note to say thank you for everything you have done

Fig 196
Two samples of rigid regularity

Regular and natural
Such writers have a good degree of balance and self-discipline with a sense of harmony and organisation.

Regular and natural	
Positive traits	*Negative traits*
Endurance in mundane tasks	Indifferent emotional response
Resistance to stress	Restricted range of interests
Stable	Boring
Orderly behaviour	Unresponsive
Calm	
Methodical	
Reliable	

Rigid regularity (Adult writing only) see fig 196
In these people a disciplined sense of duty and obligation dominates their feelings and expression of any excitability, amounting to a dull personality.

Such people tend to be dependent upon their work and so do not develop any outside interests in which they can relax. Because of their pedantic, limited views they lack friendship and affection – a self-imposed loneliness.

Rigid regularity

Positive traits	*Negative traits*
Predictable	Inflexible
Strong sense of duty	Unimaginative
Conscientious	Lack of vital drive
	Lack of emotional response
	Compulsive habits
	Slow and cumbersome

IRREGULAR WRITING

An irregular script shows variation and disproportion in at least two of the four relevant factors, but will include the middle zone letters.

Depending upon the degree of irregularity, these writers are adaptable, but because of their poor self-discipline they do not have the same degree of control over their emotions as the regular writer.

They are sensitive to their own and others' feelings. You should assess the script's level of irregularity along with the rhythmic quality (see next chapter).

Slightly irregular script (fig 197) (one or two of the four factors)
These writers are in control of their emotional response to exciting stimuli and possess a balanced expressiveness of personality. They also have the flexibility to enjoy life and their varied interests which the rigid writer lacks.

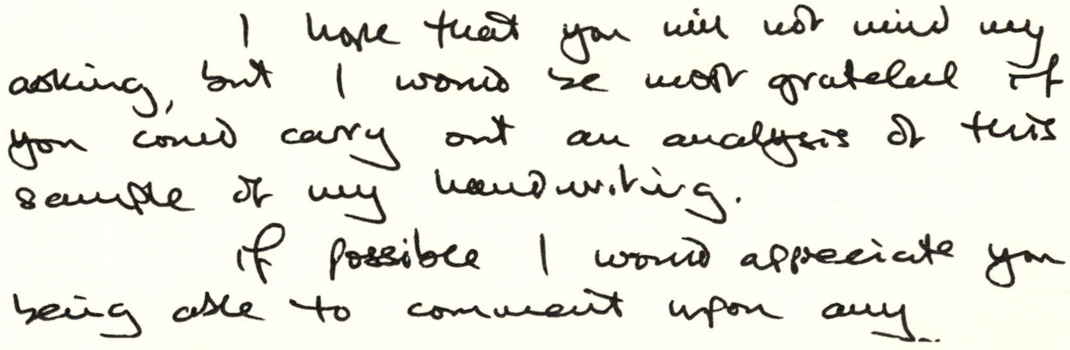

Fig 197
Slightly irregular script

Irregular script (fig 198) (three or four factors, including the middle zone where variation is likely to be very noticeable)
These writers possess only a superficial control over their emotions. They are excitable and easily thrown by awkward situations.

The irregular writer is not a contented person; he needs the constant variety of stimulating friends and ideas he can put into practice. He becomes moody and restless when restricted in any way. However, he does not easily stagnate.

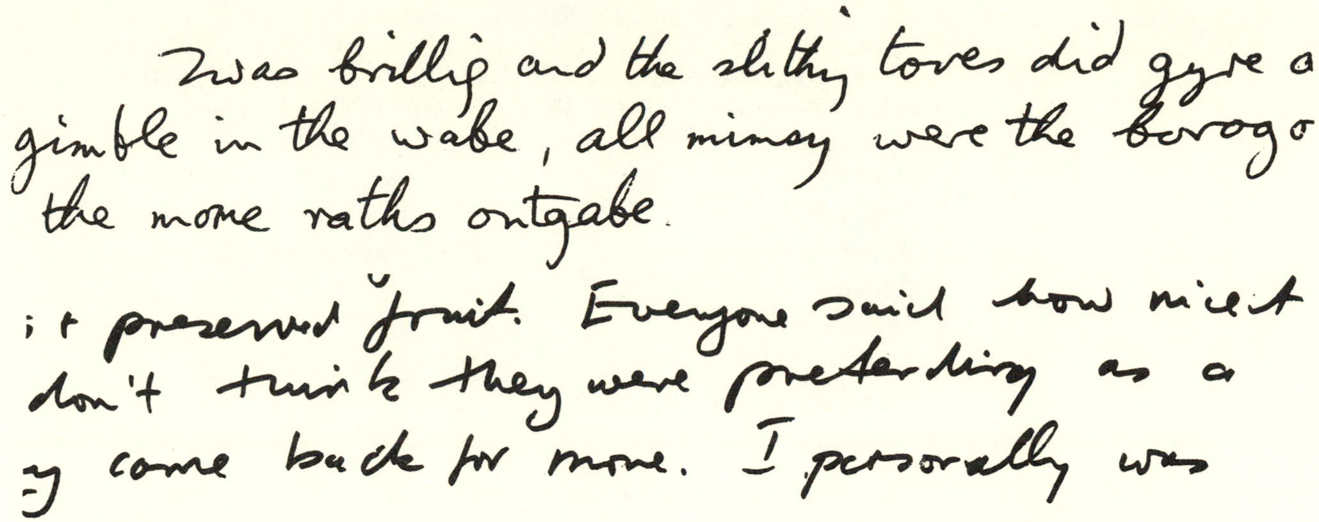

'Twas brillig and the slithy toves did gyre a gimble in the wabe, all mimsy were the borogo the mome raths outgabe.

it preserved fruit. Everyone said how nice it don't think they were pretending as a y come back for more. I personally was

Fig 198
Samples of irregular scripts

Irregular writing	
Positive traits	*Negative traits*
(High to medium Form Level)	*(Low Form Level)*
Emotional but flexible response	Irritable
Open-minded attitude	Restless
Creative mind	Excitable
Lively personality	Moody
Passionate display of feelings	Inconsistent
	Indecisive
	Poor self-discipline
	Lack of concentration
	Impulsive behaviour

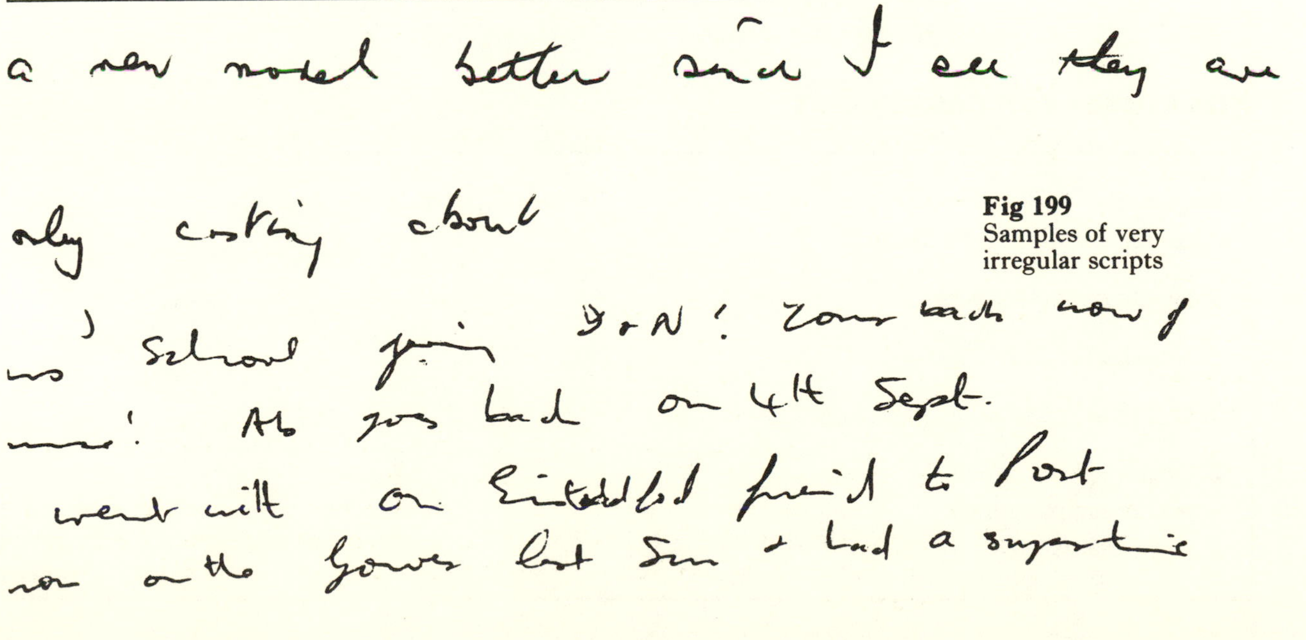

a new novel better since I see they are

only costing about

Fig 199
Samples of very irregular scripts

Very irregular script (fig 199) (All four factors, though some-times the distance between the lines may be fairly regular.)
(High to medium Form Level with consistent pressure)

Positive traits	*Negative traits*
Imaginative mind	Intolerance of stress
Fresh, novel ideas	Intolerance of routine
Artistic	
Inventive	
Love of the unusual	
Striving for individuality	

Low Form Level (with inconsistent pressure)

Distracted

Weak willpower

Confused thinking

Very unpredictable

Dominated by strong emotional feelings

Will waste time and effort

Seldom satisfied

Inconsistent behaviour

ZONES

Where irregularity is evident in a particular zone, that zone represents the dominant area of restlessness: in the upper zone – intellectual dissatisfaction or restlessness; in the middle zone – emotional and social restlessness, and in the lower zone – strong natural drives, and sexual sensitivity, with the desire for exciting stimuli.

WORKSHEET FOR REGULARITY

Regularity (How regular are the following?)	Interpretation
1 Height of small letters	
2 Variation of slant	
3 Distance between downstrokes	
4 Distance between lines Any particular zone? Any other factors	

Chapter *17* | Rhythm

The rhythm of writing indicates the writer's life force and individual versatility; how he co-ordinates his energy, thinking and feeling. Everyone has a rhythmic quality of a sort, whether 'good' or 'bad'.

GOOD RHYTHM

A good rhythm – see the two samples given in fig 200 – is neither too tight nor too loose. The tension and release pattern (i.e. pen pressure and control) is balanced to show equilibrium. It is not bound by inhibition and neurotic conflicts which would restrict the personality and thus the rhythmic flow of the script.

There will also be original forms, simplicity, a fairly spontaneous tempo, intelligent spacing and legibility.

A good rhythmic quality will be noticeable whichever way the writing is held to view – sideways, upside down or even in a mirror. Doing this can, in fact, help you to assess rhythm until you gain experience, because you are not distracted from the overall impression by the actual text.

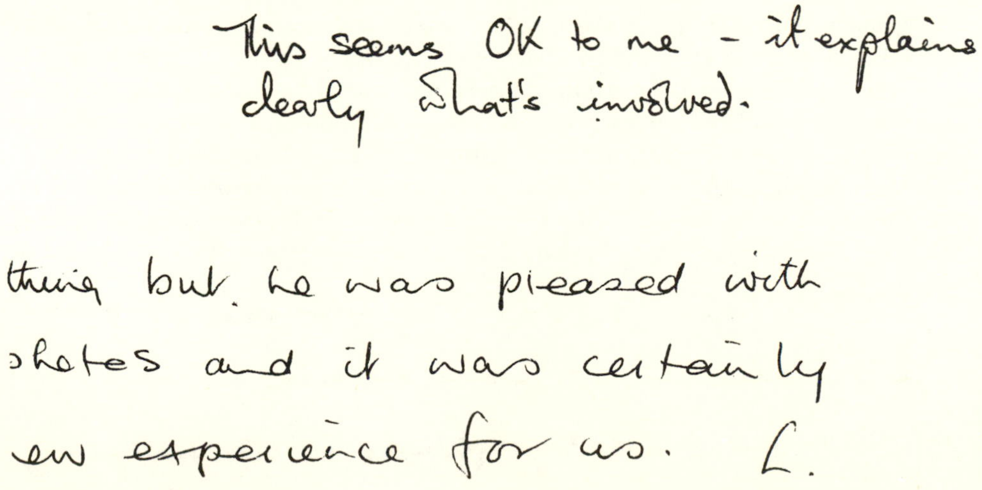

This seems OK to me – it explains clearly what's involved.

thing but. he was pleased with whotes and it was certainly an experience for us. L.

Fig 200
Two examples of good, harmonious rhythm

Good rhythm (i.e. harmonious)
Aesthetic appreciation
Good mental health and balanced personality
Inner harmony and equanimity
Controlled impulses and emotions
A readiness to gain experience
A tolerance of reasonable pressure
An ability to make well-adjusted relationships
Harmonious co-ordination between thinking and feeling

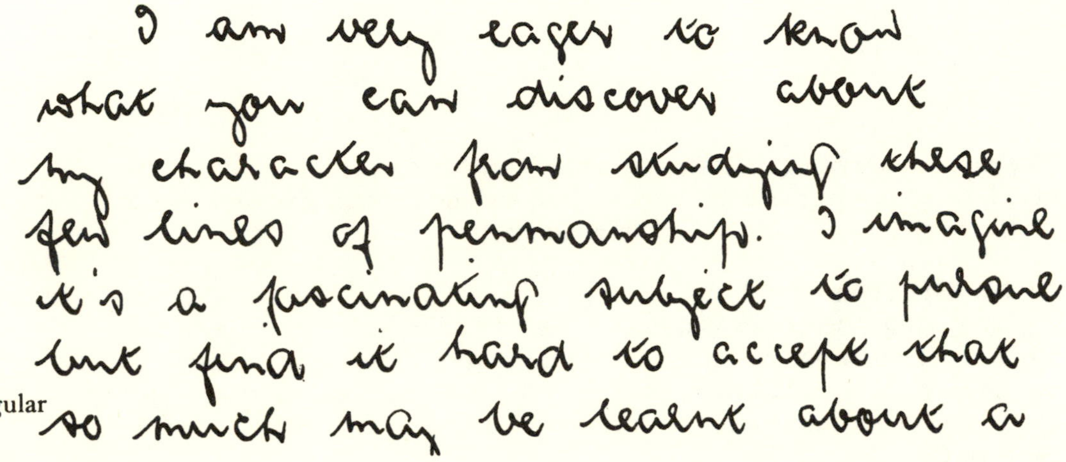

I am very eager to know what you can discover about my character from studying these few lines of penmanship. I imagine it's a fascinating subject to pursue but find it hard to accept that so much may be learnt about a

Fig 201
Rather rigid, but
rhythmic and regular
rhythm

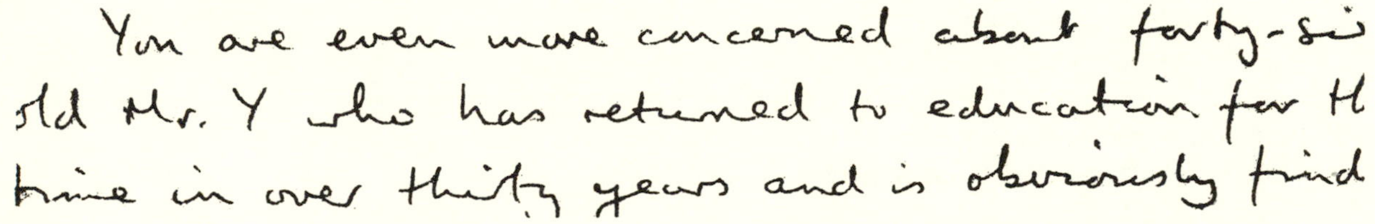

You are even more concerned about forty-six old Mr. Y who has returned to education for th time in over thirty years and is obviously find

Fig 202
Samples of arrhythmic,
but harmonious rhythm

Good rhythmic script is the result of order and control in the mind. Poor rhythm in handwriting and inconsistency can be the result of (a) *impatience, carelessness or nervous tension*, sometimes caused by the writer's thoughts flowing too quickly for steady co-ordination of brain and hand; or (b) *where writing is not frequently practised*, resulting in clumsy movements and slowness, brought about by concentration, not only on the contents but also on the way it is being written, which, for practised writers, is automatic; and (c) *there is the intelligent but physically handicapped writer* who finds the act of

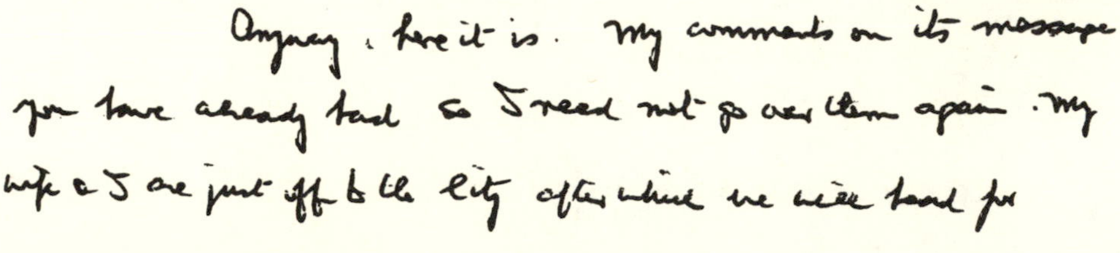

Anyway, here it is. My comments on its message you have already had so I need not go over them again. My wife & I are just off to the city after which we will head for

writing painful and difficult. There will be in this case stiffness in the letter formation and shakiness in the strokes, but some originality will be present which would be absent in an intellectually restricted copybook handwriting.

Rhythmic and regular (but rigid) (fig 201)
Here the writer's lifestyle is reserved and bound by tradition from which he is unlikely to deviate. His interests and activities are confined to mundane pursuits with which he feels safe. He is not prepared to take a risk even if its potential has been proved reliable – hence the low quality of his personal achievements.

ARRHYTHMIC but harmonious and with good Form Level (fig 202):

> Doesn't comply fully with traditional methods
> High degree of interest in life
> Individuality

POOR RHYTHM (i.e. inharmonious) – see samples, fig 203

Poor rhythm
> Emotional sensitivity
> Prone to stress and tension
> Insecure feelings
> Impatient
> Nervous temperament – easily upset
> Unrealised conflicts and complexes
> Inability to adjust to relationships easily
> Inconsistency
> Always ready with an excuse for failure
> Cannot fulfil his creative aims
> (in script with original forms)

Fig 203(i)
Samples of poor rhythm, inharmonious

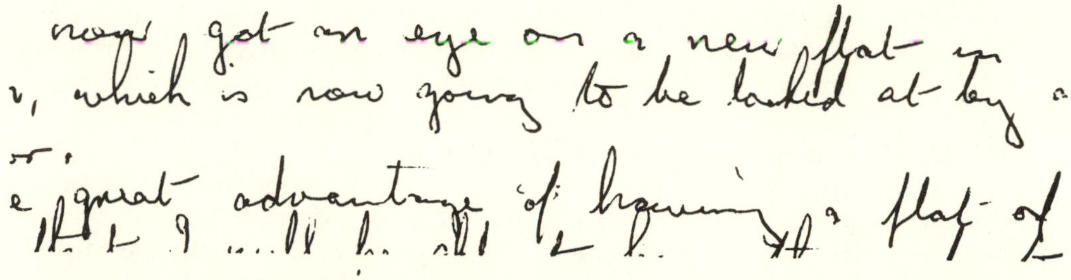

Fig 203(ii)
Sample of poor
rhythm, inharmonious

[handwriting sample]

DISTURBED RHYTHM (below standard and inharmonious – very irregular) (fig 204)
This type of rhythm indicates people whose internal conflicts are such that they are unable to participate in life without complaints or grievances. Because of their personal dissatisfaction they lack friendships which they so urgently need but which they are unable to sustain. They can be neurotic and compulsive in their habits.

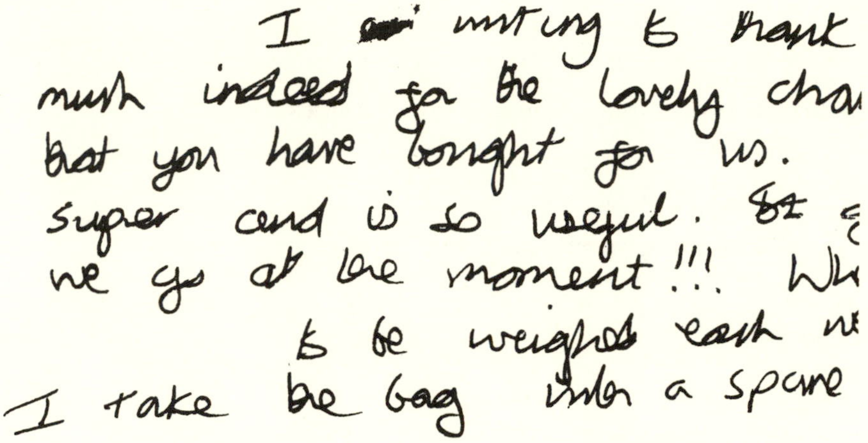

Fig 204
Samples of disturbed
rhythm

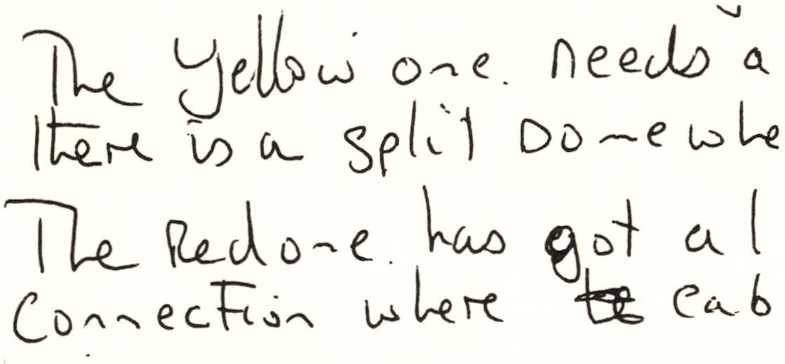

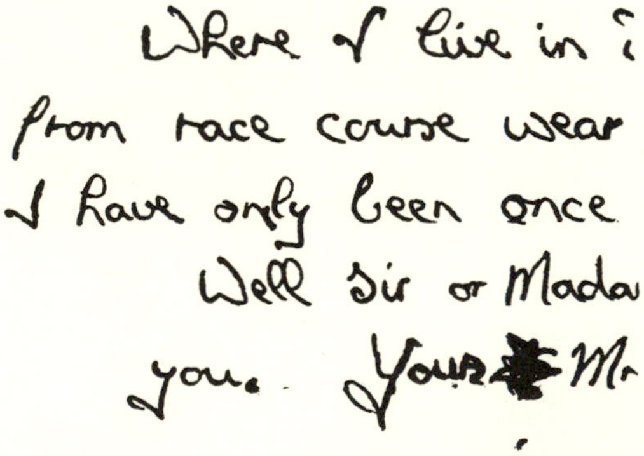

[handwriting samples]

WORKSHEET FOR RHYTHM

Rhythm (Good/arrhythmic/poor)	Interpretation
Special features	

Chapter *18* | Capitals

Someone once told me that in astrology the rising sign (or ascendant) tells us how someone enters the room. Does he creep into the room praying no-one will notice him or make an impressive entrance, as much as to say, 'Look, I'm here!'? Such is the first capital letter of your sample (fig 205).

The size and width of the capital letters in general will tell you something about the writer's self-esteem, or lack of it. This applies particularly to the personal pronoun, 'I', which is dealt with in the next chapter.

Someone writing the name or initials of a person they feel strongly about – be it positive or negative – may reflect those feelings by producing larger or smaller capitals than usual.

You must always remember that no letter has an absolute value in itself, but must be balanced by all the other factors.

LARGE CAPITALS
Where the capitals are taller than the upper zone extensions (and possibly wider), the writer is seeking status, considering himself worthy of attention,

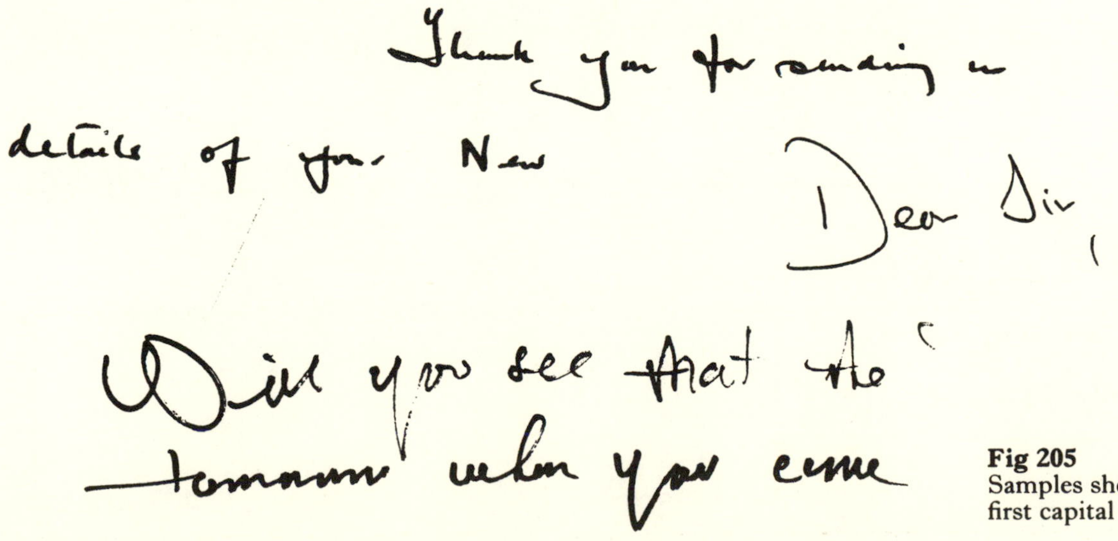

Fig 205
Samples showing large
first capital letter

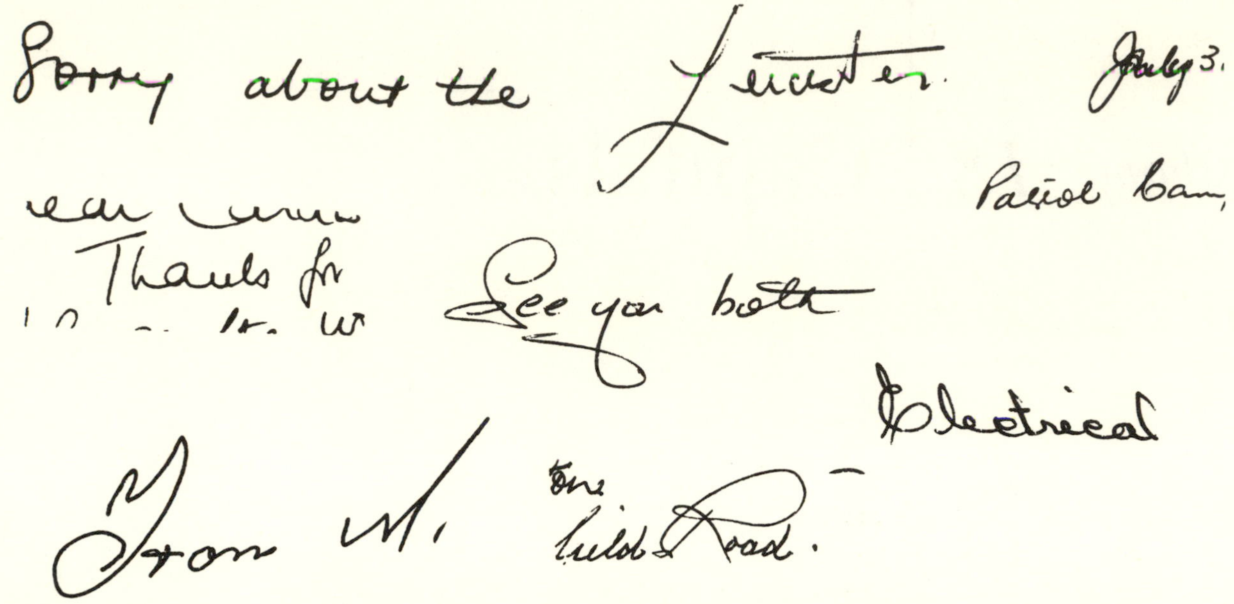

[handwritten samples]

Sorry about the Leicester.   July 3.

Patrol Car,

Thanks for   See you both

Electrical

From M.   Childs Road.

Fig 206
Samples of scripts showing capitals taller than the upper zone extensions

and he portrays an air of authority (fig 206). Whether this emerges as refined behaviour or vulgar expression depends upon the quality of the script.

Large ornamentation
Crudity is found in artificial forms and ornamentation of a lower Form Level writing. Large capitals, ornate and overdone, reflect an ostentatious personality endeavouring to be larger than life, or compensating for an inferiority complex which he cannot genuinely overcome, to reinforce his self-esteem.

SMALL CAPITALS
Much smaller capitals (fig 207), usually narrow, are a sign of a low ego type personality, self-effacing, unassuming, shy, timid and sympathetic to the needs of others. These are found in the script of an intellectual who prefers to remain in the background and has no need for arrogant vanity.

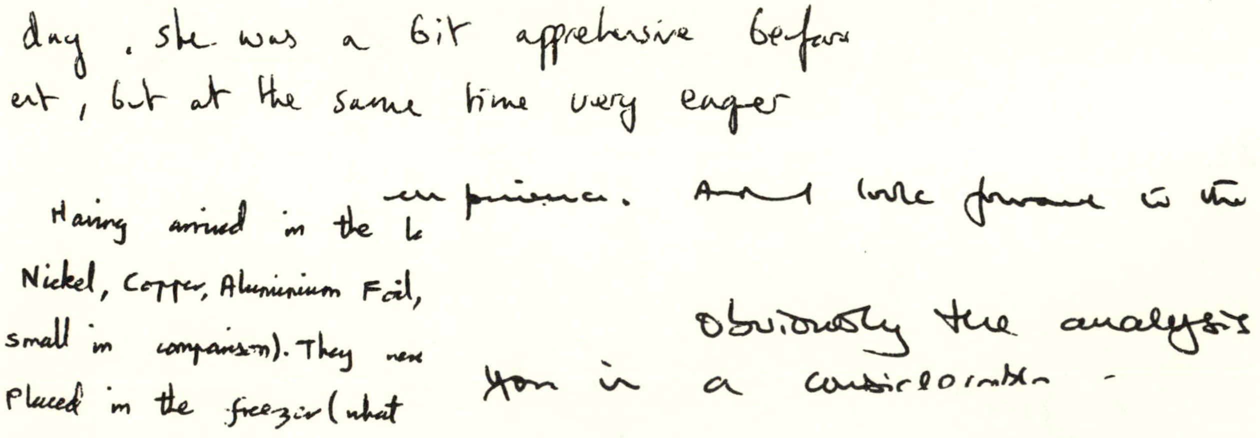

[handwritten samples]

day. she was a bit apprehensive before ent, but at the same time very eager

Having arrived in the   experience.   And I look forward to the

Nickel, Copper, Aluminium Foil, small in comparison). They were placed in the freezer (what   Obviously the analysis

You in a   considerations -

Fig 207
Samples of scripts with smaller capitals

Sincerely   : Lakeland

IN THE WRONG PLACE

Capitals found in the wrong place, such as inside words (fig 208), point to a person who over-reacts and attaches importance to matters of little consequence.

TOO MANY CAPITALS

In the case of many words unnecessarily beginning with capital letters, the writer is compulsive with an unintelligent conception of what is, and what is not, important and is therefore unreliable unless under supervision. It is also likely that where pressure is heavy or the stroke pasty, he would be too intense under emotional pressure because he is too easily swayed by his own feelings to be objective.

Here are some more possible combinations:

Narrow and tall capitals (fig 209)

Sensitive, emotional, inhibited, introverted

Aspirations towards spiritual awareness

Ambitious, but restricted by reserve

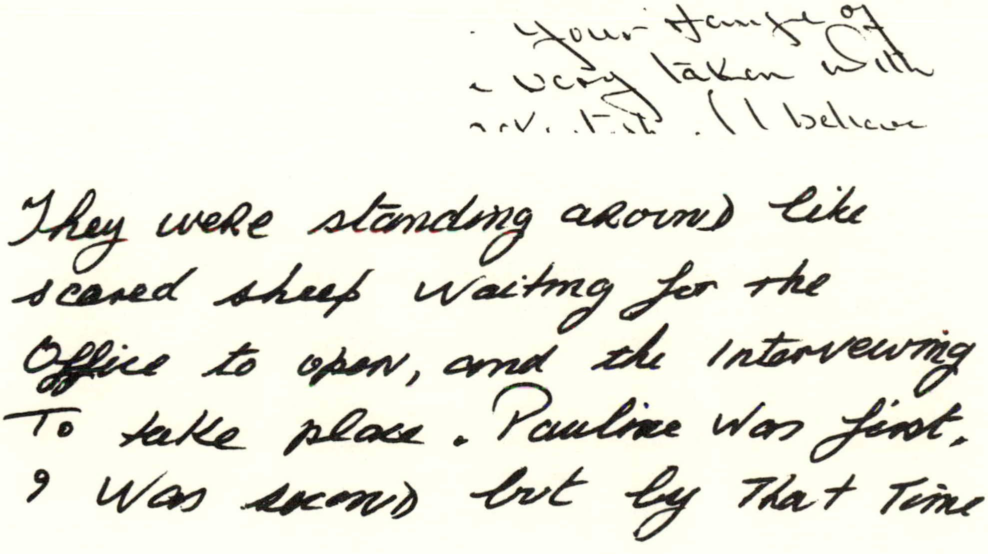

Fig 208
Scripts with capitals inside words

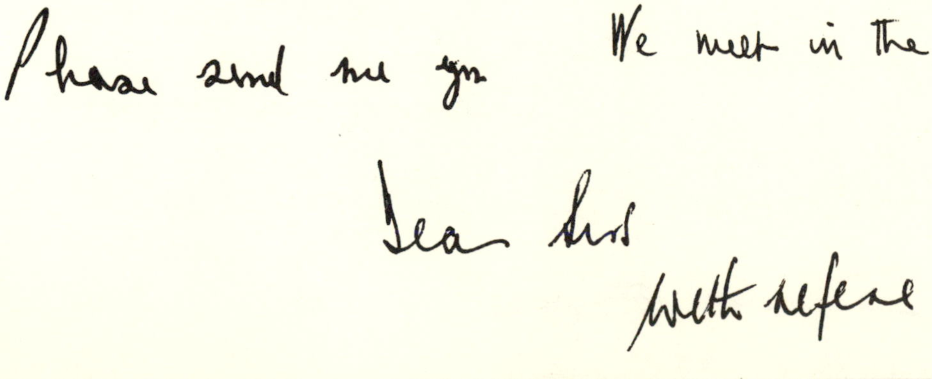

Fig 209
Four sample scripts with tall, narrow capital letters

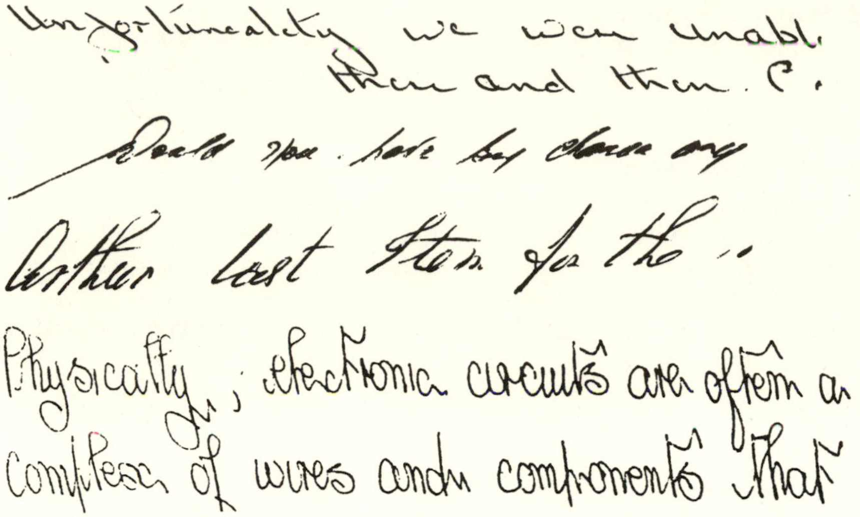

Fig 210
Samples showing
narrow capitals

Narrow, but normal height in relation to script (fig 210)
     Disappointment
     Restraint
     Suspicious nature
     Careful

Wide (fig 211)
Self-reliant, Imaginative, Outgoing personality

Embellished, ornate (depending upon Form Level) (fig 212)
Maintaining an image of individual importance usually a shallow
personality over-compensating for inferior inner feelings

Touched up, or amended to appear taller (fig 213)
     Desire for improvement
     Feelings of anxiety

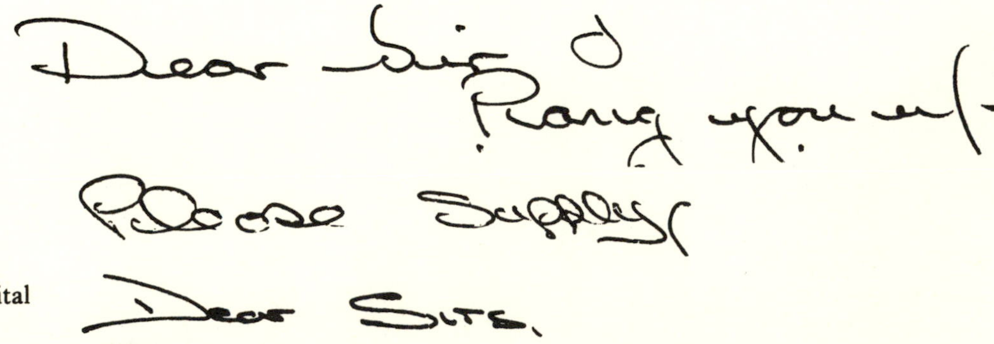

Fig 211
Samples of wide capital
letters

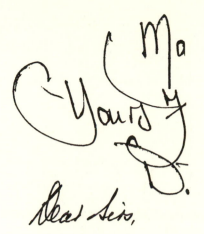

Fig 212
Scripts showing embellished, ornate capitals

Fig 213
Amended capital

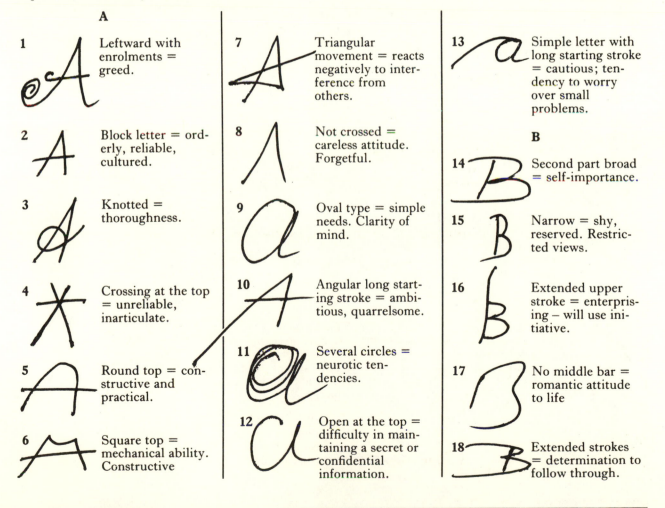

The following are a few representations of types found in each letter of the alphabet; the variety of course is infinite.

A

1 Leftward with enrolments = greed.

2 Block letter = orderly, reliable, cultured.

3 Knotted = thoroughness.

4 Crossing at the top = unreliable, inarticulate.

5 Round top = constructive and practical.

6 Square top = mechanical ability. Constructive

7 Triangular movement = reacts negatively to interference from others.

8 Not crossed = careless attitude. Forgetful.

9 Oval type = simple needs. Clarity of mind.

10 Angular long starting stroke = ambitious, quarrelsome.

11 Several circles = neurotic tendencies.

12 Open at the top = difficulty in maintaining a secret or confidential information.

13 Simple letter with long starting stroke = cautious; tendency to worry over small problems.

B

14 Second part broad = self-importance.

15 Narrow = shy, reserved. Restricted views.

16 Extended upper stroke = enterprising – will use initiative.

17 No middle bar = romantic attitude to life

18 Extended strokes = determination to follow through.

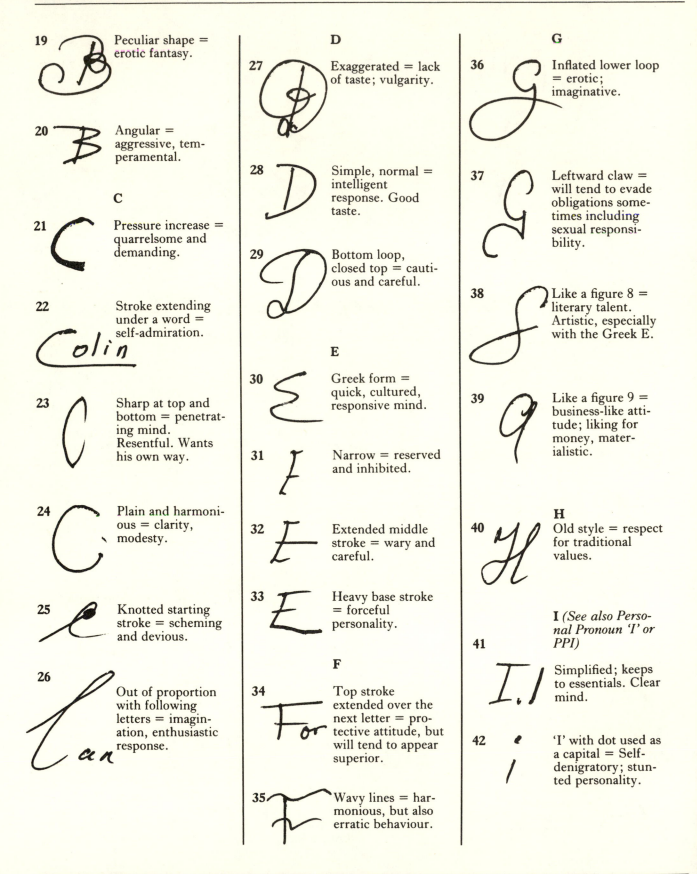

19 Peculiar shape = erotic fantasy.

20 Angular = aggressive, temperamental.

C

21 Pressure increase = quarrelsome and demanding.

22 Stroke extending under a word = self-admiration.

23 Sharp at top and bottom = penetrating mind. Resentful. Wants his own way.

24 Plain and harmonious = clarity, modesty.

25 Knotted starting stroke = scheming and devious.

26 Out of proportion with following letters = imagination, enthusiastic response.

D

27 Exaggerated = lack of taste; vulgarity.

28 Simple, normal = intelligent response. Good taste.

29 Bottom loop, closed top = cautious and careful.

E

30 Greek form = quick, cultured, responsive mind.

31 Narrow = reserved and inhibited.

32 Extended middle stroke = wary and careful.

33 Heavy base stroke = forceful personality.

F

34 Top stroke extended over the next letter = protective attitude, but will tend to appear superior.

35 Wavy lines = harmonious, but also erratic behaviour.

G

36 Inflated lower loop = erotic; imaginative.

37 Leftward claw = will tend to evade obligations sometimes including sexual responsibility.

38 Like a figure 8 = literary talent. Artistic, especially with the Greek E.

39 Like a figure 9 = business-like attitude; liking for money, materialistic.

H

40 Old style = respect for traditional values.

I *(See also Personal Pronoun 'I' or PPI)*

41 Simplified; keeps to essentials. Clear mind.

42 'I' with dot used as a capital = Self-denigratory; stunted personality.

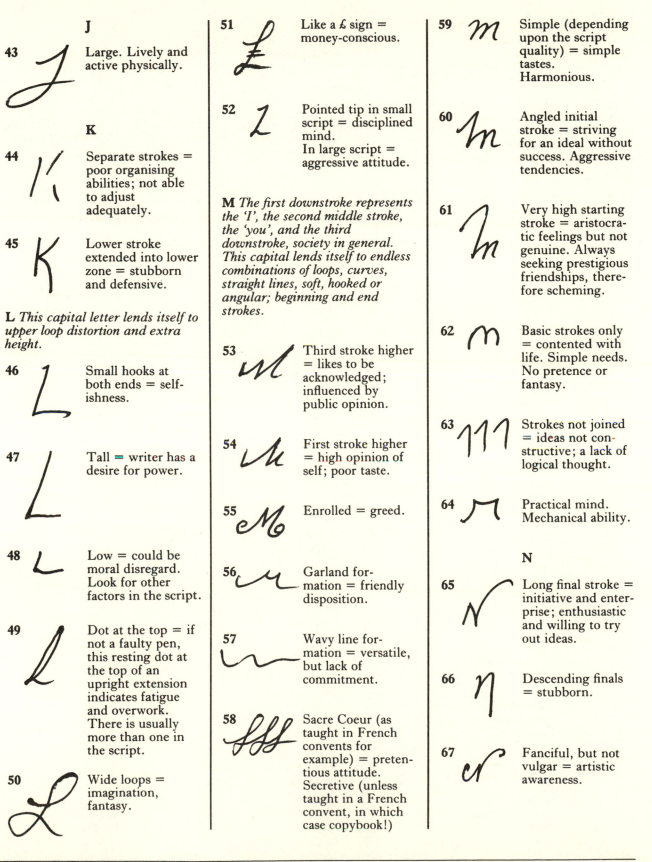

J

43 Large. Lively and active physically.

K

44 Separate strokes = poor organising abilities; not able to adjust adequately.

45 Lower stroke extended into lower zone = stubborn and defensive.

L *This capital letter lends itself to upper loop distortion and extra height.*

46 Small hooks at both ends = self-ishness.

47 Tall = writer has a desire for power.

48 Low = could be moral disregard. Look for other factors in the script.

49 Dot at the top = if not a faulty pen, this resting dot at the top of an upright extension indicates fatigue and overwork. There is usually more than one in the script.

50 Wide loops = imagination, fantasy.

51 Like a £ sign = money-conscious.

52 Pointed tip in small script = disciplined mind.
In large script = aggressive attitude.

M *The first downstroke represents the 'I', the second middle stroke, the 'you', and the third downstroke, society in general. This capital lends itself to endless combinations of loops, curves, straight lines, soft, hooked or angular; beginning and end strokes.*

53 Third stroke higher = likes to be acknowledged; influenced by public opinion.

54 First stroke higher = high opinion of self; poor taste.

55 Enrolled = greed.

56 Garland formation = friendly disposition.

57 Wavy line formation = versatile, but lack of commitment.

58 Sacre Coeur (as taught in French convents for example) = pretentious attitude. Secretive (unless taught in a French convent, in which case copybook!)

59 Simple (depending upon the script quality) = simple tastes. Harmonious.

60 Angled initial stroke = striving for an ideal without success. Aggressive tendencies.

61 Very high starting stroke = aristocratic feelings but not genuine. Always seeking prestigious friendships, therefore scheming.

62 Basic strokes only = contented with life. Simple needs. No pretence or fantasy.

63 Strokes not joined = ideas not constructive; a lack of logical thought.

64 Practical mind. Mechanical ability.

N

65 Long final stroke = initiative and enterprise; enthusiastic and willing to try out ideas.

66 Descending finals = stubborn.

67 Fanciful, but not vulgar = artistic awareness.

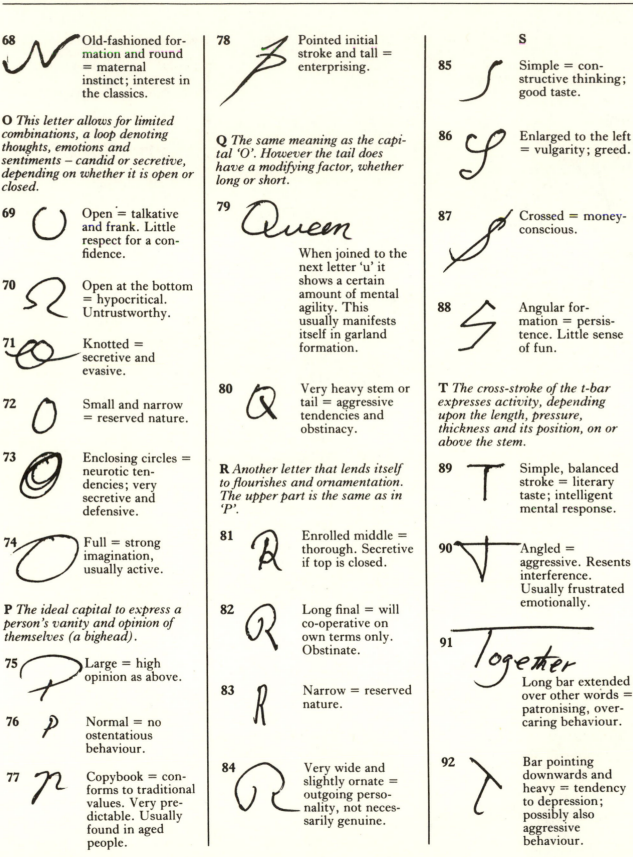

68 Old-fashioned formation and round = maternal instinct; interest in the classics.

O *This letter allows for limited combinations, a loop denoting thoughts, emotions and sentiments – candid or secretive, depending on whether it is open or closed.*

69 Open = talkative and frank. Little respect for a confidence.

70 Open at the bottom = hypocritical. Untrustworthy.

71 Knotted = secretive and evasive.

72 Small and narrow = reserved nature.

73 Enclosing circles = neurotic tendencies; very secretive and defensive.

74 Full = strong imagination, usually active.

P *The ideal capital to express a person's vanity and opinion of themselves (a bighead).*

75 Large = high opinion as above.

76 Normal = no ostentatious behaviour.

77 Copybook = conforms to traditional values. Very predictable. Usually found in aged people.

78 Pointed initial stroke and tall = enterprising.

Q *The same meaning as the capital 'O'. However the tail does have a modifying factor, whether long or short.*

79 When joined to the next letter 'u' it shows a certain amount of mental agility. This usually manifests itself in garland formation.

80 Very heavy stem or tail = aggressive tendencies and obstinacy.

R *Another letter that lends itself to flourishes and ornamentation. The upper part is the same as in 'P'.*

81 Enrolled middle = thorough. Secretive if top is closed.

82 Long final = will co-operative on own terms only. Obstinate.

83 Narrow = reserved nature.

84 Very wide and slightly ornate = outgoing personality, not necessarily genuine.

S

85 Simple = constructive thinking; good taste.

86 Enlarged to the left = vulgarity; greed.

87 Crossed = money-conscious.

88 Angular formation = persistence. Little sense of fun.

T *The cross-stroke of the t-bar expresses activity, depending upon the length, pressure, thickness and its position, on or above the stem.*

89 Simple, balanced stroke = literary taste; intelligent mental response.

90 Angled = aggressive. Resents interference. Usually frustrated emotionally.

91 Long bar extended over other words = patronising, over-caring behaviour.

92 Bar pointing downwards and heavy = tendency to depression; possibly also aggressive behaviour.

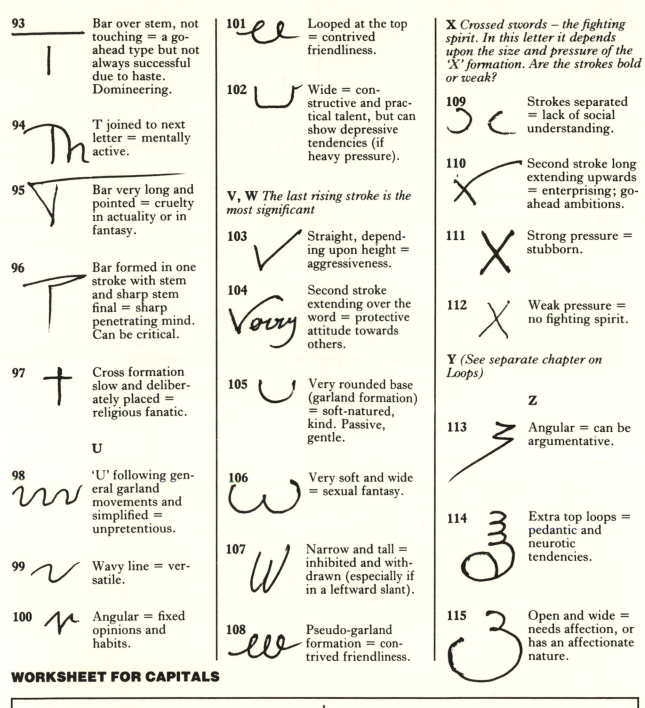

93 Bar over stem, not touching = a go-ahead type but not always successful due to haste. Domineering.

94 T joined to next letter = mentally active.

95 Bar very long and pointed = cruelty in actuality or in fantasy.

96 Bar formed in one stroke with stem and sharp stem final = sharp penetrating mind. Can be critical.

97 Cross formation slow and deliberately placed = religious fanatic.

U

98 'U' following general garland movements and simplified = unpretentious.

99 Wavy line = versatile.

100 Angular = fixed opinions and habits.

101 Looped at the top = contrived friendliness.

102 Wide = constructive and practical talent, but can show depressive tendencies (if heavy pressure).

V, W *The last rising stroke is the most significant*

103 Straight, depending upon height = aggressiveness.

104 Second stroke extending over the word = protective attitude towards others.

105 Very rounded base (garland formation) = soft-natured, kind. Passive, gentle.

106 Very soft and wide = sexual fantasy.

107 Narrow and tall = inhibited and withdrawn (especially if in a leftward slant).

108 Pseudo-garland formation = contrived friendliness.

X *Crossed swords – the fighting spirit. In this letter it depends upon the size and pressure of the 'X' formation. Are the strokes bold or weak?*

109 Strokes separated = lack of social understanding.

110 Second stroke long extending upwards = enterprising; go-ahead ambitions.

111 Strong pressure = stubborn.

112 Weak pressure = no fighting spirit.

Y *(See separate chapter on Loops)*

Z

113 Angular = can be argumentative.

114 Extra top loops = pedantic and neurotic tendencies.

115 Open and wide = needs affection, or has an affectionate nature.

WORKSHEET FOR CAPITALS

Capitals (Large/small, narrow/wide, embellished, etc) (Compared with the samples above.)	Interpretation

The capital 'I' (personal pronoun 'I')

Chapter 19

The personal pronoun 'I' relates to the self-image – this is how the writer sees himself, his needs, his values and his self-importance. It is the symbol of the inner centre of his conscious self. This capital letter is unique to the English language. It is very important in the total assessment of the personality concerned.

It should be compared with the general script factors as well as other capitals, and certainly be compared with another capital 'I' not relating to the self, if there is one, even if it is joined to another letter. For example, '*I* was in *I*reland last week'. This personal symbol can change rapidly if there is a change in personal circumstances such as trauma, illness or an increase in self-esteem.

The personal pronoun 'I' should be evaluated in relation to:

1 Pressure
2 Size and slant
3 Form of the letter
4 Fullness and leanness
5 The spacing before and after the letter.

Any difference from the general script is a particularly significant indication of the level of self-esteem. The following examples should give you a good idea of how to assess this letter.

1 *where can I go*

PPI much taller = over-compensated inferiority complex.

2 *where can I go*

PPI much smaller = lack of self-confidence inhibiting progress.

3 *where can I go*

Pressure much heavier = strain and tension; compulsive habits.

4 *where can I go*

Pressure very much lighter = personality weakness. Inhibited response to life. Inferiority feelings are not compensated and therefore will dominate, causing submission.

5 *where can I go*

Right slant 'I' in leftward script = the need for involvement is negated by shyness and fear of failure.

6 *where can I go*

Left slant 'I' in rightward script = in spite of active participation, caution governs the approach to others, resulting in feelings of isolation.

7

PPI 'I' complicated and enriched = feelings of greatness and self-worth. Often overcompensation for an inferiority complex.

8

PPI 'I' narrow and simple = natural response, no affectation. Cultured. Writer wishes to be seen as he actually is.

9

'i' for 'I' = lack of self-esteem; sign of a stunted personality.

10

'I' enrolled = greed.

11

'I' forms very angular = critical, hostile, probably of self.

12

'I' of old-fashioned type = not compulsive or rash. Dated attitude. Considers all moves before carrying them out.

13

'I's of different styles in one script = flexible approach but unpredictable.

14

'I' as counter-stroke which starts at bottom = inclination to rebel.

15

'I' as straight finishing stroke = independent.

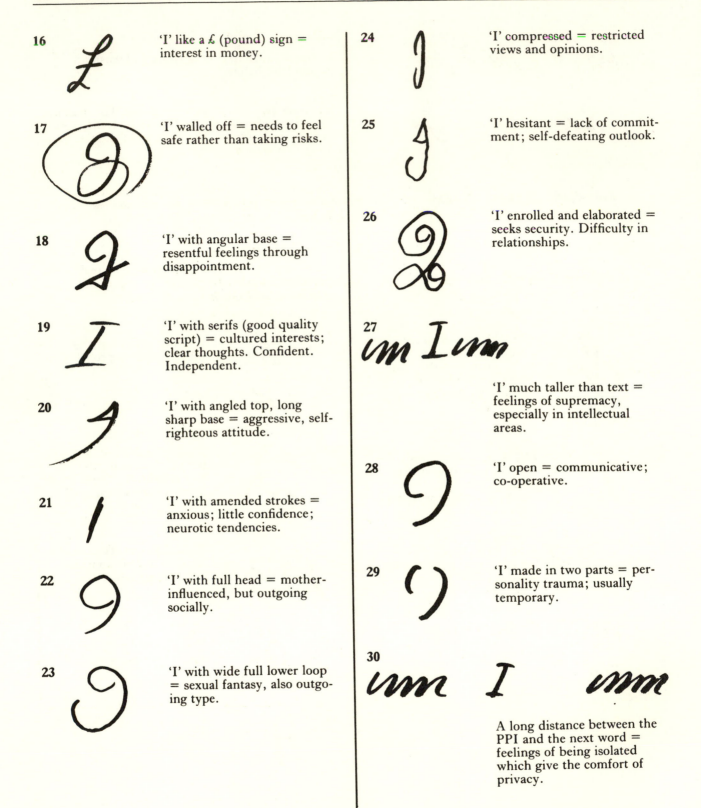

16 'I' like a £ (pound) sign = interest in money.

17 'I' walled off = needs to feel safe rather than taking risks.

18 'I' with angular base = resentful feelings through disappointment.

19 'I' with serifs (good quality script) = cultured interests; clear thoughts. Confident. Independent.

20 'I' with angled top, long sharp base = aggressive, self-righteous attitude.

21 'I' with amended strokes = anxious; little confidence; neurotic tendencies.

22 'I' with full head = mother-influenced, but outgoing socially.

23 'I' with wide full lower loop = sexual fantasy, also outgoing type.

24 'I' compressed = restricted views and opinions.

25 'I' hesitant = lack of commitment; self-defeating outlook.

26 'I' enrolled and elaborated = seeks security. Difficulty in relationships.

27 'I' much taller than text = feelings of supremacy, especially in intellectual areas.

28 'I' open = communicative; co-operative.

29 'I' made in two parts = personality trauma; usually temporary.

30 A long distance between the PPI and the next word = feelings of being isolated which give the comfort of privacy.

31

Very near to the following word = inability to be alone; afraid of solitude.

32

'I' very rightward = a need of personal intimate contact with others.

33

'I' very leftward = aversion to the social scene. Feelings of guilt.

To evaluate a personal pronoun 'I' of unusual appearance, you should decide what the dominant factor is. Make a note of this now and then, when you have finished assessing the whole script, you should have enough information to help you to decide on the significance of this letter. This private self-image may be quite different from the public, social image.

I should again emphasise that, like the other factors in the handwriting, the personal pronoun 'I' is part and parcel of the *global* view of the *whole* personality and, although very important, should not be given too great a significance.

WORKSHEET FOR PERSONAL PRONOUN 'I'

PPI (Assess PPI in relation to other letters of the script, on the following points:)	Interpretation
Pressure	
Size	
Slant	
Form	
Fullness/leanness	
Spacing, before and after	
Special features	
Dominant factor	

Chapter 20 | 'i'-dots and 't'-bars

All handwriting analysis books will have a chapter on 'i'-dots and 't'-bars. This book is no exception. However, unlike some authors, I feel that they are useful only to confirm other factors and are not particularly significant in themselves.

Heavy dots and bars
A heavy 't'-bar and 'i'-dot will be evident in aggressive handwriting which has much pressure, angular forms and connections, and a fast tempo.

Light dots and bars
Light 't'-bars and 'i'-dots go with other emotionally sensitive features such as low pressure, fine strokes, a round script and a slow to moderate tempo.

'i'-DOTS
'i'-dots should be evaluated according to
1 their location in relation to the downstroke
2 the significance of rightward and leftward movement
3 whether they are placed high or low.

The following give some examples, frequently found, but of course the variety is again infinite:

1		Accent form, in good Form Level script = critical mind. Quick intelligence.
2		Weak dot = little self-confidence, easily led by others. Low vitality.
3		*'i'-dot omitted* poor quality script = careless, lazy, forgetful. good quality script = expedient, decisive, resourceful.

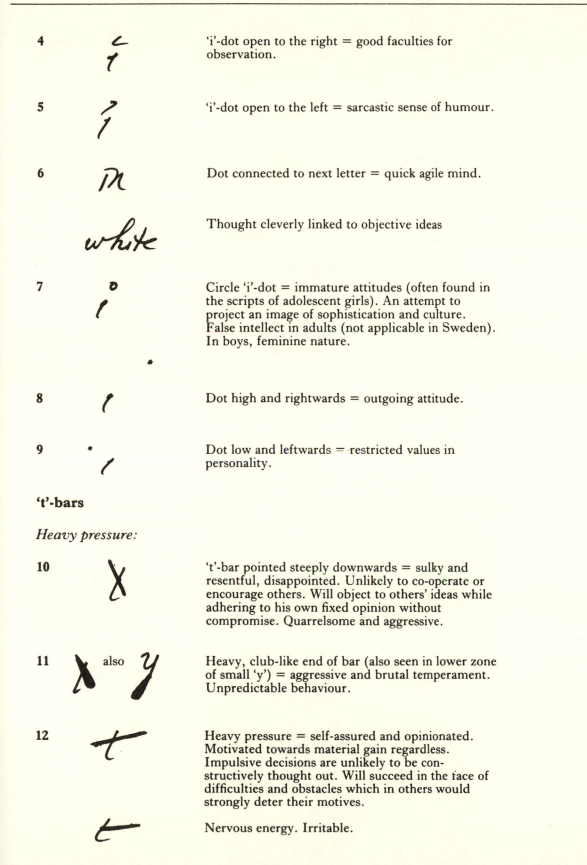

4   'i'-dot open to the right = good faculties for observation.

5   'i'-dot open to the left = sarcastic sense of humour.

6   Dot connected to next letter = quick agile mind.

Thought cleverly linked to objective ideas

7   Circle 'i'-dot = immature attitudes (often found in the scripts of adolescent girls). An attempt to project an image of sophistication and culture. False intellect in adults (not applicable in Sweden). In boys, feminine nature.

8   Dot high and rightwards = outgoing attitude.

9   Dot low and leftwards = restricted values in personality.

't'-bars

Heavy pressure:

10   't'-bar pointed steeply downwards = sulky and resentful, disappointed. Unlikely to co-operate or encourage others. Will object to others' ideas while adhering to his own fixed opinion without compromise. Quarrelsome and aggressive.

11   Heavy, club-like end of bar (also seen in lower zone of small 'y') = aggressive and brutal temperament. Unpredictable behaviour.

12   Heavy pressure = self-assured and opinionated. Motivated towards material gain regardless. Impulsive decisions are unlikely to be constructively thought out. Will succeed in the face of difficulties and obstacles which in others would strongly deter their motives.

Nervous energy. Irritable.

13   Detached bar from stem = prone to fantasy. Ideals unrealistically applied.

14   Double bar = neurotic anxiety. Very unsettled.

15   Short, detached bar = ready to accept a challenge and try new projects. Likes to move with the times and is realistically motivated (particularly with rightward slant).

Light pressure:

16   *'t'-bar very low*
in copybook forms = conformist. Predictable. Cautious, timid. Lacking in self-confidence.
in small script = ability to concentrate on small details. No flexibility.
with threads = will take evasive action. Will not be pinpointed.

17   Leftward joined bar with small middle zone and wide right-hand margin = very self-conscious. Reserved. Fear of social contact. Inferiority complex dominates.

18   Leftward bar not joined = strongly influenced by past events; indecisive.

Lack of bar (usually with leftward slant which adds to the intensity) = very seldom finishes what he sets out to achieve; dissatisfaction all round, but no incentive to alter the situation.

19   Rising bar in good quality script = imaginative mind. Some ambition but lacks the willpower and stamina to carry it out. A person who tries but with little persistence.

20   Long bar on looped stem = sensitive, especially to criticism; fickle. Refined manner. Home lover. Affectionate.

21   Wavy bar = too frivolous to be reliable (probably compensating for lack of confidence).

Normal pressure, 't'-bar and stem:

22   Regular = even application to tasks. Reliable in finishing them.

23   Rising = aims for success and usually wins through.
Realistic ambition and ideas.

24   Hooks on bar on initial and end strokes (usually with rightward slant) = determination.

25   Downward stroke of bar = depressed. Could be quarrelsome and act contrary to convention.

26   Sharp end, 'tent' stem = can be sarcastic and very indiscreet. Argumentative.

27   't'-bar high and detached from stem (usually with large middle zone) = social interests dominate. Ambition and persistence.

28   Sharp ending of bar (with rightward slant) = quick response mentally and physically. Nervous energy; not totally reliable with minute details.

29   't'-bar high, touching the stem (with rightward slant) = ability to lead and take control. Realistic application to rules and regulations but must be assured they are effective.

30   Whip-like bar = erratic and unpredictable.

31   Leftward = jealous and suspicious nature. Disappointment in life.

32   Knotted = resistance; obstinacy
Small knot = thorough

33  Star-shaped = very sensitive to criticism. Indecisive and repressed.

34  Long triangular stroke = objects to interference and becomes aggressive if questioned.

35  't'-bar joined to next letter = agile mind; quick thinker.

36 ꞏꞏꞏ A mixture of bars all in one document = conflicting thoughts and emotions; never sure or satisfied.

WORKSHEET FOR 'i'-DOTS AND 't'-BARS

	Interpretation
'i'-dots heavy or light location rightward/leftward movement high or low special features **'t'-bars** heavy or light location (low, high, on top, centre, detached, right/left-of downstroke) Slant (up/down) length (short/long) Other features (loops, hooks, mixed etc)	

PART THREE

. . . and deeper

Chapter *21* | Symbolism

Symbolised meanings, formed during early childhood, can often persist into adult life, although we usually discard them well before maturity. They are, however, only repressed and can reveal themselves many years later.

These scribbled patterns of childhood – the urge for playful movements – are often symbolised in adult signatures. When using graphological procedure and psychological knowledge, they can be useful pointers.

For instance, openness to the right – the future or father – and the left – the past or mother – are very significant, indicating, for instance, blocks to progress through the mother's or father's over-dominant influence.

A symbol in handwriting rarely illustrates the precise meaning. If you find one you must try to find its connection to the writer's personality or circumstances. It is important to remember they are not just irrelevant movements, but representations of our unconsciousness seeking expression. In most of those symbols only an intuitive interpretation can be arrived at and assessed accordingly to the basic movement and shape, but it must be done with care and not, as was once thought, as one sign of one meaning only, irrespective of the other script factors – a dangerous practice resulting in a misjudgement of the writer.

No symbol should be ignored: there is usually a reason for its appearance in a spontaneously produced script.

Pictorial forms manifest themselves in a signature which is always unique to the writer. Some self-explanatory symbols unrelated to other signs in the script can be explained relatively easily – for instance, heart-shaped circles in love letters (fig 214). Symbols connected with sport or a profession (fig 215) simply indicate that the writer takes a very active part, even if only in the imagination (wide loops) in this. You should first try to exclude all other meanings, however. If in doubt, the student graphologist should omit sexual symbols in an analysis.

Sexual symbols can be seen in the script of a sexually repressed writer. They are often in the shape of a particular article or part of the body that has been unhealthily restrained over the years.

In most cases there is no tangible way to establish symbolic meaning with the writer unless the context of the text points to it. He is unlikely to admit his *your aunty did say you are a lonely person and I would love to be your girl friend if you would let me.*

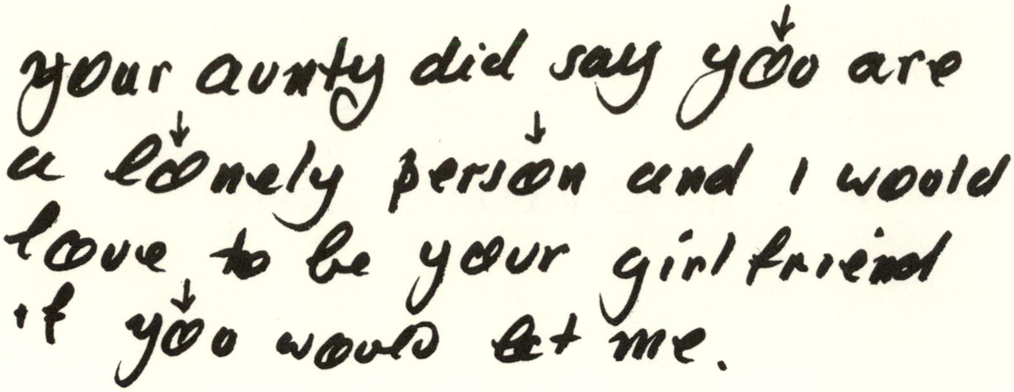

Fig 214
Heart-shaped circles

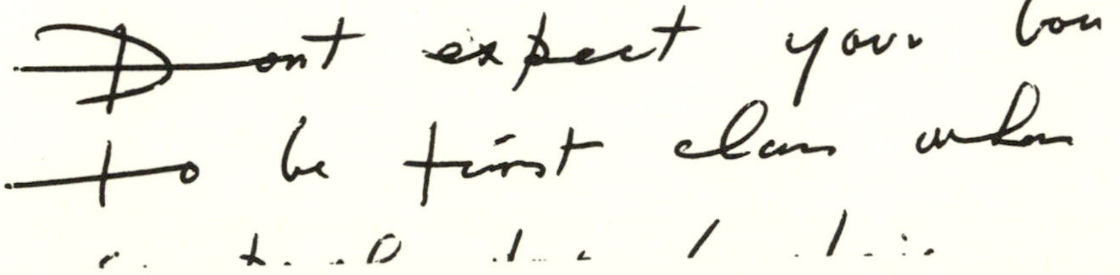

Dont expect your bou to be first class when...

Fig 215
Archery symbols

weaknesses, even to those he knows well, otherwise they would not have been repressed in the first place. If they come to light through graphology, however, it may help him to recognise them and to adjust to his inner needs and desires.

Even if his sense of morality prevents him from practising his yearnings he can benefit from the freeing of those unconscious blocks, perhaps being able to find some other outlet or expression for them.

Fig 216
Grossly abnormal
script

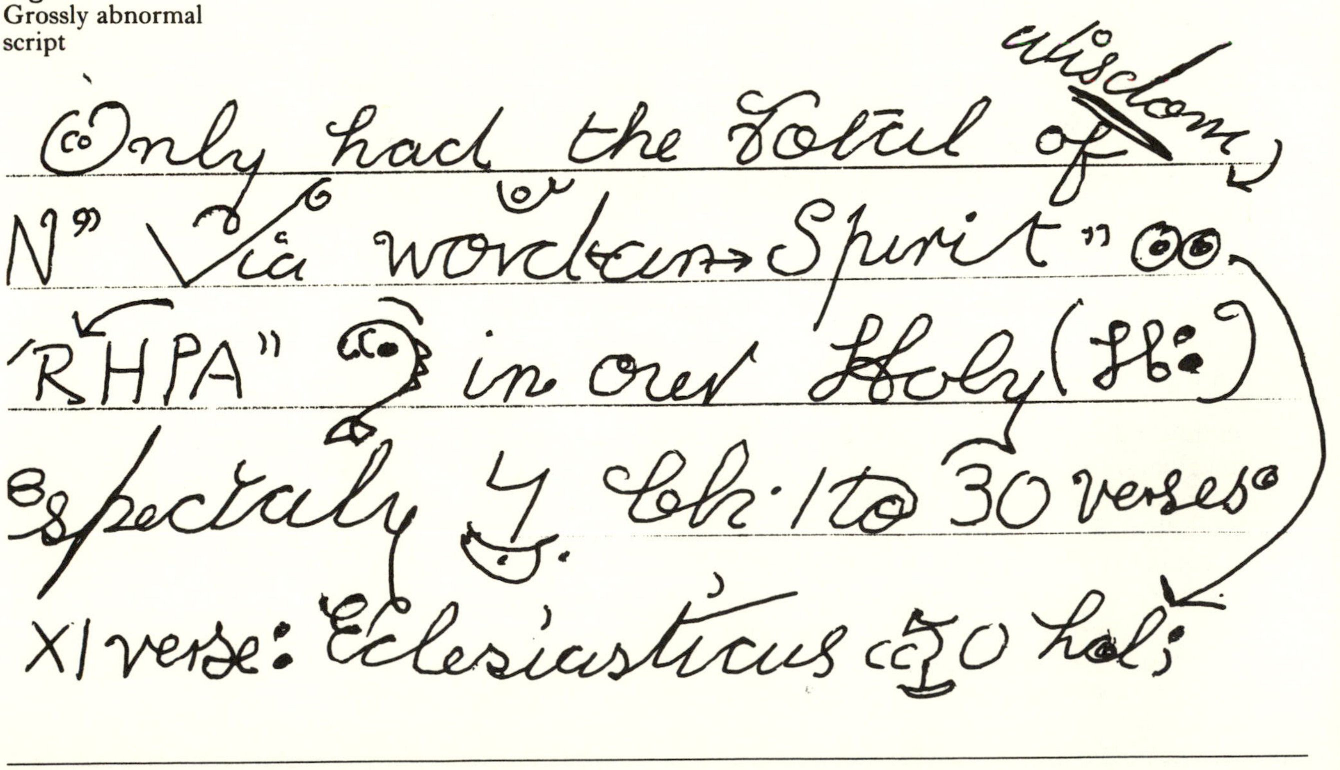

Only had the total of Wisdom) N" Via wordan Spirit " oo "RHPA" in our Holy (fb) especialy 4. ch. 1 to 30 verses XI verse: Eclesiasticus 50 hol;

Symbols must not be searched for where none exist. A text full of pictorial symbols is symptomatic of an abnormal personality in need of treatment (fig 216).

For further reading on symbols I would recommend Tom Chetwynd's book, *A Dictionary of Symbols* and C.J. Jung's *Man and his Symbols*.

WORKSHEET FOR SYMBOLISM

Symbolism	Interpretation
If any	

Chapter 22 | Signatures

Most graphologists find that when they are in company, and their interest (whether professional or amateur) in handwriting is revealed someone will immediately say 'You can do mine', promptly write a signature and then wait for the revelation to follow.

It must be stressed that a signature on its own without a sample of the writer's normal script should not be assessed because there can be – and there often is – a difference between the two.

The general script represents what the writer is and the signature represents the image the writer wishes to project to others.

An ego symbol can be contrived for show; should the individual's view of himself alter in some way for any reason, his signature will most likely alter accordingly. The change may be minor, but psychologically significant in terms of projection of the personality.

The development of the writer can, in fact, be assessed in relation to the signature changes over a period of years as each new phase is reached. Generally, most signatures remain unaltered throughout the writer's mature and settled life until old age takes its toll and the hand becomes less stable, but the basic structure remains constant.

A person in the public eye such as an actor or pop star has two signatures, one for his private life and one for his autographs. The autograph will be stylised and at variance with the private one; even so, it is still graphologically valid to outline the image he projects to his following.

A child's signature should not be analysed until maturity, when the confines of school have been left behind. He will then, hopefully, be making his own way in the world, developing his signature and script as he progresses. How the signature manifests itself during this period depends upon the realisation of his ambitions and ideals in relation to his self-image. Dissatisfaction and disappointment would most likely weaken his signature, whereas the complete attainment of his efforts would strengthen it. A disappointed person may try to save face by putting on a façade of lightheartedness and subconsciously flourish his signature which would then be at variance with his script – revealing to the graphologist that he is falsely representing his inner self. When the signature and the body of the script are very alike, there is little discrepancy between the writer's private and public life.

A signature on a cheque can be written with less self-consciousness than that on a letter, because you are not writing to another, but to an establishment. However, a bank employee may be more aware of the importance of a signature where money is involved and will dutifully write his own cheques with professional clarity.

When a signature is just a mark of identification, to be recognised rather than read, then a wavy line or a scribbled mark is usually sufficient, but this is not enough for a graphologist and you should ask for a proper signature.

THREADLIKE SIGNATURES

On an official letter or document, a threadlike signature (fig 217) is the mark of a manipulator who can turn any situation to his own advantage and way of thinking, often a business-like person who has little time for the subordinate. Such people are elusive and avoid commitment easily. They are very good at making shrewd assessments of situations and people and at adopting the appropriate action to dominate and control them subtly. This often points to a flighty type, for instance a speciality salesman whose only ambition and function is to move in and sell regardless, then retire quickly. There will also be secondary threads in the general writing (fig 218).

In contrast is the salesman who is conscientious and willing to provide a service on a regular basis as well as take an order. His signature might also be a thread, but would have definition, as in a primary thread, or a wavy line with pressure (fig 219). (See also chapter 13 on forms of connection.)

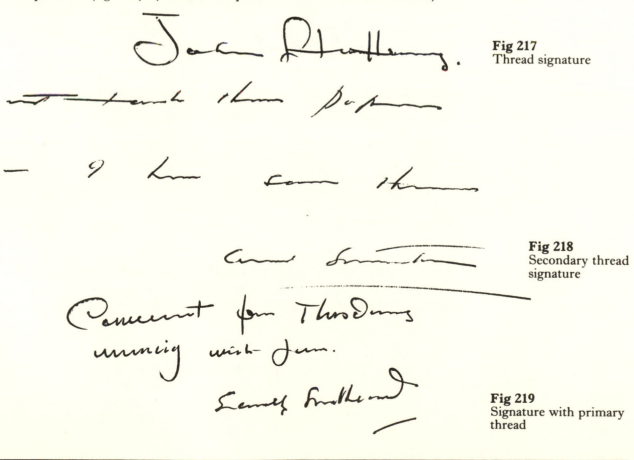

Fig 217
Thread signature

Fig 218
Secondary thread
signature

Fig 219
Signature with primary
thread

The following are factors which give a general guide:

SIZE

Signature *larger* than the general script (fig 220)
The writer is exhibiting an image of importance and stature in a desire to be recognised in some way.

Signature *smaller* than the general script (fig 221)
This individual is maintaining a low profile of modesty and humility. It could also be a measure of self-protection due to inhibition and shyness. Normally this is a sign of low self-esteem.

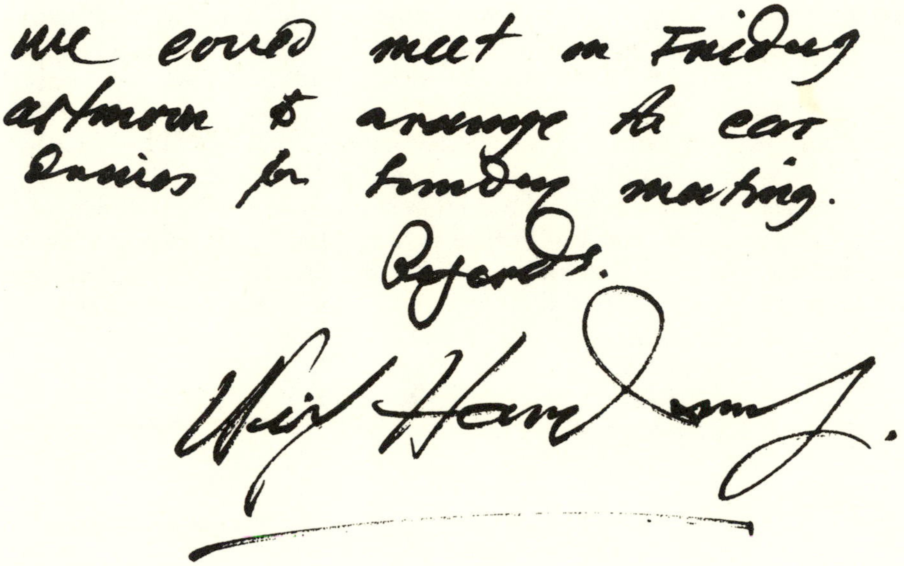

Fig 220
Signature larger than script

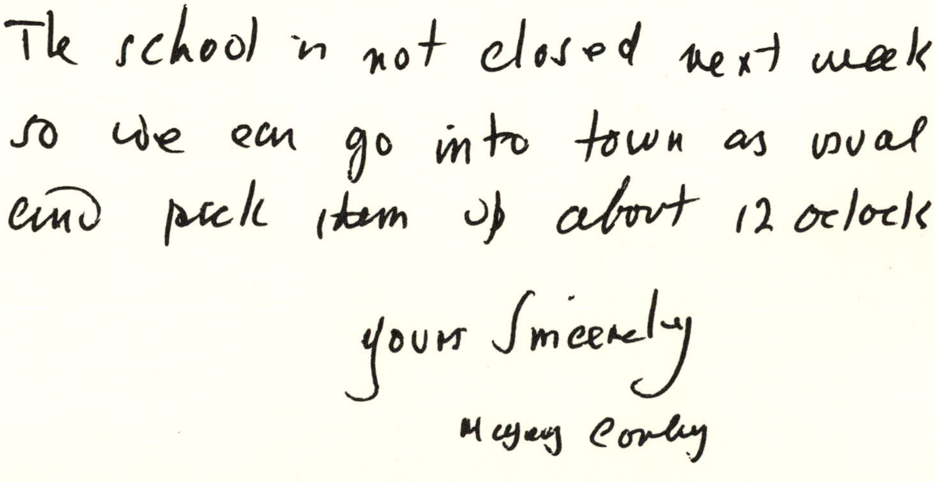

Fig 221
Signature smaller than script

SPEED

A *fast* signature in a slowly written script (fig 222)
An element of calculation present, a desire to be understood – hence the clear and slowly written message from a person whose signature is well known to the recipient.

A *slow* signature in a fast script
A person involved with the lawful aspects of a signature, i.e. a bank manager, lawyer etc. who is aware of the importance of a signature in a document as a legally binding commitment.

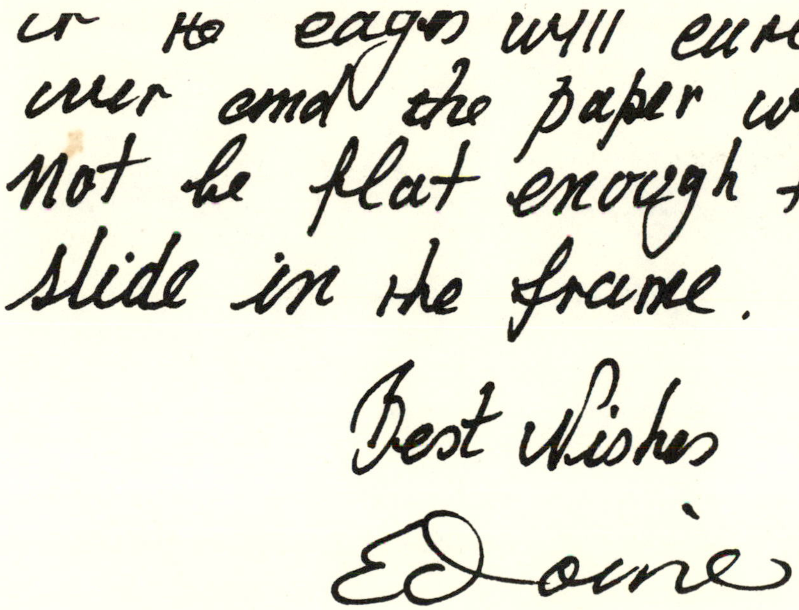

Fig 222
Slow script, fast signature

LEGIBILITY

A *legible* signature written naturally with a lively tempo (fig 223)
The writer is ready to honour her commitments; a sincere and reliable person, with a good balance of expressiveness in personality.

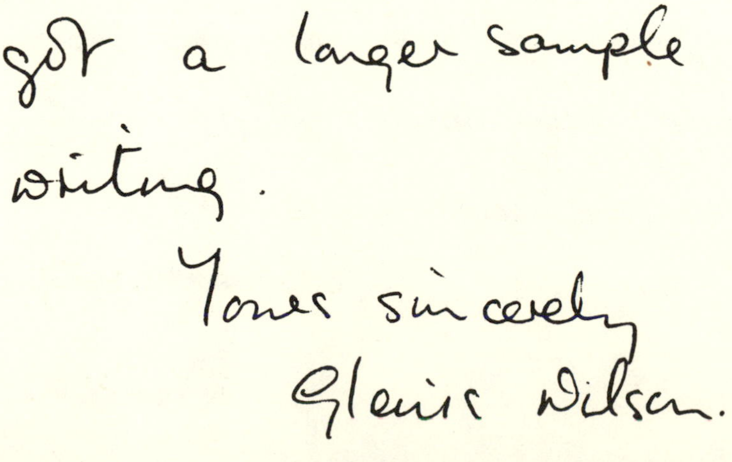

Fig 223
Legible signature

A *completely illegible* and complicated signature (fig 224)
A vain character who considers himself superior. An ostentatious and standoffish manner may prevent him getting promoted, causing an even more flamboyant signature to compensate – a vicious circle.

Fig 224
Illegible signature

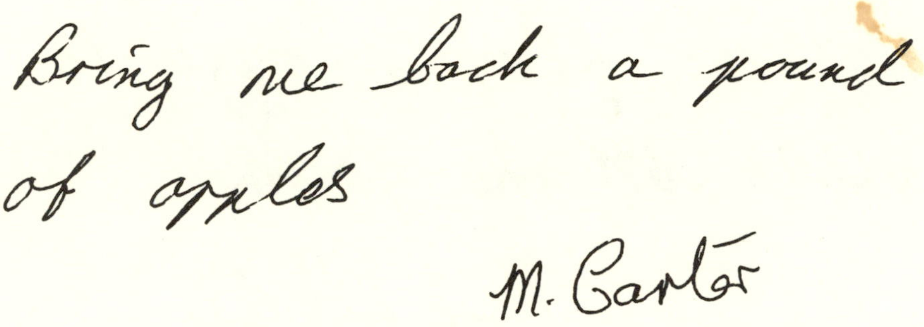

Fig 225
Rightward slant with
upright signature

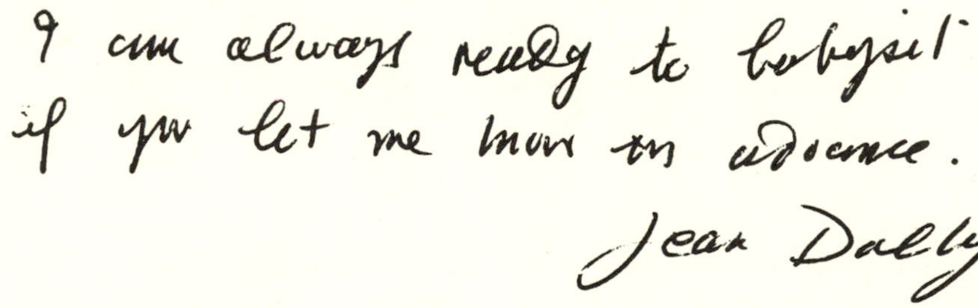

Fig 226
Upright script with
rightward signature

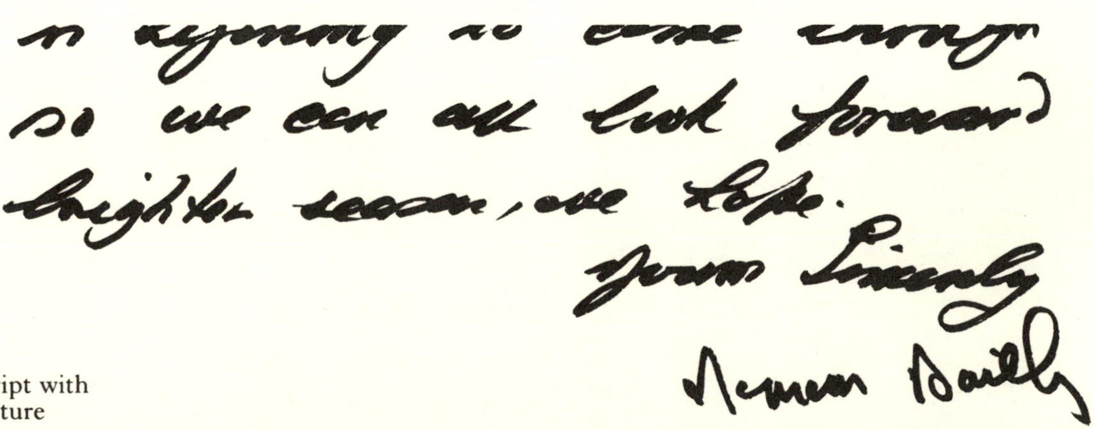

Fig 227
Rightward script with
leftward signature

SLANT

The slant of a signature can be different from that of the script.
When the script is rightward and the signature upright (fig 225), the writer has a façade of reserve. Underneath he is warmly responsive but his circumstances force him to adopt an aloof, dignified exterior. (In fig 225, note the leftward last letter).

When the body of the writing is vertical and the signature is rightward, (fig 226) we have a reserved person with a desire to convey warmth, and extrovert behaviour, but in actual contact there is a barrier of introversion causing restraint.

A *rightward slanting script with a leftward signature* (fig 227), indicates a barrier often due to fear. There is a need to gain this person's confidence when his natural friendliness will break through. Even so, for appearances' sake, the response will be controlled.

A *leftward script with a rightward signature* (fig 228): because of an occupation which entails meeting others on an amiable basis this introspective writer is compelled to project an outgoing manner which is innately unnatural. There is tension in this level of friendship, the lack of intimacy causing some hostility. However, an equally shy and inhibited person would have a better understanding of this person and is more likely to succeed in establishing a genuine rapport. Like attracts like.

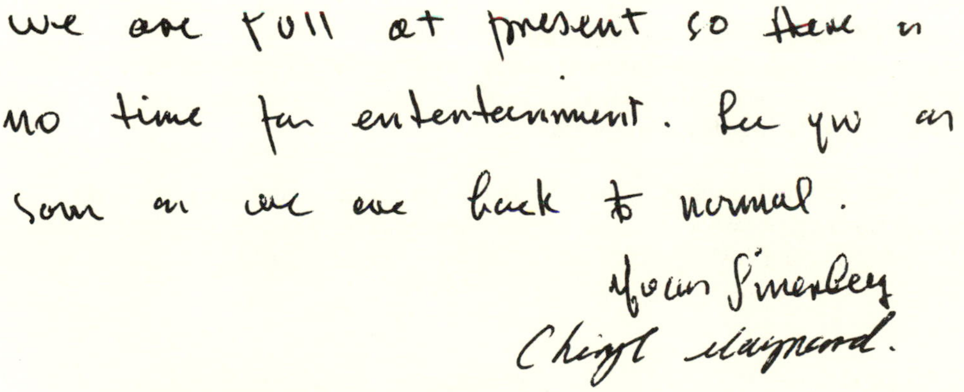

Fig 228
Leftward script with rightward signature

FIRST NAME AND FAMILY NAME

The graphologist should check that there is no difference in the writing of the first name and the surname.

   This could be seen particularly in the case of an unhappily married woman. Her married name could be written with less care, indicating her feelings about the marriage.

   The forename is associated with the writer's early life or experiences. If this is larger, smaller, weaker or stronger than the second name, then there are subconscious memories, good or bad, affecting the writer emotionally and being reflected in the script.

Forename which is larger and with stronger pressure (fig 229)
Pleasant memories of former times dominate and cannot be suppressed.
These people can act childishly and reject responsibility.

Small forename, larger surname (fig 230)
Early life experiences and traumas cannot be repressed either, but the writer
has a more adult attitude to commitments and responsibilities. In a woman,
this denotes also a satisfactory married or single state, with no desire to put
back the clock.

Fig 229
Larger forename or
first name than
surname

Fig 230
Smaller forename than
surname

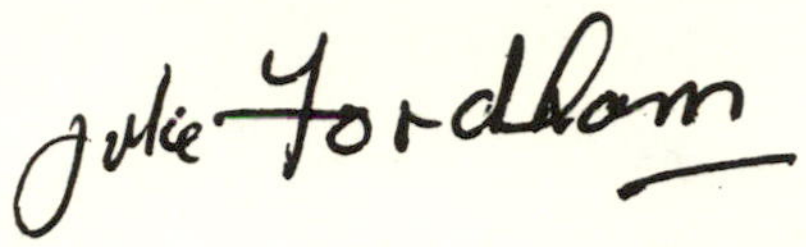

OTHER FEATURES TO CONSIDER

Cancelled out signature finishing leftwards (fig 231)
This writer is very low in self-esteem and has no desire to carry on with life as
it is. (Look also for heavy pressure.)

A circled signature or one boxed in (figs 232 and 233)
Such samples indicate in each case a crossed-out ego – self. Here the writer is
dissociating himself from social contact with others – a self-imposed loneliness and resignation. Also he could be contemplating committing suicide.
   Look for leftward slant (withdrawal), pressure disturbances (disordered
mind); also falling lines (depression).

Signature with a weak crossing through (light pressure) (fig 234)
A cry for help possibly. The writer is in need of assurance that in time all will
be well. Tender loving care from someone close is desired.

Fig 231
Cancelled-out signature

Fig 232
A circled signature

Fig 233
A boxed-in signature

Springboard initial strokes (fig 235)
A need for continuous advancement in business and social circles. Active drive; aggression.

Fig 234
A weak crossing-through of signature

Fig 235
Strong initial strokes

Signature with an extra long and heavy-pressured 't'-bar (fig 236)
Needs constant involvement in social activity.

Fine penmanship (harmonious) (fig 237)
An individual with respect for traditional values, but who tends to hide under a façade of great respectability. Usually slow in action, the spontaneity being curbed by deliberation and for appearances' sake – depending upon the degree of ornamentation.

Fig 236
Strong rightward stroke

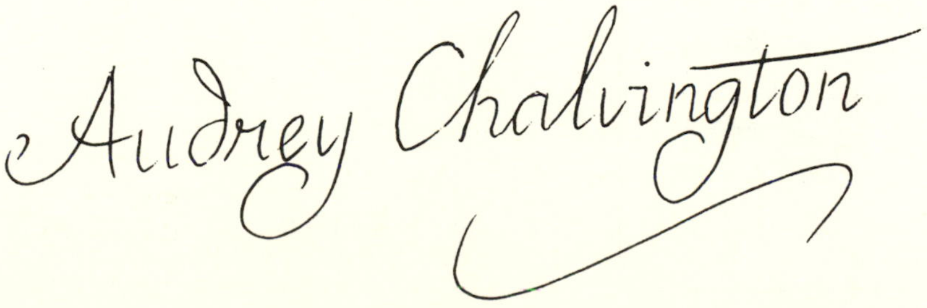

Fig 237
Signature of fine penmanship

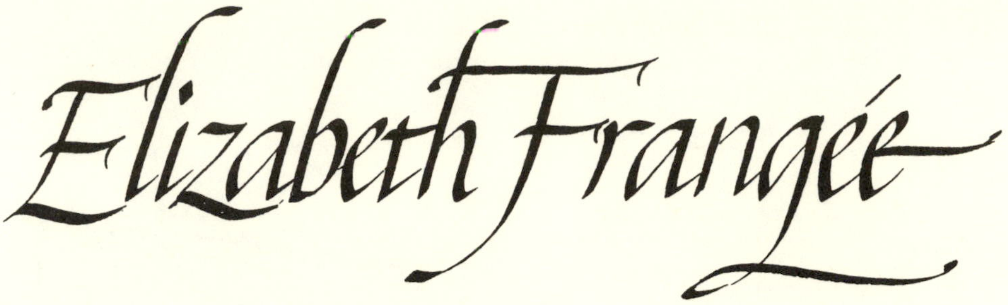

Fig 238
Calligraphic signature

Elizabeth Frangée

Calligraphic signature (fig 238)
The truly artistic calligraphic signature and script is simple, with no surplus strokes or ostentation (the latter indicate a person who is putting on an act).

A full signature written in one continuous movement (fig 239)
Logically orientated but probably under conditions of tension and stress, or the writer is not willing to be interrupted in his thoughts.

A full stop after a signature
A conventional attitude. If this is very heavy the attitude is opinionated and obstinate.

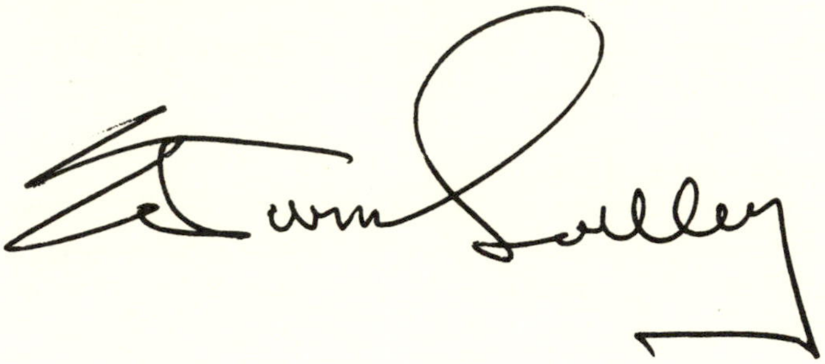

Fig 239
Forename and surname joined

THE PLACING OF THE SIGNATURE
All the rules of spacing apply generally (see chapter 3)

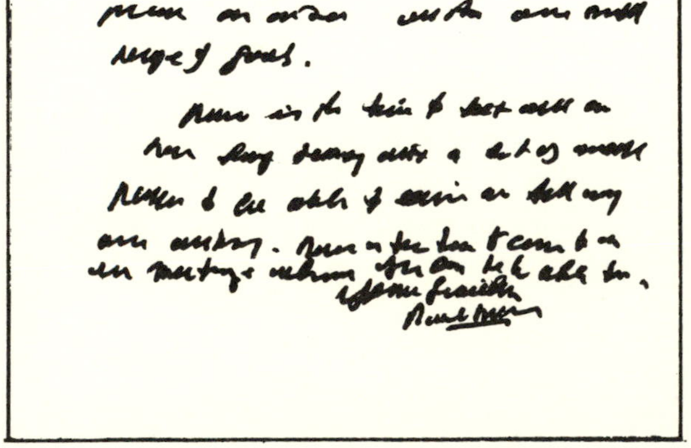

Fig 240
Very close to the text.
The writer here is identifying with the recipient too closely, without regard to his privacy.

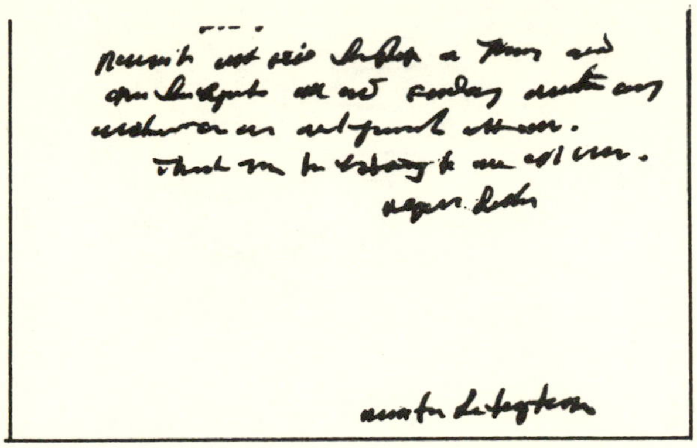

Fig 241
Very low, leaving ample space above.
A tendency towards depression, also an anxious attitude towards the recipient – probably afraid of the response to the message; or without any desire to be associated with him socially (a withdrawal sign). Isolation and insecure feelings with a lack of self-esteem.

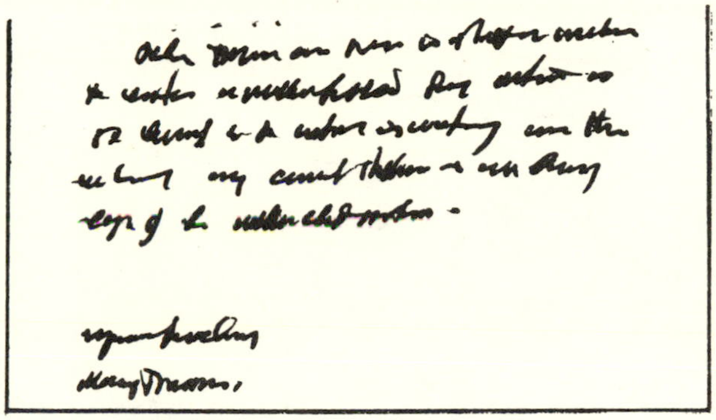

Fig 242
Very low and placed leftwardly.
Acute lack of self-respect.
Anxiety, fear and inhibition to the state of neurotic tendencies.
Inclinations of suicide if also circled.
In a business letter the leftward placing is normal procedure but should not be too low, as in this case.

THE UNDERSCORE

With regard to its length, firmness and formation this is an indication of self-emphasis.

Where there is no underscore this indicates not so much a lack of ambition and assertion, but an attitude which is not demanding, or where recognition is unnecessary for the projection of the personality. See the illustration for the various meanings.

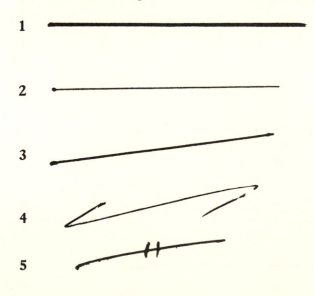

1   *Thick and long* = aggressive drive towards progress

2   *Normal pressure* = good self-confidence but not exaggerated

3   *Strong and rising, not too short or too long* = ambitious

4   *Hooks at both ends* = needs recognition

5   *Crossed* = money-conscious

6 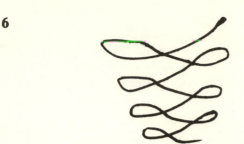   *Decorated, ornate* = affected and narcissistic

7    *Short and light* = no strong drive

8    *Several strokes* = self-assertive and over-bearing attitude – no compromise.

9   *Double stroke* = affectation, need for attention.

WORKSHEET FOR SIGNATURES

Signatures	Interpretation
In relation to the rest of the script Size Speed Legibility Slant Pressure First name/family name dominant Other points (e.g. cancelled out, circled, full stop)	
Placing of signature	
Underscore	

Chapter 23 | Stimulus or motive words

Examples of these are 'God', 'Mother', 'Father', 'Death', 'Sex', or the name of a person or subject and they can be identified in that a single word or passage is written at a different speed and pressure from the rest of the script.

This so-called 'stimulus word' causes an emotional association or conflict and is penned with extra care, anxiety, or release. Something holding the person back, calling for greater conscious concern, love or hate or some other impediment or conflict causes the writer to deliberate, and use more pressure and less speed. Or the writer may react to the word or name that causes him displeasure or embarrassment by evading the issue in a quick flourish, using less pressure and more speed than normal. This can point to psychological distress, and should be taken into consideration if relevant to the type of assessment being prepared.

WORKSHEET FOR STIMULUS OR MOTIVE WORDS

Stimulus/motive words (*Clues*: different speed pressure etc.)	If there are any it is probably enough just to point them out.

The influence of stress and tension

Chapter *24*

A certain amount of stress and tension is necessary in our lives – it provides the stimulus for action, the problems to solve. Without it we would progress through states of boredom to depression and despair or would have to create a crisis to make us feel alive again. To some extent we do this anyway when life becomes monotonous, the way we choose depending on our personality and conditioning.

Too much stress and tension, however, is a well-recognized evil of our times, and much has been written on the subject. Left unchecked it can ruin careers, break up relationships and cause illness, perhaps even death.

Symptoms of stress and tension range from vague feelings of restlessness and insecurity to aches and pains, headaches, sweating, constricted breathing, nausea and anxiety attacks.

Some people seem to be more prone to stress than others. The perfectionist is at risk because he cannot tolerate disorder and strives constantly for the impossible. But we are all prey to the major crises of life – death of loved ones, loss of job, financial worries, sexual problems, illness and other major changes. Even positive change can trigger stress – a new home, a better job or public acclaim.

Fig 243
Examples of scripts showing indication of stress

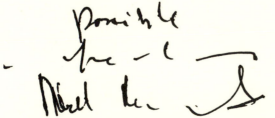

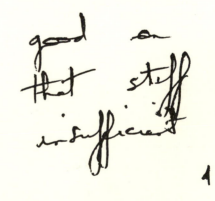

There are many ways to defuse stress. A change in attitude is often enough and there are several methods of relaxation and meditation to explore.

Realizing that you are stressed is the first step, of course, and this is where the graphologist can help.

When you find several indications of stress in a script (see the list on page 180), you should warn the writer. Tell him which area of his life is being neglected or under strain (the zones indicate this) and give any other clues you can based on the individual points in the writing, making any advice you give positive and constructive. The last thing he needs is dramatic warnings from you which will frighten the life out of him and plunge him into extreme anxiety, so be gentle.

Fig 243
Examples of scripts showing indication of stress

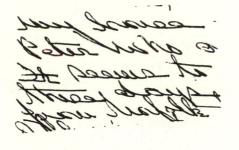

WORKSHEET FOR STRESS AND TENSION

Indications of stress in handwriting	√
1 Excessive pressure in all or any zone.	
2 Small middle zone compressed between a large upper and lower zone.	
3 Disturbed rhythm.	
4 Rigid strokes.	
5 Sudden weaknesses in a dominant pressure.	
6 Extreme smallness, especially in a very leftward-slanting script.	
7 Extreme connection of words.	
8 Touching up of many letters and overstroking.	
9 Carefully formed but cumbersome slowly written letters (an attempt at style).	
10 Extreme narrowness, cramping and covering strokes.	
11 Falling lines of writing.	
12 Downwards tiling.	
13 Abrupt terminals.	
14 Much underlining.	
15 Secondary (pressureless) threads.	
16 Narrow left margin with a very wide right margin.	
17 Large gaps inside words.	
18 Heavy starting strokes.	
19 Heavy angular strokes.	
20 Very narrow, tall upper zone extensions.	
21 Ovals made with two or more circles.	
22 Irregular base line.	
23 Columning (where each word appears under another deliberately, as the lines progress: see chapter 3 on spacing).	
24 Excessively wide lines of writing.	
25 Letters missing.	
26 Resting dots on indentation where the writer has momentarily paused, during the forming of a letter. Seen through a magnifier.	
27 Marked irregularity.	
28 Filled in loops in pasty writing.	
29 Trembling stroke formations.	
30 Very large capitals.	
31 Very small signature in relation to the script.	
32 Very small personal pronoun 'I', or 'i' to replace it.	
33 Signature circled round the outside.	
34 Excessive punctuation in a heavy-pressured script.	
35 Letters formed in more than one stroke, where normally one stroke is suffcient.	
36 Very wide word spacing, but narrow letter spacing.	
37 Excessively variable slant.	
38 One zone out of all proportion in size.	
Total	

The more stress there is in the writer, the more the factors are prominent and the more there are of them.

The writing will always be heavy on the tension side of the tension and release scale.

Most business people are under pressure and many can thrive on it successfully. The angular writer can survive pressure far more and for longer than the garland or thread writer, who would snap under the strain. However the thread (or wavy line) writer would avoid the stress somehow where possible.

Chapter 25

Colour of ink and paper

COLOUR OF INK

The colour and shade of the ink used by the writer can also be taken into consideration.

Blue/black   A moderately masculine colour favoured by business people with no desire to be exceptional or pretentious.

Weak blue/black   Usually used with a fine nib. These writers often belong to the artistic group known for their sensitive temperament and serious attitude to literature and music.

Black   The bolder type of writer likes this colour, used mainly with a broad nib or a felt-tip pen giving a thick stroke effect. It indicates power and a serious, forceful attitude.

Royal blue   A feminine colour liked by sociable and affectionate people. They are understanding and willing to help others.

Turquoise   A ladies' ink colour, but also liked by men who have a desire to improve, particularly in artistic pursuits.

Green   Symbolic of harmony, flexibility and strong mental development. These writers have a desire to be individual and distinguished. They may also tend to show off.

Violet   Usually found with a coloured writing paper, the writer wishing to be trendy. Liked by theatre people.

Red	If used for ordinary letter writing, it indicates a pedantic and pompous person who is also dependent on having friends with professional standing, and is willing to be generous only to be seen as such. Also used by professional people to mark or make notes that are conspicuous. Unless used in an ostentatious manner, red ink is not to be overestimated. Red is symbolic of anger and aggression which in graphology will also show in heavy pressure, angular connections etc.
Brown	Used by artistic, professional people, e.g. calligraphers and designers possessing an air of authority.

If possible, always enquire if the ink used is that regularly used by the writer and that it is not just a random choice of the moment. (See chapter 32.)

THE PAPER

It is now possible to buy coloured writing paper of a good quality, with matching envelopes.

The person who wishes to portray a façade of good taste often chooses a colour that, to the sensitive person, is offensive, such as bright red or green or black, using white ink.

To the person who has a desire to be slightly unconventional the softer shades will appeal – particularly pink to those who wish to extend their feminine front and are loving in nature.

The ordinary writer with no ostentatious intent will keep to white, cream or grey knowing that good taste is shown in the type of paper rather than the actual shade.

The discerning writer will choose a medium to heavy weight paper made by the quality manufacturers and he avoids economy pads for important letters.

WORKSHEET FOR COLOUR OF INK

Colour of ink, paper *(kind of paper, pen etc)* Writer's own choice? Used normally?	*Interpretation*

Chapter 26 | Dishonesty and unreliability

Handwriting is a valid expression of our whole being reflecting the values we extend to our everyday activities. Where do we draw the line in disclosing a person as 'dishonest'? Do we brand him as unreliable, not to be believed or trusted in a financial situation? Irresponsible in other ways and situations? Dishonesty in what respect and to what degree?

When compiling a graphology report to be sent to someone other than the writer himself, you must be extremely careful both in your preparatory work and in choosing your words for the report. Think of the consequences.

You will have to do a complete breakdown of all the writing factors before you can make an assessment. It takes many years of practical experience to delve to this depth with confidence.

In reports for personnel selection in particular you will be expected to give some rating for honesty and reliability, whether the employer asks for it directly or not.

You should study all the factors below carefully and in relation to each other. There should be at least five to bring an indication of 'dishonesty' into the assessment.

The following individual signs of unreliability are the major pointers, along with the specific trouble spots when applicable.

1 Slow script

Rigid copybook forms, but in which other factors show a graphically mature writer, with a sharp mind and sound physical co-ordination, the writing being contrived for effect. Usually a feature of suspected forged scripts. A false presentation of facts.

2 Shark's tooth and covering strokes together (see fig 244)

Indicating a writer capable of secretiveness and deceit. Shark's tooth is also an indication of someone capable of (but not necessarily doing) sharp practice deals.

Fig 244

3 Flat arcades with secondary thread, also possible pressureless garlands

A writer open to influence, with no definite values on which to build a straightforward lifestyle.

4 Disturbed pressure pattern – not attributable to physical difficulties

A light and dark mixture of exaggerations and pressureless forms. Inconsistently applied – overcompensation for weak willpower and instability.

5 Enrolments

Complicated letter forms (not genuinely calligraphic). Deliberate approach to obscure reasons and confuse issues.

6 Other letters produced instead of those intended (not dyslexic), often with threads

Avoidance of definite commitment.

7 Touching up without improvement (amendments)

Often found in the upper zone when the writer is trying to make reality match his hopes by indirect means due to failure in meeting his own requirements. Conversely, this could be an attempt to make a good impression. Nervousness will cause frequent starts to a letter.

8 Blotched and muddy script with resting dots and unnecessary punctuation

Unreleased inner tension, causing strain and anxiety with possible uncontrolled activity and aggression.

9 Leftward-tending strokes on terminals

Very selfish attitude.

10 Important parts of letters missing (no other signs of carelessness)

The writer is distracting attention from himself. It is not what he says, but what he does not say that is important.

11 Marked initial emphasis

A desire to make a good impression.

12 Small ovals open at the base

The writer will act contrary to convention and is open to selfish demands.

13 Extreme narrowness or covering strokes

Concealment, anxiety, self-protective attitude. No progressive involvement with others through fear of becoming too involved personally.

14 Indistinct and ambiguous letters

Disregard for others.

15 Marked difference between signature and script, especially with exaggerated flourishes

Variance between what he really is and how he wishes to be seen, whether in private life or in business – usually both.

16 Marked constantly changing slant in poor rhythmic script

Unresolved inner conflicts and inability to face reality.

17 Incomplete terminals (downstrokes not returning to the base line)

Unwilling to face up to reality or a definite course of action.

18 Mixed connective forms

Indication of a weak character.

19 Blurred and misshapen numbers in an artificial-looking script (for instance on 5 or 3)

The ransome note trick – hoping the smaller figure will be mistaken for a higher one: to mislead.

20 Illegible script (especially on an envelope)

Not wishing to make himself clearly understood – a lack of consideration.

21 Arcades, concealing strokes, leftward, slow script

Not reliable in his statements.

22 Threads inside words – or a squiggle instead of a letter – **(poor Form Level especially)**

Elusive and insincere. Essential parts of communication left out or filled with vague non-essential matters.

WORKSHEET FOR DISHONESTY/UNRELIABILITY

Dishonesty/unreliability		*Interpretation*
1		
2		
3		
4		
5		
6		
7		
8		
9		
10		
11		
12		
13		
14		
15		
16		
17		
18		
19		
20		
21		
22		
(N.B. There must be more than 5 to indicate dishonesty)	**Total**	

PART FOUR

The heart of
the matter

Chapter 27 | Speed

The speed or personal tempo of the writer begins to gain fluency at school when school work increases or wherever notetaking is required.

A quick script, though not a hasty one, must develop without the loss of legibility. Everyone has their own tempo, but because we are not machines we have emotional upsets from time to time and these will affect our writing.

Like a piece of music, the speed with which the individual writes across the paper reflects the tempo of his thinking and his actions.

Where the temperament of the person is very lively, then more discipline is required to maintain a positive regular rhythm.

A high quality script is a matter of experience and dexterity which will be reflected in the simplicity of the letter forms. The mature, intelligent writer moves along the line, saving time in straightforward, graceful movements, individually creating his own short cuts, thinking of the subject matter rather than the style of writing. The speed assessment, then, reveals the spontaneity of the writer, plus his sincerity – does he really mean what he is saying in the message?

A naturally slow person would not write intelligently and legibly if he tried to write faster than his normal pace and physical capability. It is therefore the writer's natural speed which counts. It does not have to be quick for a positive evaluation. Take the case of a person suffering from a physical disability which slows down his movements and consequently his writing tempo. Intelligence would still show in the originality of the script, as would his sincerity in the simplicity of the letter forms, which may, in recognition of his disability, produce a shaky stroke quality, possibly with a loss of pressure.

One must also remember a dyslexic, who cannot remember images and who will also write slowly, through hesitation, which will show in the form of frequent pen lifts from the paper, and reversed letters or misshapen numbers – a characteristic of this condition.

The spontaneity which goes into a script is commensurate with the amount of energy the writer applies to his everyday tasks, and with his inner resources, which drive him to greater activity through ambition and enthusiasm.

Should the writing show irregular, unstable forms of connection such as secondary threads and hasty, neglected letters and words, the person is excitable and full of nervous tension – wasted energy – not a good recommendation for reliability.

Any form of unnecessary stroke is contrary to quick, fluid, intelligent writing. What, at first glance, suggests a speedy tempo can on closer examination, show impeding factors such as ornamentation, long initial strokes, abrupt end strokes, totally disconnected script and devious adjustments that take extra time and effort to produce. Such a writer spends (but not necessarily wastes) time before beginning any activity. The graphologist should assess whether the writer needs time to elaborate for negative personal effect, or is being careful to produce a positive, desired result, such as calligraphy requiring skilful manipulation – or somewhere in between to give a good impression for a genuine reason? Often in this case the first few lines are carefully written but as the missive progresses the writer's natural pace takes over and the letter takes on a more spontaneous flow. In another instance the speed can be excessive with no care taken over legibility, the writer's motive being to get to the end quickly. There would be threads, no punctuation and over-corrected words with wide spacing. Should the envelope be written in the same scrawl, then the writer is unconcerned about delivery.

Speed, coupled with pressure, regularity, rhythm and Form Level (of which speed is an essential component) enable the experienced graphologist to construct a personality sketch of the person's spontaneity and energy level, along with any inhibiting factors impeding progress and also revealing his reliability and integrity.

How does he react under stress? Does he, after a moderate beginning, lose control of the script formation and allow the handwriting to deteriorate into an illegible scrawl? This type of writer would be unable to cope under intense competition or while experiencing other stress factors which are a part of life.

A handwriting can be deceptive in the case of speed. For this reason all the following factors must be taken into consideration. (Those who do not wish to go to this length should look for rightward movement and continuity.)

SPEED

Quick factors	Slow factors
1 Connection	
Fully connected with normal rightward end strokes.	Disconnected letters, blunt end strokes, leftward endings.
2 Form of connection	
Garland, wavy line, thread.	Angle, arcade, concealing strokes.
3 Width	
Broad, natural spacing between words and letters.	Narrow spacing and letters, leftward-tending end strokes.

Quick factors	Slow factors
4 Pressure Rhythmic and light to average; consistent throughout.	Heavy, inconsistent pressure; filled in loops.
5 Regularity Irregularity.	Very regular in a slow writing style.
6 'i'-dots and 't'-bars Omitted; or rightward placed; connected to the next letter.	Leftward placed. Connection broken to form the dot or 't'-bar before continuing. Carefully placed over the top of the 'i' and the 't'-bar placed on the upright.
7 Left margin Widening as it progresses down the page.	Narrowing as it progresses down the page, or being placed very precisely in line.
8 Rightward slant Rightward and consistent.	Leftward and varying slant.
9 End strokes Endings to the right.	Abrupt endings or leftward-tending.
10 Simple letter formations Uncomplicated and simple forms of lettering.	Complicated forms; ornamentation.
11 Direction of the lines Rising.	Falling.
12 Firmness of the stroke Clean and clear, firm strokes.	Broken tremors or disintegrating strokes.

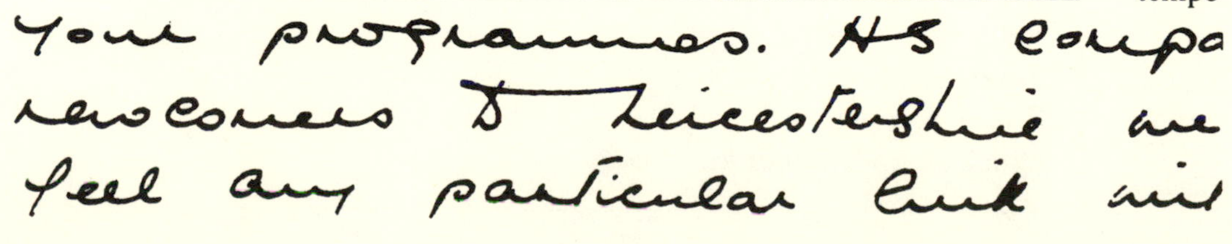

Fig 245
Example of a lively tempo

Your programmes. As compa rewcomers to Leicestershire we feel any particular link and

QUICK SPEED

To indicate sincerity and reliability, a very quick writing must be simple and legible, which would also point to a positive Form Level speed section, to be studied next.

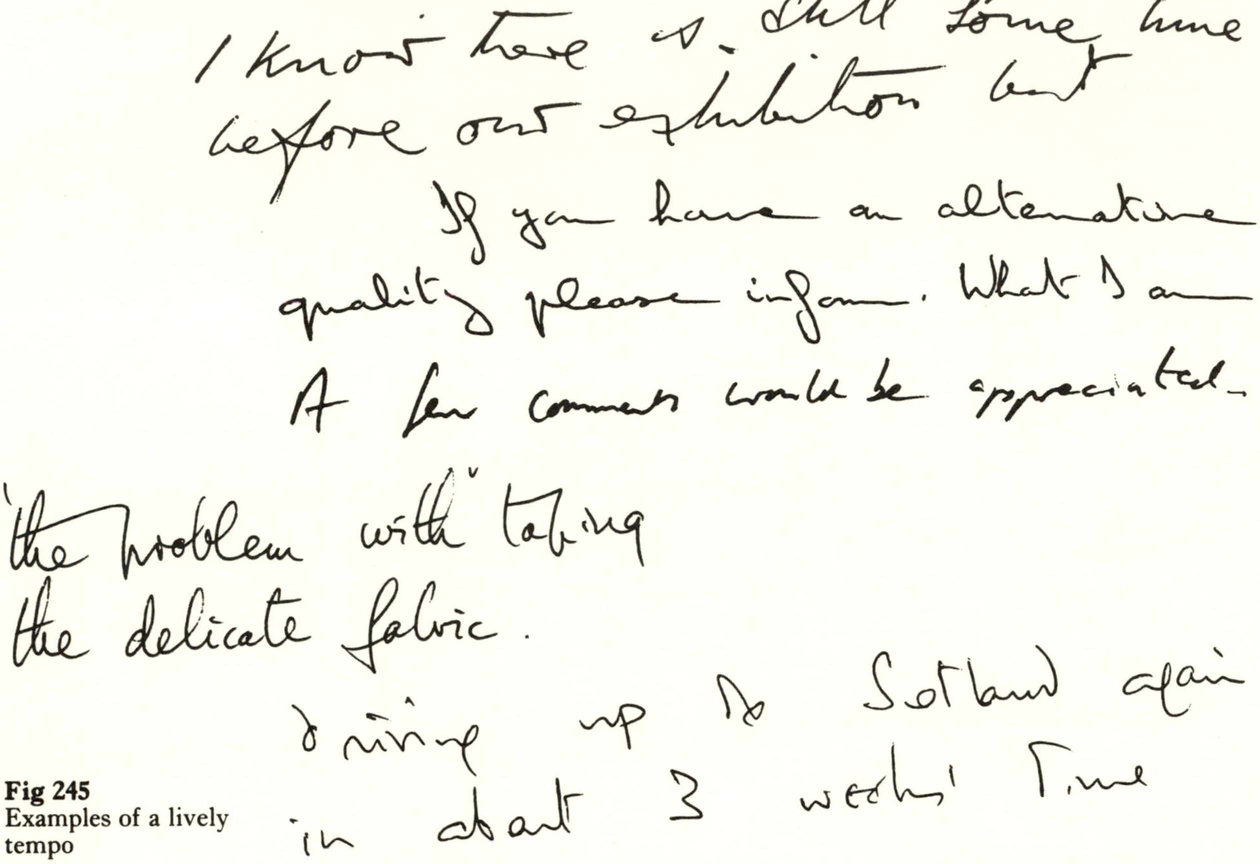

Fig 245
Examples of a lively tempo

Quick (fig 245)

Legible	Illegible
Positive traits	*Negative traits*
Self-assurance	Impatient
Initiative and interest in most things	Irritable
Agility – particularly mental	Unreliable
Spontaneity	Temperamental
Extroversion	Restless
Industriousness	Superficial
Purposeful drives	Easily distracted
Flexible	Inconsistent behaviour
Reliable	
Sincere	
Progressive action	
Quick assimilation of knowledge	

MEDIUM SPEED

On average, this is the tempo normally found in most handwriting.

Medium – *Smoothly fluent rather than hurried* (fig 246)
Sincere
Reliable
Well organised and integrated
thinking processes
Regular habits – predictable
Not a quick thinker, but
thorough and careful

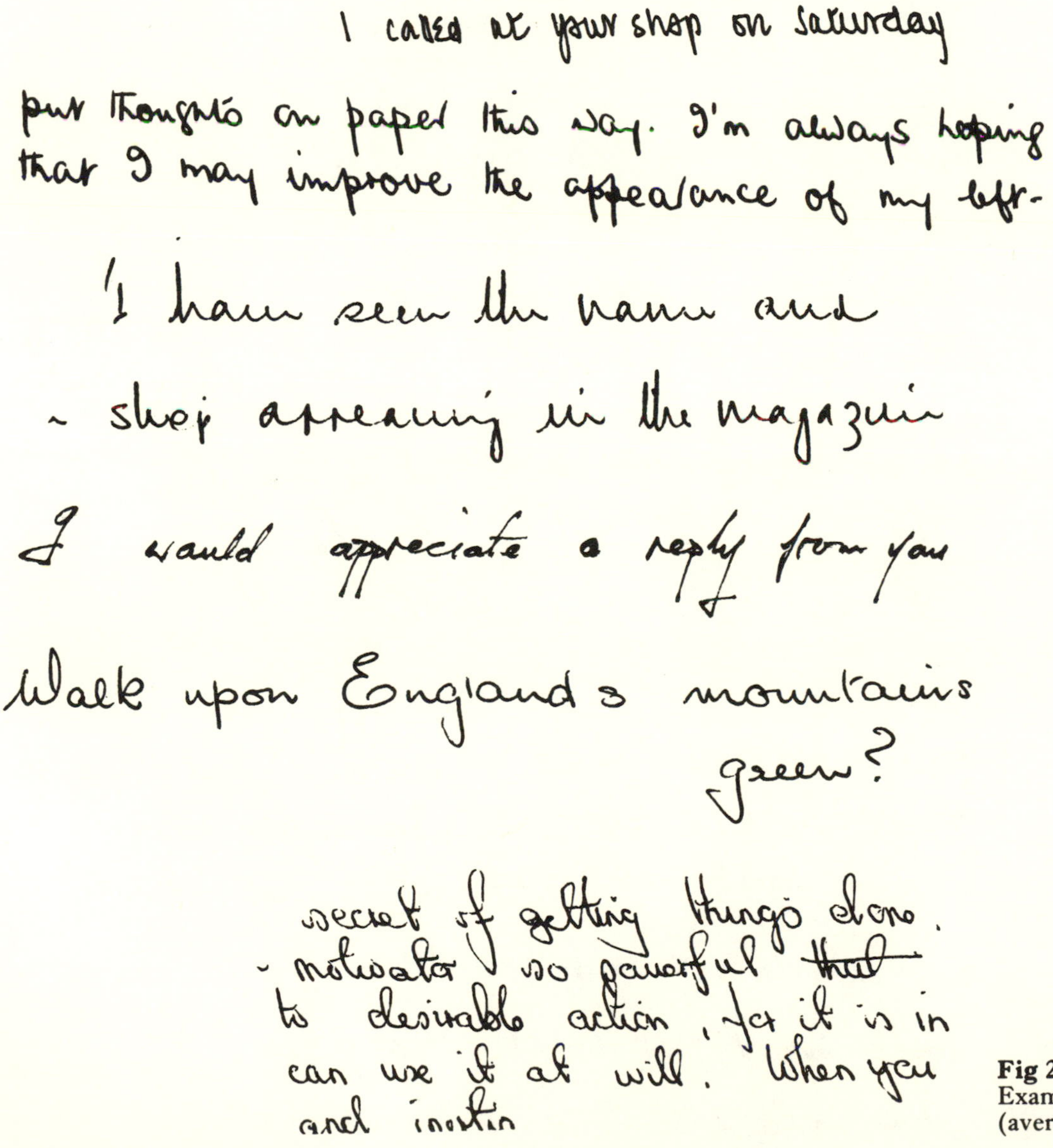

I called at your shop on Saturday

*put thoughts on paper this way. I'm always hoping
that I may improve the appearance of my left-*

I have seen the name and

~ shop appearing in the magazine

I would appreciate a reply from you

*Walk upon England's mountains
green?*

*secret of getting things done.
~ motivator so powerful that
to desirable action, for it is in
can use it at will. When you
and inertia*

Fig 246
Examples of medium
(average) speed

SLOW SPEED

A very slow speed is not often encountered unless the writer is infirm or old; therefore great care must be taken over the various factors to ensure that they are all genuine.

Slow

Average Form Level	*Poor Form Level*
Steady	Inactive
Careful	Lazy
Self-controlled	Slow thinker
Considerate	Weak willpower
Cautious	Dull temperament
Introvert tendencies	Inflexible
Passive	Slow reactions
	Insecurity

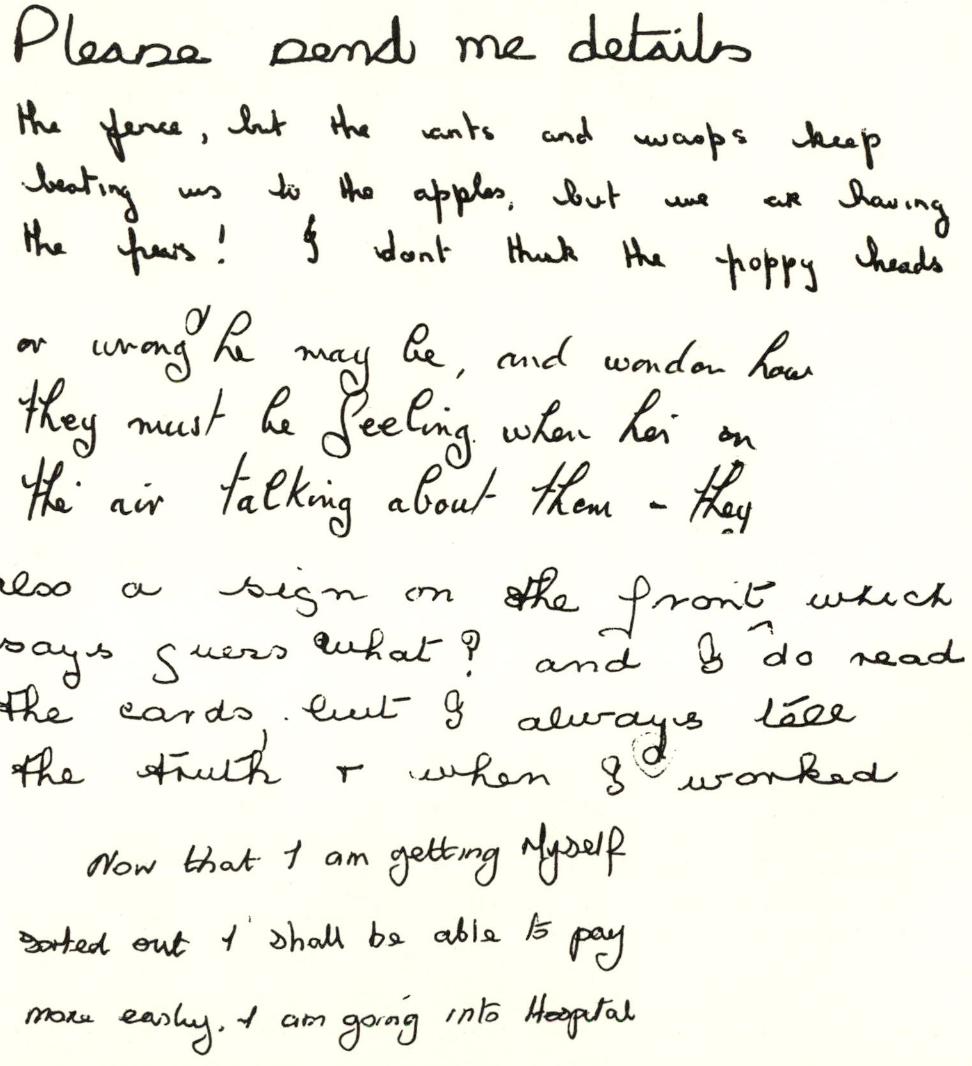

Please send me details

the fence, but the ants and wasps keep beating us to the apples, but we are having the pears! I dont think the poppy heads

or wrong he may be, and wonder how they must be feeling when her on the air talking about them — they

also a sign on the front which says guess what? and I do read the cards. but I always tell the truth r when I worked

Now that I am getting Myself

sorted out I shall be able to pay

more easily. I am going into Hospital

Fig 247
Examples of slow
handwriting

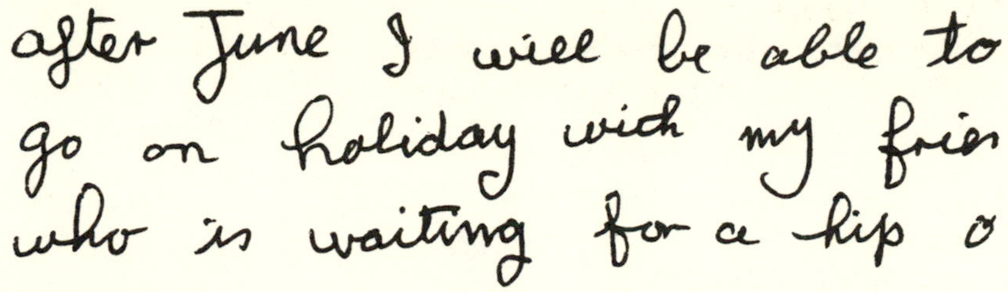

after June I will be able to go on holiday with my frien who is waiting for a hip o

Fig 247
Examples of slow handwriting

OTHER FACTORS

False, stylised writing – Pedantic viewpoints or a desire to deceive

Shakiness (Ataxia)   – Poor co-ordination and illness

Retouched strokes   – Feelings of anxiety

Slow copybook style
Often a lack of education and self-confidence results in a slow copybook style writer who will be a reliable manual worker.

Fraud
A slow writer with criminal or fraudulent intent finds it virtually impossible to copy a script in a more versatile and higher quality handwriting, without it having a slow, laboured appearance. A naturally fast writer with graphic maturity, but also criminal intent, produces an unnatural-looking script if trying to copy a slow handwriting, by holding back his own natural flow – but he would be more successful than the example above in escaping detection by anyone other than an experienced graphologist.

It is important to remember always that the tempo of the writing reflects the personality of the writer.

NUMERICAL ASSESSMENT
For those requiring a more accurate speed assessment, the method below can be used, following the format already explained but awarding points from 0 (very slow) through to 4 (very fast). This sample table refers to fig 248.

1	Degree of connection	4
2	Garland forms	3
3	Broadness	3
4	Pressure	2
5	Irregularity	3
6	Placement of 'i'-dots and 't'-bars	3
7	Left margin	4
8	Rightward slant	2
9	End strokes	3
10	Simplicity of letter forms	4
11	Direction of lines	3
12	Firmness of stroke	4
	Total	38

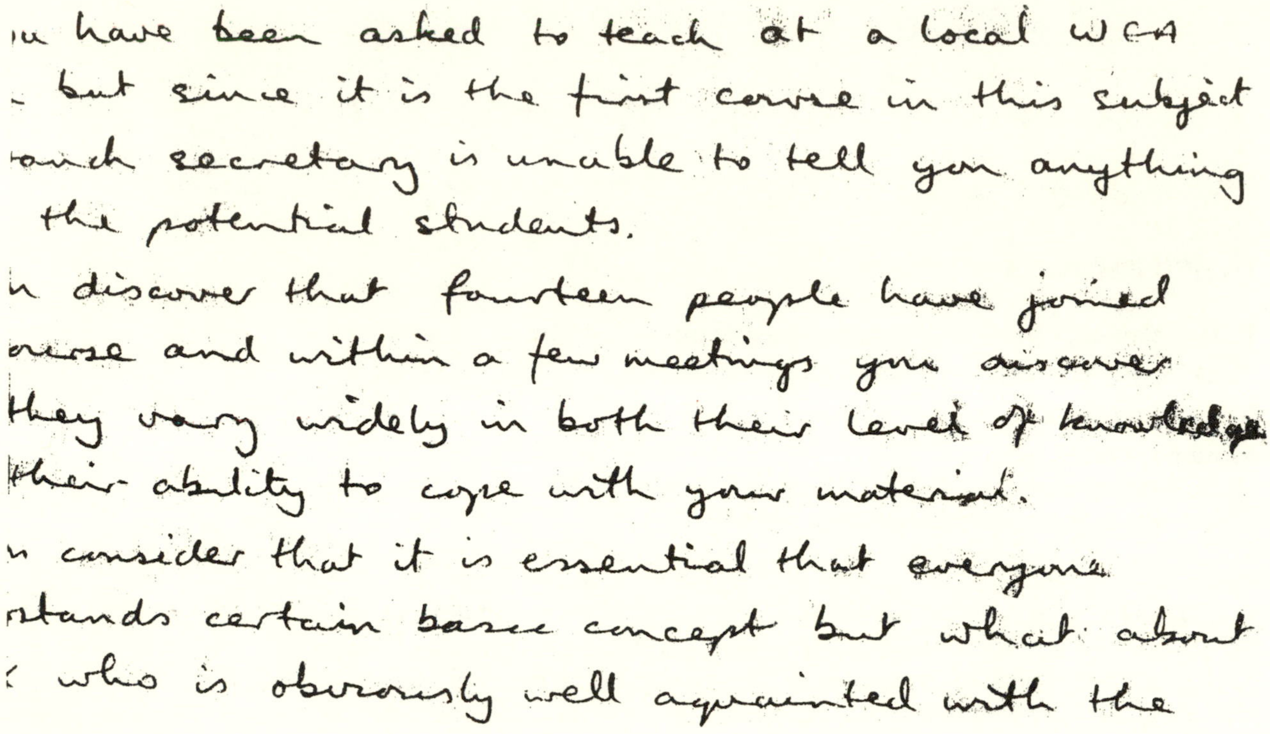

u have been asked to teach at a local WEA

- but since it is the first course in this subject

ouch secretary is unable to tell you anything

the potential students.

u discover that fourteen people have joined

ourse and within a few meetings you discover

they vary widely in both their level of knowledge

their ability to cope with your material.

u consider that it is essential that everyone

stands certain basic concept but what about

who is obviously well aquainted with the

Fig 248
(See speed assessment table)

The maximum number of points would be $12 \times 4 = 48$. The total of the above, taken from example 248 is 38 out of 48. The average marks are 28: therefore this sample of handwriting is fast and a good Form Level.

WORKSHEET FOR SPEED

Speed	*Quick*	*Medium*	*Slow*
1 Degree of connection			
2 Form of connection			
3 Width			
4 Pressure			
5 Regularity			
6 'i'-dots and 't'-bars			
7 Left margin			
8 Slant			
9 End strokes			
10 Simplicity			
11 Direction of the lines			
12 Clarity of the stroke			
Total			
Overall:			

ALTERNATIVE, NUMERICAL, SPEED WORKSHEET

Speed assessment of example in fig 249

1	Degree of connection	2
2	Garland forms	2
3	Broadness	2
4	Pressure	3
5	Irregularity	2
6	Placement of 'i'-dots and 't'-bars	2
7	Left margin	2
8	Rightward slant	1
9	End strokes	2
10	Simplicity of letter forms	4
11	Direction of lines	4
12	Firmness of stroke	4
	Total	30

A high average tempo and medium Form Level

Fig 249

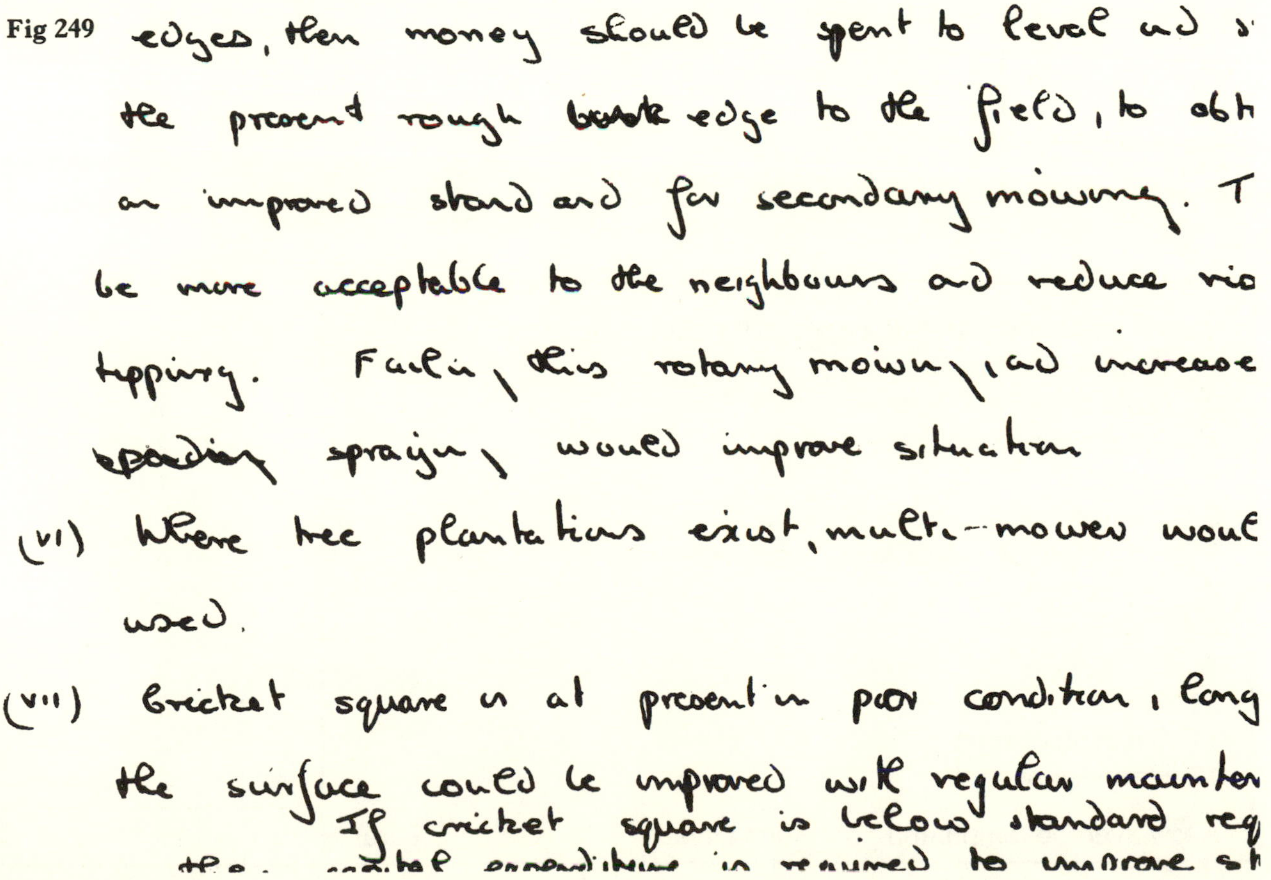

edges, then money should be spent to level and s

the present rough bank edge to the field, to obt

an improved stand and for secondary mowing. T

be more acceptable to the neighbours and reduce vio

tipping. Furti, this rotary mowing, and increase

spending spraying, would improve situation

(vi) Where tree plantations exist, multi-mower woul

used.

(vii) Cricket square is at present in poor condition, long

the surface could be improved with regular mainten

If cricket square is below standard req

the capital expenditure is required to improve st

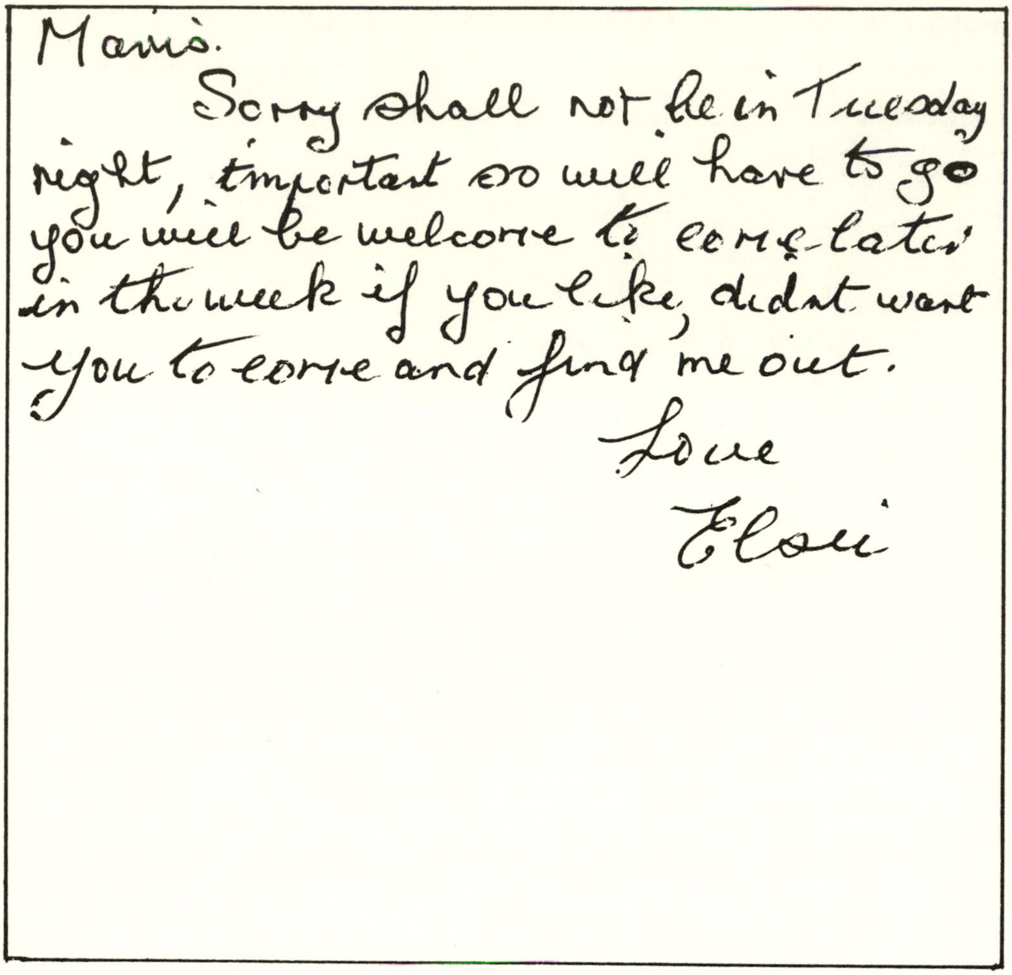

Mavis.
    Sorry shall not be in Tuesday night, important so will have to go you will be welcome to come later in the week if you like, didnt want you to come and find me out.
                    Love
                        Elsie

Fig 250
(Note also the
top and
bottom margins)

Speed assessment of example in fig 250	
1 Degree of connection	3
2 Garland forms	1
3 Broadness	2
4 Pressure	1
5 Irregularity	2
6 Placement of 'i'-dots and 't'-bars	3
7 Left margin	2
8 Rightward slant	2
9 End strokes	3
10 Simplicity of letter forms	2
11 Direction of lines	2
12 Firmness of stroke	2
A low average tempo and poor Form Level **Total**	25

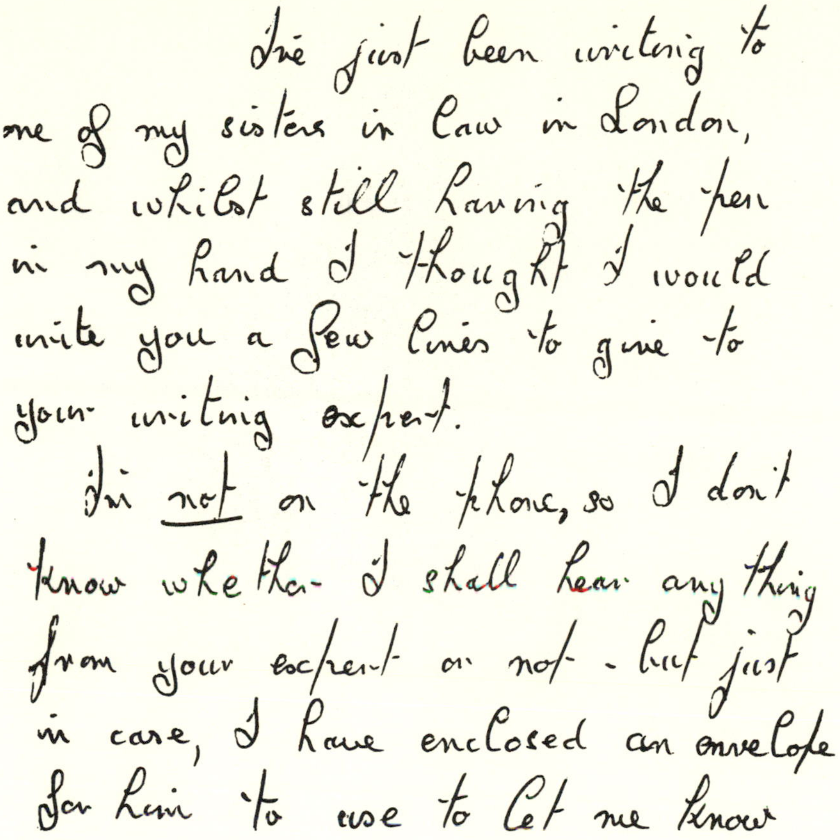

I've just been writing to me of my sisters in Law in London, and whilst still having the pen in my hand I thought I would write you a few lines to give to your writing expert.

I'm not on the phone, so I don't know whether I shall hear anything from your expert or not - but just in case, I have enclosed an envelope for him to use to let me know

Fig 251

Speed assessment of example in fig 251	
1 Degree of connection	1
2 Garland forms	1
3 Broadness	2
4 Pressure	2
5 Irregularity	2
6 Placement of 'i'-dots and 't'-bars	2
7 Left margin	2
8 Rightward slant	3
9 End strokes	2
10 Simplicity of letter forms	1
11 Direction of lines (Falling ends)	1
12 Firmness of stroke	2
A slow handwriting, with poor Form Level **Total**	21

To summarise:

Under 15	Very slow	**31–35**	Fairly fast	**41–45**	Very fast
16–24	Slow	**36–40**	Fast	**46–48**	Excessively fast
25–30	Average				

Chapter 28 | Form Level

Depending upon the individuality, intelligence and sincerity of the writer, there must be some overall means of distinguishing between positive and negative indications in the script being examined.

For instance, in one handwriting, with irregular, uneven spacing of letters, words and lines but also quickly executed with original and simple letter forms, this would point to a flexibly minded, reliable worker; while in another script with irregular, uneven spacing but with overloaded forms, slowly written and ornamented, it would indicate a time-waster, unduly concerned with personal presentation – probably as a compensation for an inferiority complex and therefore unreliable and insincere. The Form Level would be rated 'low'. This does not imply that all low Form Level writers are unreliable; they make good manual operators for example, who will take orders without argument. The only way to gain experience in recognising the relevant Form Level is by constant practice.

The ability to determine Form Level is of prime importance because all your other evaluations depend on this most important factor. In general, the higher the standard of the writing and spacing, the more positive is the interpretation of the other factors.

A slow, copybook form of handwriting (fig 252), projecting very little originality or intellectual leaning, will be written by a monotonous, stereotyped and unimaginative individual, content to observe rather than take part – to follow, not to lead; thus this will merit a fairly poor Form Level, which does not imply law-breaking or dishonest tendencies but is just plain and commonplace – a mundane character.

There are three main considerations to a Form Standard conclusion: *speed, spacing* and *originality*, based on Robert Saudek's method which has been proven over many years to be reliable when correctly applied.

SPEED

Speed and naturalness are an indication of spontaneity. For this factor you should check out all the writing trends relating to released impulses such as rightwardness, broadness, connectedness, extended end strokes, garland forms and simplicity. Refer to chapter 27 on speed to help you with this.

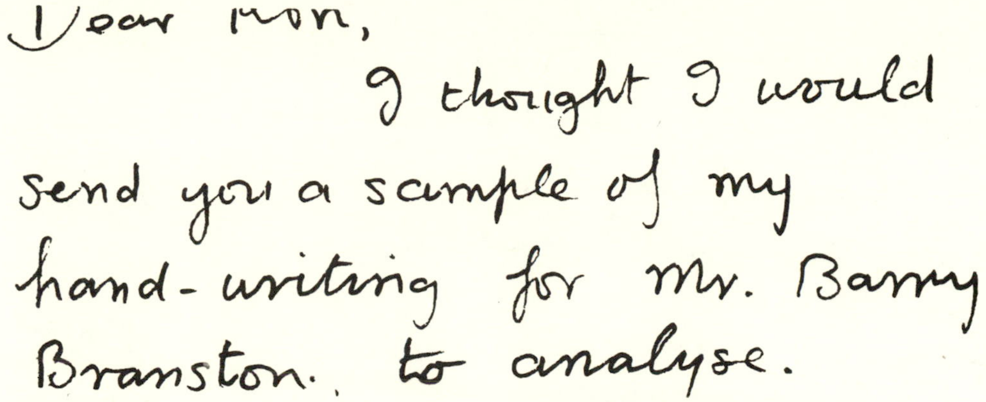

Dear Mum,

I thought I would send you a sample of my hand-writing for Mr. Barry Branston. to analyse.

Fig 252
A slow, copybook form
of handwriting

SPACING

Spacing, as an indication of the writer's intelligence, is in three parts, in relation to approaching problems, and the common sense in handling them.

You should check:

(a) the general arrangement of the text, with regard to the formation of the *margins*, of which there should be an all round sufficient spatial layout that is not inadequate or excessive. (See chapter 3)

(b) the spacing between the *words*, which should be realistically and evenly distributed for a natural appearance. (See chapter 3)

(c) the space between the *lines* of writing, which should be harmoniously balanced and constant in relation to the size of the words.

ORIGINALITY

Originality of letter forms (deviation from the school copybook script) with emphasis on the graceful quality of the letter forms, simplicity and legibility are an expression of the writer's productive ability and intelligent ideas.

A creative and logical thinker will write without adornment where possible but not to the point of neglect (fig 253). If there is neglect, then, depending upon the degree, the writer might be careless, inexact, accident-prone and disorganised (fig 254). Where the spacing is also in disorder, there is disturbance in the intellectual sphere, and comprehension is confused. Haphazard use of time and effort is also indicated (fig 255).

Fig 253
A script showing a
creative and logical
thinker – lucid, without
adornment

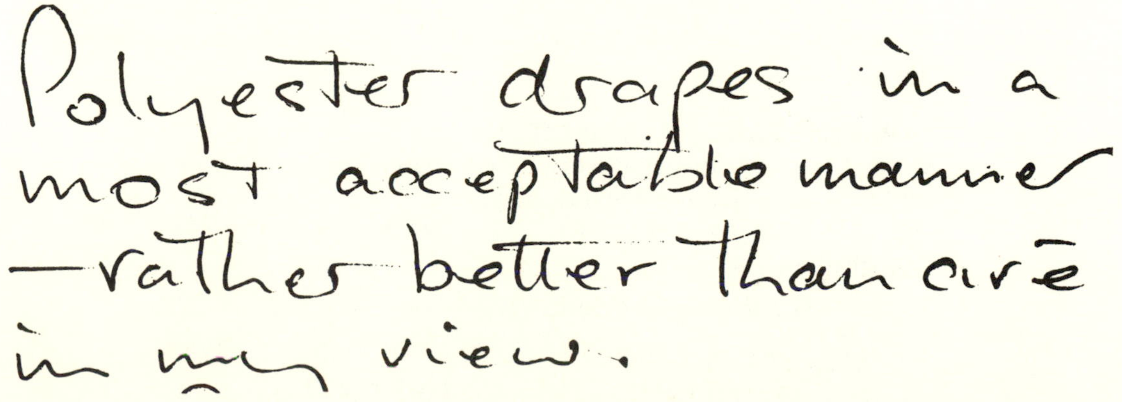

Polyester drapes in a most acceptable manner —rather better than are in my view.

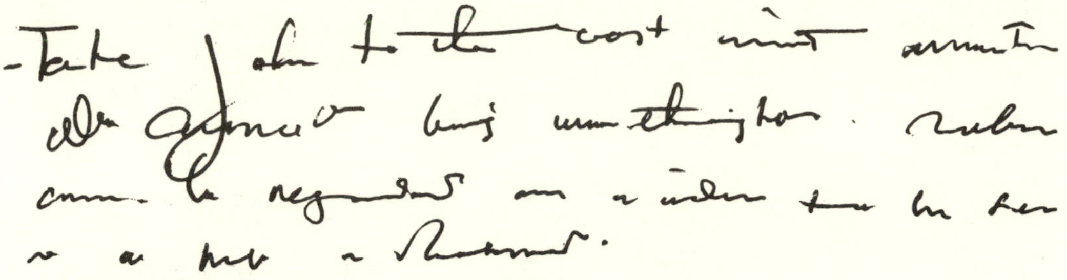

Fig 254
A script showing
neglect –
(disorganisation,
inexact etc)

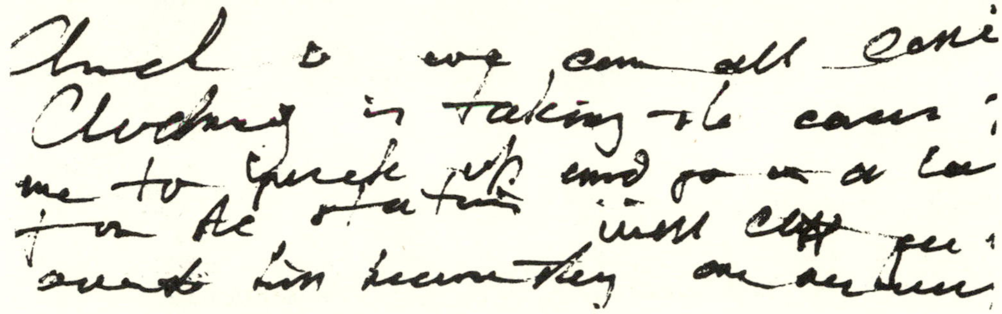

Fig 255
Examples showing
spacing in disorder –
(intellectual
disturbance etc)

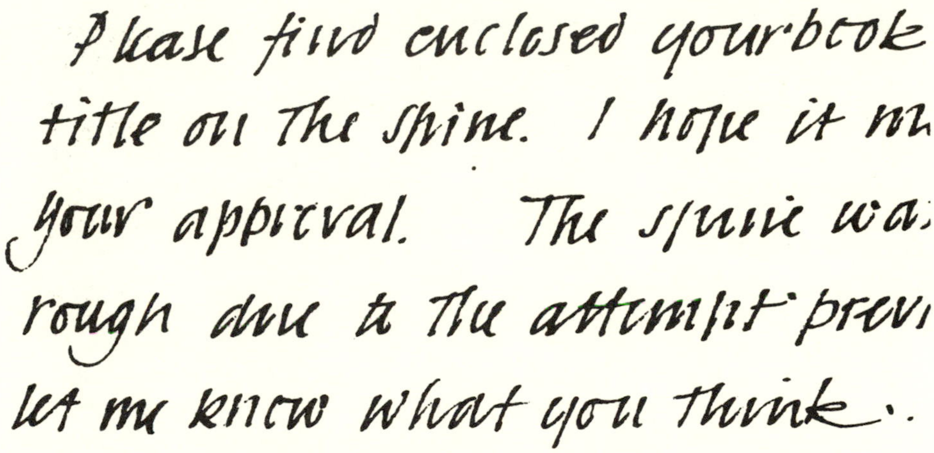

Fig 256
Script showing
natural, artistic
accomplishment,
unforced and with
spontaneous flow and
tempo

Naturalness in handwriting is for self-expression, not a means of showmanship. But if the writer is artistically adept, a calligraphic style of script is a genuine aesthetic accomplishment, part of that individual and appears natural, with a spontaneous flow and tempo (fig 256). A good quality script always looks unpretentious, from a medium to a very high standard.

COMMON SENSE EVALUATION
First, I have illustrated and evaluated various scripts' Form Level, to begin with just using common sense judgement based on the factors above.

Fig 257 – a poor Form Level	Below average (fig 261)
Fig 258 – an average Form Level	Average (not shown)
Fig 259 – a fairly high Form Level	Above average (fig 262)
Fig 260 – a high Form Level.	Fairly high (not shown)
	High (fig 263)

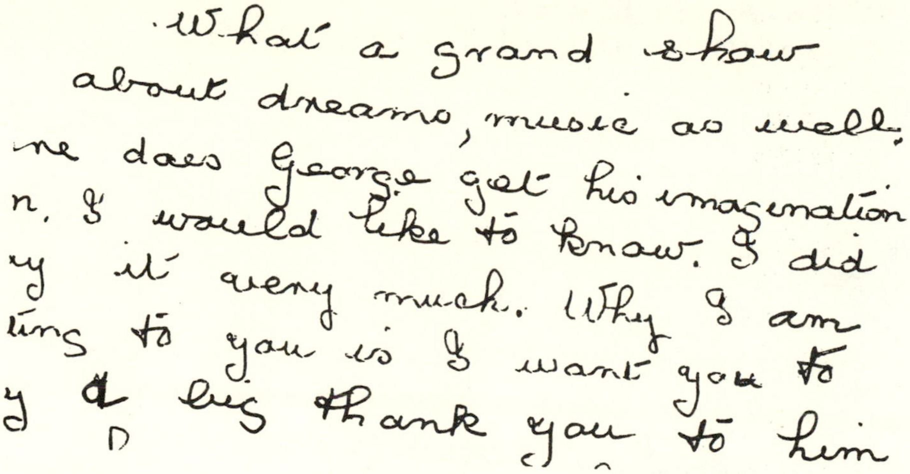

What a grand show
about dreams, music as well,
ne does George get his imagination
n. I would like to know. I did
y it very much. Why I am
ting to you is I want you to
y a big thank you to him

Fig 257
A low Form Level

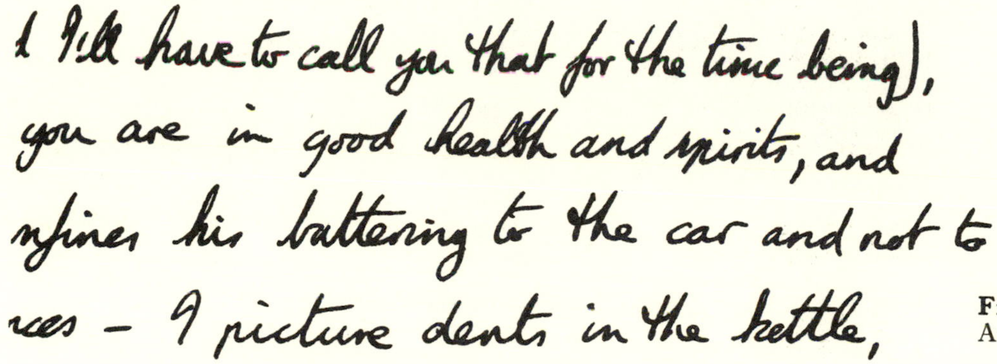

1 I'll have to call you that for the time being),
you are in good health and spirits, and
nfines his battering to the car and not to
ces — I picture dents in the kettle,

Fig 258
An average Form Level

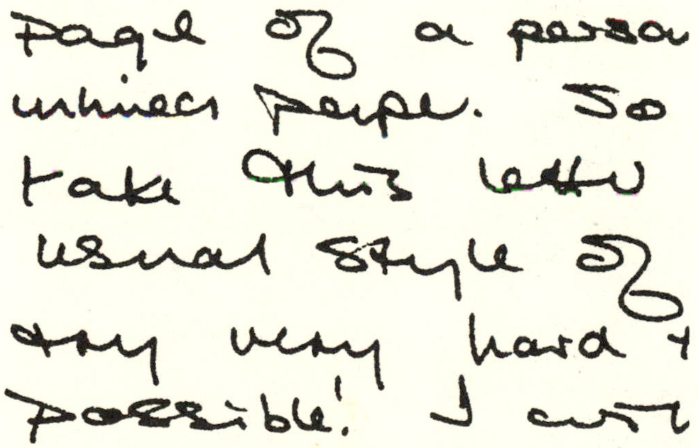

Page of a persa
unhinecs peupe. So
take this letter
usual style of
try very hard &
possible! I writ

Fig 259
A fairly high Form
Level

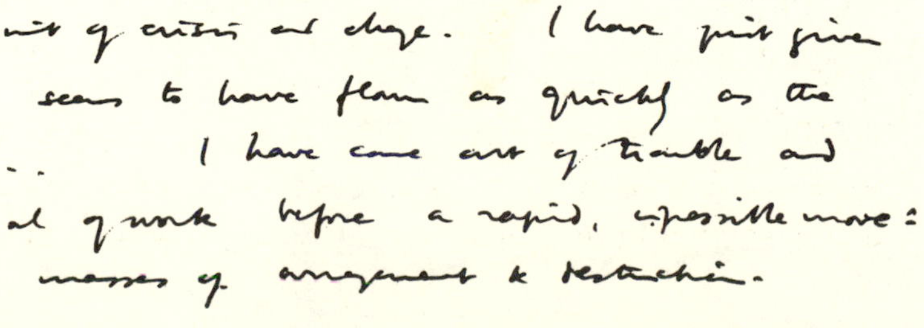

nt of critics and clergy.   I have just give
seem to have flown as quickly as the
I have come out of trouble and
al quandy before a rapid, impossible move:
messes of amusement & destruction.

Fig 260
A high Form Level

NUMERICAL ASSESSMENT

Secondly there are three more detailed assessments.

Form Level assessment of example in fig 261

Breakdown for Form Level assessment

Speed

Connection (degree of)	2
Garlands	1
Broadness	3
Pressure (inconsistent)	2
Irregularity	2
'i'-dot and 't'-bar placement	1
Left margin (lines used as a guide)	2
Rightward slant	1
End strokes	2
Simplicity (no originality)	2
Direction of lines (guidelines)	2
Punctuation and clarity	2
	—
	22 out of 48

---

1 **Speed** rating for Form Level slow and below average, therefore *poor*.

2 **Spacing** in three parts:
 a) general arrangement and margins – average
 b) spacing between words　　　　– average
 c) spacing between lines　　　　– average

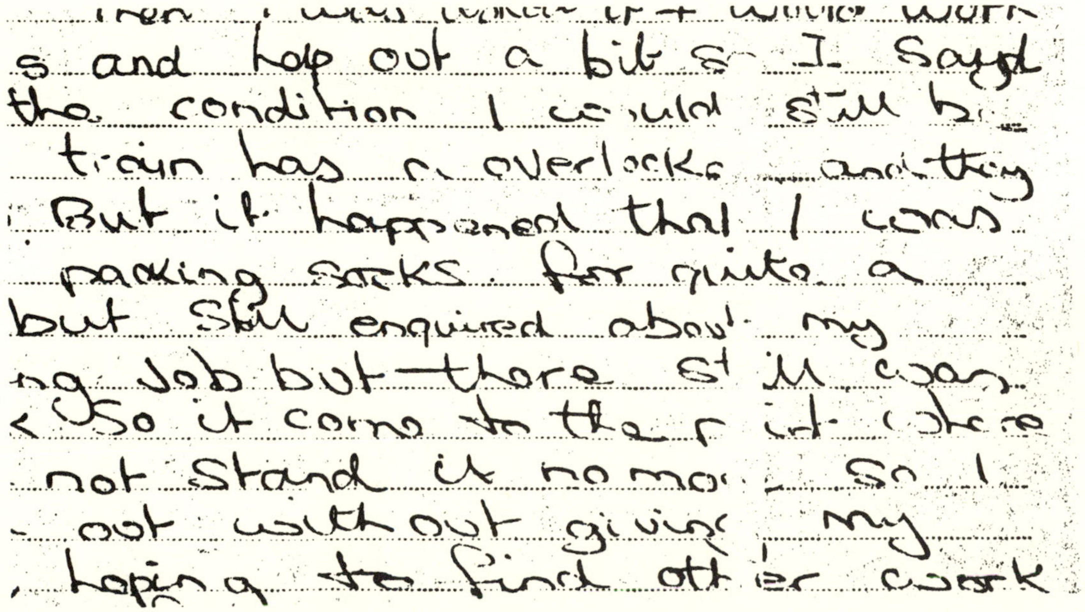

Fig 261
Below average Form
Level

Note: The majority of scripts will be found to be good in all spatial arrangement, relating to intelligent application.

3 Originality – below average
   a) degree of graceful variation – below average
   b) legibility   – average

Below average Form Level

Form Level assessment of example in fig 262
Breakdown for Form Level assessment
Speed

Connection (degree of)	3
Garlands	1
Broadness (see 'g' and 'd' forms)	3
Pressure	4
Irregularity	2
'i'-dot and 't'-bar placement	1
Left margin	2
Rightward slant	4
End strokes	3
Simplicity	2
Direction of lines	3
Punctuation and clarity	3

31 out of 48
Just above average

Fig 262
Just above average
Form Level

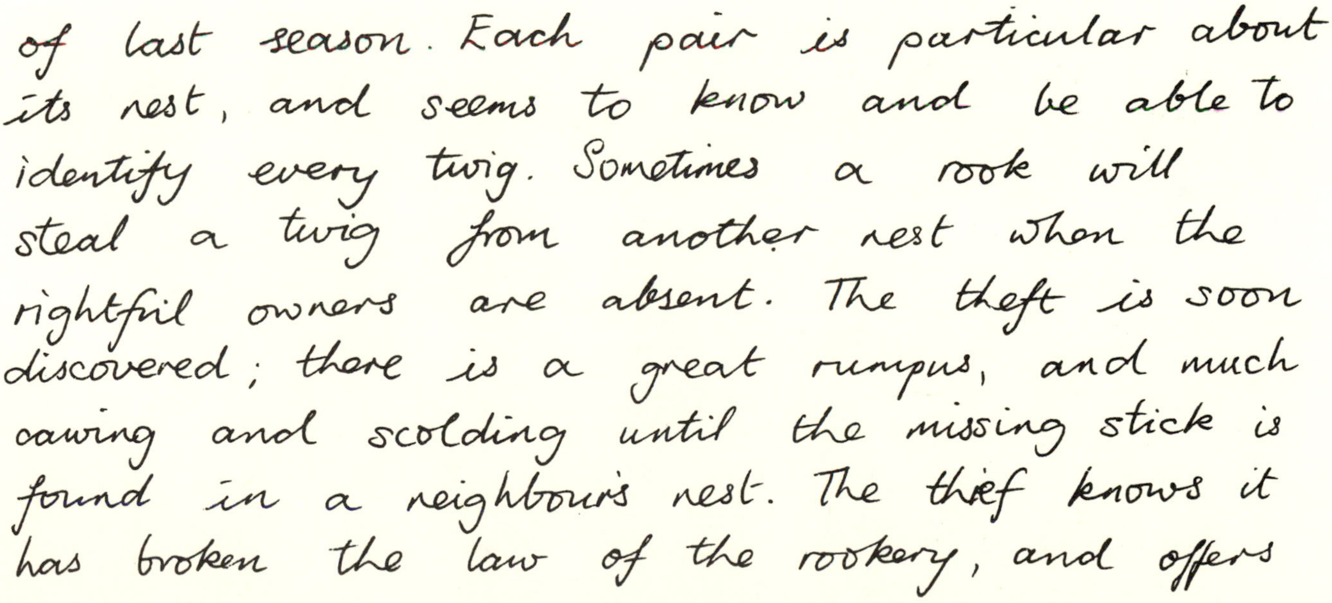

of last season. Each pair is particular about its nest, and seems to know and be able to identify every twig. Sometimes a rook will steal a twig from another nest when the rightful owners are absent. The theft is soon discovered; there is a great rumpus, and much cawing and scolding until the missing stick is found in a neighbour's nest. The thief knows it has broken the law of the rookery, and offers

1 **Speed** rating for Form Level – *just above average*.

2 **Spacing**
   a) general arrangement and margins – good
   b) spacing between words   – good
   c) spacing between lines   – very good

3 **Originality** – average
   a) degree of graceful variation – average
   b) legibility   – very good

Just above average Form Level

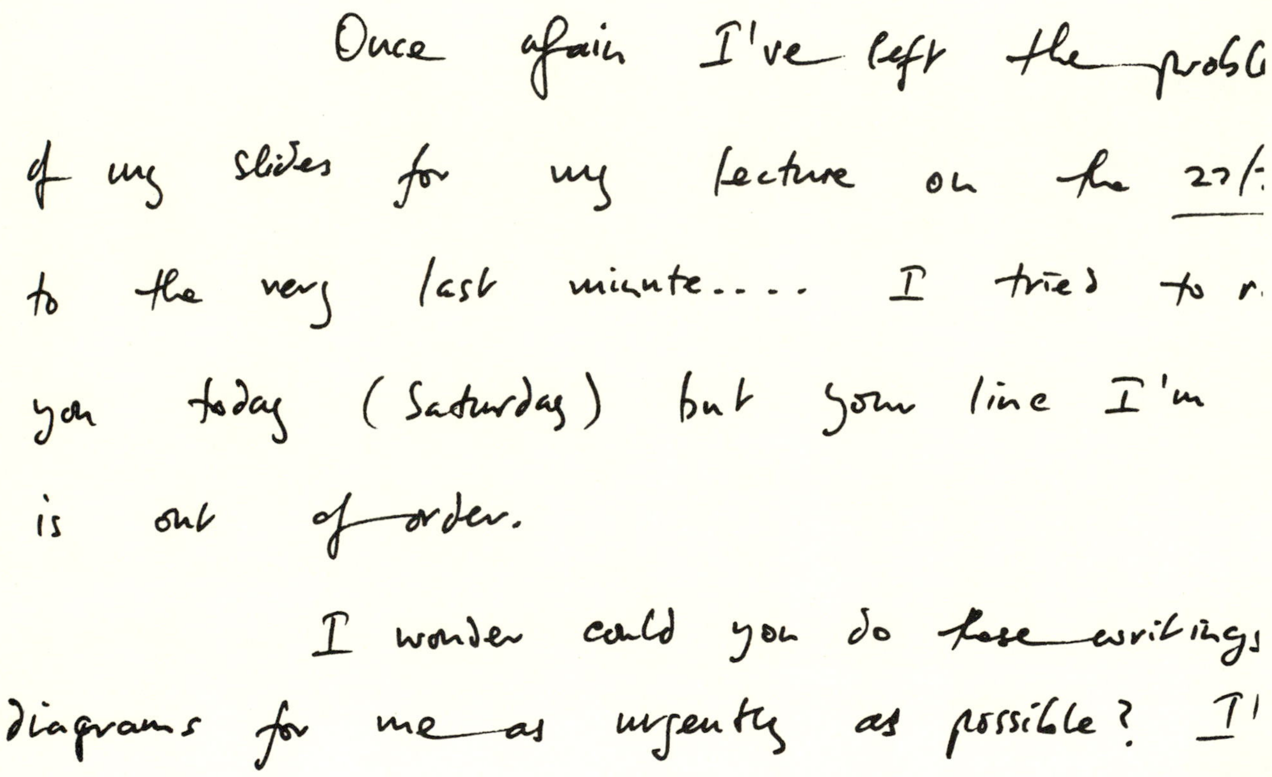

Once again I've left the probl
of my slides for my lecture on the 27/.
to the very last minute.... I tried to r.
you today (Saturday) but your line I'm
is out of order.

I wonder could you do those writings
diagrams for me as urgently as possible? T'

Fig 263
A very high Form Level,
all factors positive

Form Level assessment of example in fig 263

Breakdown for Form Level assessment

Speed

Connection (degree of)	3
Garlands	3
Broadness	3
Pressure	4
Irregularity	3
'i'-dot and 't'-bar placement (some 't'-bars joined to next letter)	3
Left margin	2
Rightward slant	3
End strokes	3
Simplicity	4
Direction of lines	3
Punctuation and clarity	4

38 out of 48
A fast writing speed

1 Speed rating for Form Level – fast: *high*.

2 Spacing
   a) general arrangement and margins – excellent
   b) spacing between words   – very good
   c) spacing between lines   – very good

3 Originality – very good
   a) degree of graceful variation – very good
   b) legibility   – very good

A very high Form Level;
all factors positive

WORKSHEET FOR FORM LEVEL

Form Level: Speed Connection, degree of Garlands Broadness Pressure Regularity 'i'-dots and 't'-bars Left margin Rightward slant End strokes Simplicity Direction of the lines Punctuation and clarity	
Total	

Assessment:

1 **Speed** rating for Form Level   = (high/med/low)

2 **Spacing**   =
  a) general arrangement and margins =
  b) word spacing   =
  c) line spacing   =

3 **Originality**   =
  Degree of graceful variation   =
  Legibility   =

Overall assessment

The Form Level is the final part of the worksheet and you can now complete the puzzle.

Go back to the beginning of the worksheets and, with the Form Level established you can select the positive and negative traits which depend on Form Level.

At the same time, if you have not already done so, you will be able to fill in any other missing 'interpretations'. For example, in chapter 2 on the three zones you may have noted that pressure will affect the interpretation, yet at that point you had not studied pressure. Now you have, and may need to add more information to this part of the worksheet.

This is the last stage of information gathering and you must remember that if you leave anything out, it will affect the accuracy of your analysis – possibly quite seriously.

With these first samples, and for some time to come, you should go through the whole book again at this stage, checking every point in the book against your worksheet.

PART FIVE

Bringing it all together

Chapter 29 | The worksheet

This is the big moment. You should now have one or more complete worksheets.

This section has been arranged in the order that you would have covered in the book, chapter by chapter; it is therefore better to work from, at this stage. However, when you are practised and confident, you will make your own worksheet layout in the order you yourself wish to work.

As a suggestion, my own worksheets are arranged in order of the following, which I find best for my needs:

1 Regularity
2 Rhythm
3 Size
4 Zones
5 Connection, degree of Connection, form of
6 Horizontal tension
7 Shading
8 Slant
9 Pressure
10 Margins
11 Punctuation
12 Spacing between words
13 Spacing between lines
14 Direction of the lines
15 Fullness and leanness
16 Width of letters
17 Covering strokes (if any)
18 Leftward and rightward tendencies

19 Initial strokes
20 Terminal strokes
21 Form of letters
22 Speed
23 Signature and underscore
24 'i'-dots and 't'-bars
25 Personal Pronoun 'I'
26 Form level (or standard)
27 Reliability factors (if applicable)
28 Tension and release (stress factors)
29 Degree of attention
    (This section deals with any characteristics not covered in the general worksheet,
    i.e. stimulus words
        symbols
        envelope if different from general spacing)
30 The analysis

At this stage you might like to compare your worksheets with the sample I have done on page 215 for fig 264.

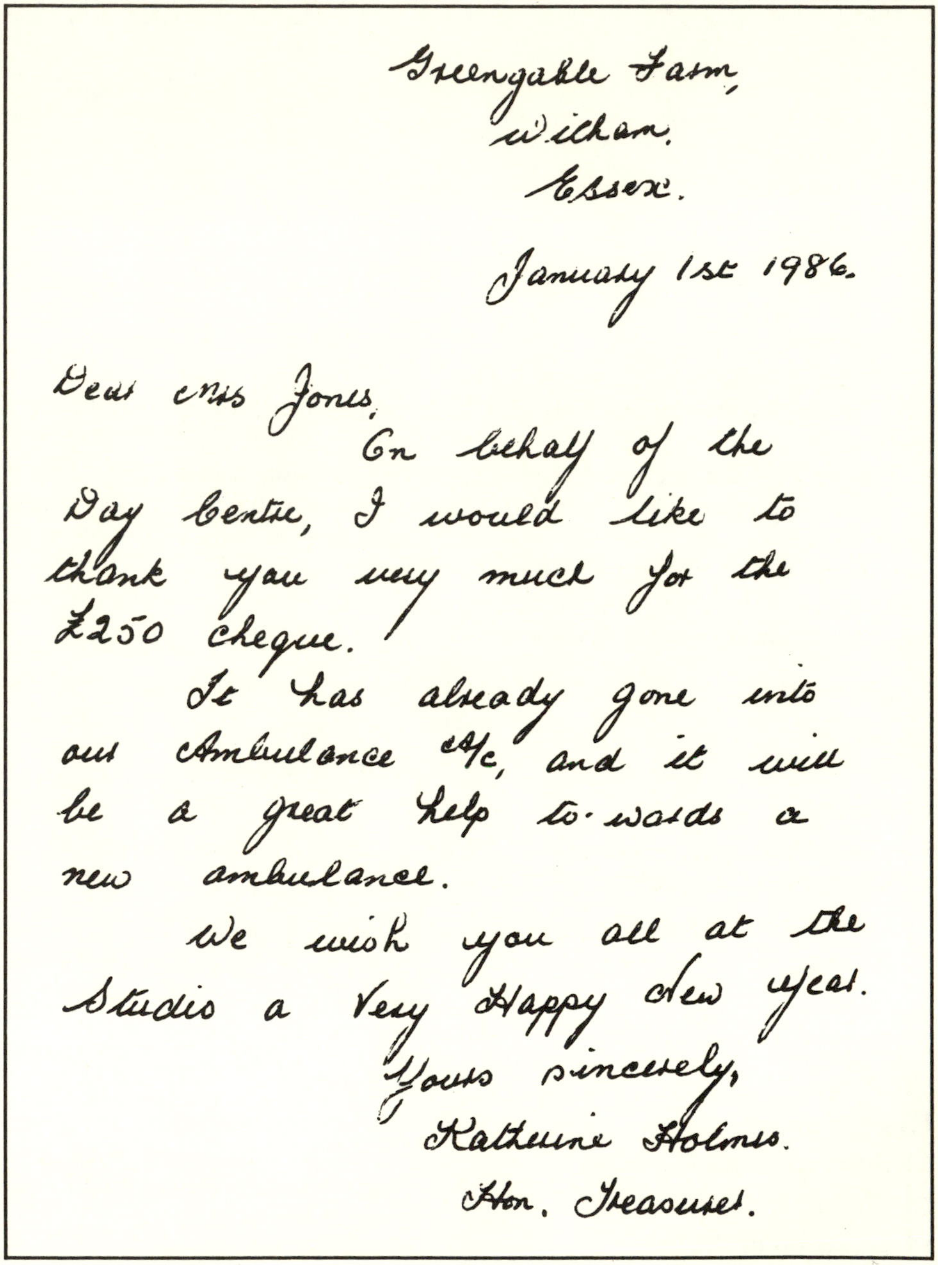

Greengable Farm,
Witham.
Essex.

January 1st 1986.

Dear Mrs Jones,
On behalf of the Day Centre, I would like to thank you very much for the £250 cheque.
It has already gone into our Ambulance A/c, and it will be a great help to-wards a new ambulance.
We wish you all at the Studio a Very Happy New year.
Yours sincerely,
Katherine Holmes.
Hon. Treasurer.

Fig 264
Female, aged 65 years.
British

WORKSHEET FOR FIG 264

Technical considerations (Tech. con.) Plain white paper; blue ballpoint pen, medium thickness	
Size Absolute (all 3 zones) = between 9 and 11mm Average 10mm = *large*, but only marginally so, 9mm being normal. (*Note:* It is the lower zone (LZ) which brings the absolute size into Large)	Whilst not being overtly extrovert or wanting to be noticed, there is a normal expression of leisure activities and self-reliance without excess. A good balance of activity and reflection. Good manual dexterity.
Zones **Upper** = between 1mm and 4–5mm. The average is 2mm, there being more of them. <div align="center">*Small*</div>(Note the extension on the capital 'N' does not count)	Realistic attitude. No strong ambitions. No dominant intellectual pursuits. Down to earth imagination regarding ideas and ideals. No fanciful wants or needs.
Middle = average 2mm throughout <div align="center">*Small*</div>	Slight self-consciousness. Good concentration. Rational behaviour. Practical routine habits.
Lower = between 3–5mm and 8mm, the average being 6mm. <div align="center">*Large*</div>(Note that although this is a sexual attitude indicator, the age of the writer must be considered).	Some materialistic concern. Practical inclinations. Fondness for average physical pursuits. A readiness to respond to stimulation in the instinctual sphere of life, on a rational level. Warm and responsive friendliness.
Layout – general margins *Left* margin = normal	Good organisational capacity. Good use of resources.
Right margin = initially slightly wide but otherwise normal.	Generosity. Slight hesitancy in formal approach to others.
Top margin = normal for the amount of text.	Not prepared to take a risk. Accurate application to tasks.
Bottom margin = normal	Not held back by the past, nor is there a fear of the future.
Summary of margins Generally normal and well laid out.	
Line spacing Clear and even, although there is one touching: 'sincerely'.	Good organisation of daily routine tasks and planning. Strong sense of justice.

Direction (slope) of lines

Slight fall and undulation.

Last paragraph = concave.

Slight feeling of tiredness when the sample was being written; however, persistence was being exercised. Realistic attitude. Sober views.

Word spacing

Consistent and well spaced.

Able to express ideas clearly and coherently. Firmly rooted convictions, and an intelligent thinker. Able to communicate and think objectively. Able to adapt to conventional circumstances. Clear judgement.

Slant

Rightward (Vere Foster-taught script), therefore copybook slant, which has not altered because it suits her personality.

Read as average.

Note the lower zone has a more dominant rightward movement.

Co-operative and amenable to friendly directions. Affectionate and sympathetic.
Socially active and able to initiate orders on a conventionally controlled level.
Can adapt to other people's moods.

Father influence in early life.
Kind and humane qualities.

Leftward and rightward tendencies
(other than actual slant)

Overall, a rightward progression with little leftwardness apart from starting strokes.

Forward looking and co-operative with others.
Not dependent on past experiences.

Connections
Degree of connection

Connected
(Note capitals are not considered)

Logical thought processes. Purposeful direction of ideas. Practical organisation. Will remain within safe limits. Co-operative; will easily follow the ideas and plans of others.

Form of connection

Copybook forms

Formal imagination. Conventional attitudes and expression of personality. Orthodox lifestyle. Needs to be accepted as normal among peer groups and would not deviate from this path.

Form of letters

Copybook

Clear thinking and coherent grasp of essentials. No ostentatious display for self-appraisal.
Normal down-to-earth attitude to all matters. No fantasy impulses other than ordinary, imaginative process. Simple tastes.

Fullness and leanness no dominant	Realistic imagination
Width and narrowness Narrow upper and lower zones; middle zone generally normal but some narrowness throughout.	Good self-control. Reserved, tactful and cautious. Economical handling of affairs.
Horizontal tension Fairly strong and well maintained	Purposeful direction of expressive impulse. Consistent working ability and continuity of effort. Logical thought procedure. Perseverance and reliability.
Pressure Normal Note in this instance, not having the original to work from, you must accept my assessment.	Average energy application in general duties and activities. Realistic self-image. Good co-ordination of mental and physical resources.

Tension and release
Mark with tick (√) or cross (×) where relevant

Contraction		**Release**	
Regularity	√	Fluctuation	
Smallness overall		Largeness overall	√
Slowness	√	Fast tempo	
Heavy pressure		Lack of pressure	
Disconnection		Connected	√
Narrowness	√	Width	
Leftwardness		Rightwardness	√
Angle and arcade	√	Garland and thread	
Narrow spacing		Wide spacing	√
Falling lines	√	Rising lines	
Circles moving inwards	√	Circles moving outwards	
Very small middle zone		Large middle zone	

6	4

The writing borders on the side of *contracted* – a good balance of tension and release, ready to be utilised when necessary to maintain an equilibrium in awkward and stressful situations.

Shading (Not to be confused with pressure) No clear dominant. Slight sharpness. Slight pastosity (pastiness). Characteristic of a copybook script.	Refined manners. Sensitive. Logical reasoning. Discriminate in friendship. Warm nature. Fairly impressionable. Prepared to conform to the majority of life's experiences. Mildly tactile-orientated; normal needs for bodily contact.
Covering (concealing) strokes Some in the upper zone, but generally copybook forms. The narrowness in the lower zone is not quite a covering stroke.	Can keep a secret. Keeps plans and ideas to herself. Personal restraint.
Punctuation and paragraphs Intelligently used.	Good common sense approach to problems. Intelligent verbal expressiveness.
Initial and terminal strokes **Initial strokes** Normal to copybook style script. A few garland forms on the 'h' etc	Is able to go into action without a great deal of inner preparation or undue hesitation. Pleasing manners.
Terminal strokes Normal to copybook script.	Good co-ordination and control of movement. Even powers of application. Normal social relations.
Regularity *Height of small letters (H.S.L)* = Fairly regular *Variation of slant (V. slant)* = Regular *Distance between downstrokes (D.B.D./st.)* = Regular *Distance between lines (D.B.L.)* = Regular	Composed and steady attitude in daily life situations. Consistent mood levels. Willing to progress steadily where friendship is concerned. Clear organisation of thoughts and ideas.

Rhythm Harmonious and controlled; slightly stilted	Good balance of emotional feelings and energy levels, with a reserved overtone, not likely to experience feelings of panic. Good control over nervous tension.
PPI (Personal Pronoun 'I') One only Same as script	Consistent private and social feelings; no discrepancy between self and others.
'i'-dots and 't'-bars *'i'-dots* fairly high and quite consistently over the stem. *'t'-bars* mainly on the stem and small to normal length.	Peaceful nature maintained. Can be painstaking and patient. Ambition kept within realistic bounds.
Symbolism	None
Signature Same as script Small Carefully written	No desire for attention or feelings of grandeur. Sincere and honest opinion of her own worth and social standing. Modest, even nature. Stable character development. Liking for conformity. Readiness to honour commitments.
Stimulus/motive words None	None
Stress and tension	None to cause problems
Dishonesty/unreliability	None

Speed (0–4 points each)

Degree of connection	3	Fluent co-ordination of movement
Garland forms	3	Sincere response to people
Broadness	2	Intelligent assimilation of knowledge at an average rate
Pressure	3	Even application of energy to tasks
Irregularity	1	Average enthusiastic response
'i'-dot and 't'-bar placement	1	Calm attitude. Reliable
Left margin	2	Caring and considerate attitude
Rightward slant	3	Well organised and integrated thinking process
End strokes	3	Regular, stable mood levels
Simplicity	2	Careful thinker
Direction of lines	3	Good self-control
Firmness of stroke	3	Average adaptability.
	29	Coherent expressive speech Prudent economical awareness.

Average tempo

Form Level

1 **Speed** assessment 29 out of 48.
   Average. (25–30)

   Average spontaneity of action and thought. Reliable and steady.

2 **Spacing**
   a) *Overall*, normal, although slight right margin narrowing.

   b) *Between words*, evenly distributed.

   c) *Between lines* – balanced and normal

   Strong common sense and basic intelligence applied to problems realistically.

3 **Originality**
   Very little deviation from the copybook script style (Vere Foster).

   An average Form Level, indicating, in this case, a positive interpretation of graphological factors.

   Average productive capacity.
   Logical application.
   A follower rather than a leader.

   A well balanced personality, with no complexes or deviant behaviour pattern.

Chapter 30 | Writing an analysis

The graphological analysis must be written clearly without unnecessary jargon. Keep it short and to the point at first, sticking to the main points about which you are sure. With experience you will be able to go into more detail. Above all, it should not be ambiguous.

If you find it difficult to write an assessment direct from the worksheet, you could try putting the information on each area onto small index cards first, or try some method of your own to organise the material into groups – social, intellectual, moral etc.

I have done a sample analysis for fig 264 (see p. 214), based on the sample worksheet in the last chapter. It should give you some idea of how an analysis should be done.

When you have read it, you should be ready to write your first analysis.

ANALYSIS OF HANDWRITING SAMPLE Fig 264

Female, age group 65 years. British. Educated UK.

This writer has very good control over her emotional response to exciting stimuli, and in awkward situations.

Her outlook is neither confined nor expansive, with no strong ambitions, except to finish what she sets out to do, following the established patterns and methods.

She is able to assimilate facts and to understand their meaning, as most people can, with an average mental standard of learning capability. She is responsive to intellectual and practical matters. Her judgement is clear. She possesses a strong sense of economical planning, along with good organisation of time, effort, thoughts and ideas, taking a factual approach to problems.

She has a good memory and is constructive in her criticism where she would bring to the fore her strong, tactful and diplomatic faculty.

Her interests are well balanced, there being no fixations or habits contrary to convention.

It will be found that her mood levels are predictable and consistent, her general behaviour sober and rational – considerate and straightforward in her dealings with others. She has no desire or intention to deceive or create a false image. Basically, she is contented and harmonious, having a reliable attitude to friendship in which she can be expected to co-operate fully. There can be, however, in some instances, a reluctance to approach people who, to her, may seem to be unconventional. While not being inflexible, there are limitations which she sets herself. For instance, she will not care to lead, but would rather follow, nor does she like spontaneous changes in routine, Once she comes to a decision, she will rarely change her mind without realistic evidence.

She is tender and sensitive, moderately able to give and receive affection. There are no domineering or aggressive tendencies in her make up. She is also patient and understanding.

She will discuss intelligently in a refined, quiet manner and apply her strong· common sense and initiative where necessary.

Her balance of manual dexterity and well founded personality mean she will work well and get on easily with others. She is always ready to honour her commitments and has a good sense of traditional values.

Stressful situations are met with a calm acceptance and a logical reasoning. They will, however, be avoided by careful discrimination when convenient to do so.

Now try to write an analysis based on one of your own worksheets. Remember to be as positive as you can in the way your phrase your words.

You can then produce this fruit of your labours to the 'subject' whose writing you have analysed. Hopefully they will be delighted and you will be encouraged to do another one, and so your interest will progress to where you will be delving into every piece of handwriting that comes your way.

Chapter 31 | Writing a report

You should always treat a handwriting analysis as a serious undertaking, whether it be brief or comprehensive. On no account should you accept an analysis until its purpose has been confirmed as legitimate. In the case of an assessment for the client's own use in order to gain self-knowledge, verify that the handwriting submitted is in fact that of the client. To ascertain that the handwriting submitted for analysis is that of the client, apart from the sample given, ask the person for another short specimen to be seen written on the spot. If it comes by post, check the writing on the envelope with the writing of the enclosed sample. It should be the same. Even capitals will have the same slant, rhythm, etc.

You should not give an analysis to anyone other than the writer unless the writer has given his or her consent.

Having accepted the writing, a strict ethical code must be followed. Depending upon the use of the report and who will see it, only the salient facts should be presented with no exaggerated statements or stretching to fit preconceived ideas.

FOR PERSONAL USE

This is an analysis, as in chapter 30. As was said then, diplomacy rather than blunt statements regarding intimate inadequacies, with constructive suggestions to put these into perspective and help to strengthen these failings will gain the confidence of the enquirer, along with his belief in graphology.

PERSONNEL

Where the report is to be examined by others, such as in personnel selection, *it should be stressed that complete confidentiality is maintained*. The use of coded identification is preferable to actual names and addresses in case an analysis falls into the wrong hands. Also in a report for recruitment, give only the details relevant to the appointment. Unless pertinent for some special reason, personal details are of no concern to the prospective employer. Needless to say, accuracy is essential.

MARRIAGE COMPATIBILITY

In the case of friendship or marriage compatibility the report should ideally be sent to both parties or, better still, discussed with the couple face to face, where any potential difficulties and differences can be talked about and hopefully resolved. There can be occasions when a future in-law has requested an assessment. In this case, only the basic points in question should be reviewed.

GENERAL GUIDELINES

To avoid misunderstandings and ambiguity your report should be free of jargon and compiled as plainly and as clearly as possible, while still retaining a professional formality.

To summarise: for accuracy and clarity in, for example, a general sketch or in personnel selection, the following headings might be used.

1 *Intellectual and spiritual area* – i.e. the way in which the writer's mind works.

2 *Social area* – his attitude to others

3 *Working qualities*

4 *Moral/sexual area* – i.e. intimate private details.

This is a proven, reliable format which will ensure that nothing essential is omitted.

Vocational guidance

Vocational guidance is often for the school leaver who asks 'What am I to do when I have to make a choice of career?'

There is also the person who wishes to change direction. Having reached middle life, he feels the need to obtain more personal satisfaction rather than just financial security. Such people usually have an idea of what they want to do, but need the assurance that they are capable of the change before they leave their present job.

There may be others who are faced with unemployment and redundancy – having change thrust upon them.

Most youngsters, having reached their third year at a higher or comprehensive school, need to choose a goal often before they really know what they want, because of taking the relevant GCSEs and 'A' Levels needed in that particular field, whether it be in the arts or sciences. They can so easily decide on something for which they are not suited. Once they settle on a course with little or no prospects, then, as they naturally develop, they become stifled.

Some people have been wrongly motivated by their well-meaning but misguided parents, to follow a family profession or trade, or a profession carrying a high status which the parents themselves wanted to do but were unable to.

Many people do not do as well as they should in a career because their personality is simply incompatible with the work. This causes 'free floating' (i.e. not knowing why), unhappiness and stress, which inhibit ability and creativeness.

Obviously we all need to express ourselves, mentally, emotionally and physically. If we can do at least some of this within our work, so much the better. The more we can use our natural interests and talents in our work the stronger incentive there is to achieve both success and profit.

There are other factors that affect adolescents in particular. A few examples are:

Over-sensitivity to criticism	Divorce of parents
Lack of security	Financial problems in the family
Awareness of world problems	Love life
Very poor job prospects	Influence of his peers
Redundancy within the family	

Vocational guidance is one area of graphological practice in which we cannot really be specific. It is difficult to pinpoint a particular career with certainty. We can only indicate the direction a person should take, comparing it with a position that would probably not be suitable.

The report not only helps in the choice of a career, however, but also indicates the basic needs of the writer. It is most important to preserve his or her self-esteem. Any limitations must be pointed out realistically and constructively, so that his natural capabilities, no matter how moderate, shine through.

When the report is being requested the graphologist should ask what specific interests, hobbies and sport the candidate has (see chapter 32). These are an indication as to whether his inclinations are towards intellectual or manual, practical pursuits. A man or woman will do best at that for which they have a natural liking.

Having completed the worksheet the graphologist should look for the following factors in particular:

Emotional balance	Social attitude
Degree of responsibility	Adaptability
Methodical mind	Tolerance
Intellectual approach to problems	Imagination
Ability to organise	Self-confidence
Ability for leadership	Accuracy of detail
Clarity of self-expression	Discretion, confidentiality
Artistic inclinations	Desire to follow, or not, the
Inhibitions	established patterns
	Ability for salesmanship

You should have a fairly wide knowledge of and access to information about a broad range of careers, the formal requirements and what is involved in each one before undertaking this kind of detailed report. Vocational guidance is an area you may choose to specialise in at a later date. Until you have studied the handwriting of those you know well who have followed successful careers, it is best to recommend the National Careers Service to the enquirer and give a more general personality analysis. (A useful book on careers, together with the requirements in professions, industry, commerce and public service, is the *Annual Careers Guide*, published by HMSO.)

Marriage compatibility

A report for marriage or friendship compatibility must be tactful; any adverse criticism, especially of the person making the enquiry, is unwelcome. Should there be difficulty in the relationship, each partner tends to blame the other and you could become pig-in-the-middle.

Always put psychological explanations into everyday, understandable language and treat the negatives constructively, helping your client to accept any problems that surface and to consider what they can do about them.

The most essential point, as with all assessments, is accuracy. You must make a full breakdown of the script for each partner. This area of graphology is very personal so the couple's sensitivity must be respected, with total confidentiality.

When you have finished the analysis arrange a meeting with the two people. Discuss trouble spots and hopefully solutions can be found, or at least the potential problems will have been explained. Obviously this is far better than trying to save a relationship which has already broken down after some minor problem has burgeoned into a major conflict.

As with vocational guidance, this is one of the speciality areas in graphology and you need to have done some special study of marriage problems to support the graphology. The Marriage Guidance Council, now called RELATE, publish a good range of books on the subject.

All graphologists should study sexual abnormalities and deviations as a graphology follow-up. I recommend *Crime and Sex in Handwriting*, by Patricia Marne.

For a personal relationship compability report, the following are the major factors:

a) Maturity and personality balance

b) Level of intolerance

c) Give and take – the ability to see each other's points of view.

There should be a slight difference but not a wide discrepancy in the following:

1   Intellectual capacity

2   Social inclinations

3   Moral principles

4   Creative talents and awareness

5   Musical appreciation

6   Ability in self-expression

7   Economic and social values

8   Spiritual leanings

9   Ambition

10 Sexual balance and a sympathetic response to the other's sensual qualities

A good marriage or friendship is a unique relationship of two people in love, the quality of which could make a seemingly unsuitable bond into a very rewarding relationship. The two concerned have intelligently accepted what would be, to others, off-putting traits. Human weaknesses, when approached with humour and tolerance, have a way of binding couples together in a lasting relationship.

The handwriting factors to be considered are as follows in relation to a full worksheet examination:

1 Form level

2 Size

3 Regularity and rhythm

4 Tempo

5 Slant

6 Connective forms – angle, garland, copybook etc.

7 General spacing

8 Shading – sharp, pastose etc.

9 Pressure

10 Lower loops for balance, length and width.

Remember that a person wants an interesting partner in life, not a shadow: ideally, a balance with slight contrasts in all areas, in which one may complement the other and use qualities to complete those which the other lacks.

Personnel selection

Personnel selection is an area in which graphology can prove invaluable to assess the skills and personalities of job applicants in order to meet the employer's needs and specifications, not only for large companies which are now aware of its contribution to the recruitment of staff, but also for the small businessman who, while being knowledgeable about his technical needs, is afraid of making an expensive mistake in his choice of staff, the employment of whom he cannot delegate to someone else. Also he rarely has the time to spend in probing the deeper motivation of a person's behaviour pattern: yet these are important considerations in building an efficient work force.

A handwriting analysis is especially useful when a shortlist has been prepared, even if other tests have been used, and there is little to choose by way of qualifications and experience between the final candidates. An assessment by an experienced graphologist will often point to one person who stands out among the others on the short list because of emotional stability, harmony in personality and general reliability. These people are often those who are industrious and capable workers but, because of nervousness and tension, tend to overcompensate and unintentionally give the interviewer an unfavourable impression. Therefore both the applicant and employer can benefit.

Before you begin the analysis, the security factor should be questioned and checked. Who is going to see the report and where will it be kept? Will it be shown to the candidate? In any event, you must take care over the wording, especially where a negative factor could cause embarrassment both to the job-seeker and the graphologist. Nothing but the relevant information should be included, particularly concerning the private life of the person under review. You must always bear in mind that what you say may well affect the rest of someone's life.

Depending upon the type of qualities and qualifications required for the job in question, the following are usually included in an assessment:

Basic personality
Aggressive tendencies
Sensitivity
Self-confidence
'Masculine'/'feminine' attitudes
Conventionality

Temperament
Emotional control
Quarrelsome, or amiable
Irrational behaviour
Compulsiveness

Intellectual qualities
Spontaneity of mental grasp
Originality
Versatility
Thinking processes
Learning ability

Working qualities
Economical awareness
Reliability
Initiative in problem-solving
Organising ability
Discretion – ability to keep a confidence
Accuracy for detail
Leadership capabilities

Social tendencies
Inhibition
Friendliness
Co-operation
Pretentiousness or sincerity
Independence, or dependence on others
Sympathetic response to others, or lack of it

Moral qualities
Integrity (including financial)
Truthfulness
Malicious intent
Immaturity
Susceptibilities to influence

Chapter 32 | You're on your own

By now you will be looking at every piece of writing you see in a new light. It is now up to you to decide what you want to do with this new knowledge. Many of you will be able to use it in your present career. Office memos are transformed into mines of information, rather than fodder for the litter bin; lecturers can learn far more from their students' essays than they could previously. At work and in your personal life, you have a valuable new tool which can help you to understand the people in your life and improve your relationships with them.

You may wish to take graphology further and, after three to four years of study and practice, including psychology, you could take a professional qualification and make it your career.

SUGGESTED PROCEDURE

Accepting a sample
1 At least one sheet of script
  At least 15 lines long
  Full signature
2 Establish legitimacy – of writer
                        – of purpose
3 Fill in questionnaire (see below)

Order of work
1 Keep the envelope
2 Remember confidentiality, privacy
3 Build up the worksheet
4 Make headings appropriate for the kind of analysis/report you are doing (chapters 30, 31)
5 Write analysis/report
6 Face-to-face interview or covering letter
7 Keep records of your work – carefully

QUESTIONNAIRES

You may want to develop some kind of questionnaire to help eliminate many queries which may arise while doing an analysis.

You can fill this in yourself when enquiries come in on the phone or, if there is time, send it to an enquirer by post.

SAMPLE QUESTIONNAIRE
(Application for a handwriting analysis)

Name   (not for personnel)   *Address* (not for personnel)
Age or *Date of birth*   *Phone No* (not for personnel)
Sex   *Occupation*
Nationality   *Interests*
Sex

Purpose of the Analysis/ Report √	Own use	Personnel	Vocational guidance	Marriage compat.	Other

Name of person applying for analysis (if different from above)
Address
Phone

1   Is this the kind of paper you usually use? (If not, what?)
2   Is this the kind of pen you usually use? (If not, what?)
3   Is this the colour of ink you usually use? (If not, what?)
4   Were there any interruptions/distractions when you were writing? (children, pets etc)
5   Where were you when you wrote this? (At home, work, interview; on plane, bus etc)
6   Were you in a hurry?
7   Are you under any particular stress at the moment? (Home, work, bereavement etc – details only if you want to)
8   Are you suffering from any illness?
9   Are you dyslexic?
10 What time of day was this written?
11 If you feel your writing varies, e.g. 'best' writing and 'private' writing, would you like to enclose another sample?

If you do become a graphologist, then remember that you will build a reputation based on your success, and that success will be based on accuracy, plus your knowledge of psychology and an understanding of what makes people tick.

Whatever use you make of graphology, I trust you will use the information wisely and know that it will greatly enrich your life.

The history of graphology

In the year 120 AD Suetonius Tranquillus, the Roman historian of the first twelve Caesars, said of the Emperor Augustus, 'He does not separate his words – I do not trust him': so it seems that since actual graphic writing began there has been a link between handwriting and personality. The first recorded book on the subject was written by Alderius Prosper in the early seventeenth century, its title being *Ideographia*. This was in Bologna where a few years later, 1622, a professor of medicine also published a treatise on handwriting analysis. His name was Camillo Baldi. His work, written in Greek, had a long title, which translated is *The means of knowing the habits and qualities of a writer from his letters*.

Little notice was taken of this book, except by a few travelling entertainers who went from castle to castle giving consultations.

For the next hundred years, very little happened in the exploration of handwriting analysis. It was during the early eighteenth century when the link between writing and character became more than a game that it found some devoted followers, especially in France. In the first half of the nineteenth century, approximately 1830, a group of French churchmen came together, to make a serious study of the relationship between handwriting and character, using single letter forms as the main source of information. They were Cardinal Regnier, Archbishop of Cambrai, Bishop Soudinet of Amiens, and Abbé Flandrin (1806–81) who taught a very dedicated student, Jean Hippolyte Michon, with whom the history of handwriting analysis really begins.

It was he who in 1871, by combining the words 'grapho' – 'I write' and 'ology' – 'knowledge of' – gave the science its name, 'graphology'. The understanding of graphology at that time was controversial. Michon, however, published a comprehensive work based upon his lifetime study, which took the Continent by storm and was enthusiastically received. Tremendous sales of this work were recorded. Although graphology was termed a science, Michon still thought of it as an art. Using his intuitive observation, he compared the handwriting of thousands of people whom he knew, and recorded the graphic signs common to people with similar qualities and deficiencies. This was really a catalogue of signs and rules, each having a fixed meaning based on his own experience. He made no attempt to explain why people had different styles, or to connect them psychologically. He was later branded as 'just an interpreter of signs'. He held the opinion that a sign's absence denoted the opposite quality to that indicated by its presence.

Graphologists now know that this is not valid; but for Michon at that time, the system worked very well and was a major contribution to later research by his ex-pupil, Jules Crepieux Jamin. He recognised that the lack of a sign does not necessarily indicate a contrary quality, and in fact very seldom does; also that valid deduction could only be made from existing material, overall graphic evidence to be co-ordinated as a whole.

Crepieux Jamin asked Alfred Binet, a French physician and psychologist – the founder of modern intelligence testing (IQ tests) – to examine the realiability of graphology, relating it to his own psychological methods of testing character. The results of these tests were excellent, and generated further enthusiasm and research into what other learned men and women called 'The science of the future'.

French graphologists were the dominant leaders in the field until the end of the nineteenth century. About 1880, three German scholars approached the subject from a purely psychological viewpoint. They were Dr Wilhelm Preyer, a child psychiatrist and professor of physiology, Dr George Meyer, a psychiatrist and Dr Ludwig Klages (of Zurich), a philosopher. The three undertook extensive research, printed papers and wrote books that were accepted in psychology establishments.

It was Dr Klages who became the leading force in Germany with a credit of five books on the subject of handwriting analysis. He was the first to create a system of working out a character assessment by the method now known as 'Form Level', based upon the quality from a very high to a very low general standard of writing and spacing: natural impulses and rhythm on the one hand, and mental discipline on the other. Thus he found a way to reveal both intentional and unintentional disguise, by examining changeable and unchangeable elements. Until this time, the question of natural and unnatural writing was not considered. Graphologists made correct analyses when the writing was spontaneous, but were wrong when it was forced or disguised.

I have already said that 'handwriting is really brainwriting'. Proof of this was supplied by Dr Preyer, who examined work produced by hand, mouth and foot. He also found that it was not reliable to examine a signature without the text also being scrutinised. He also made a study of the writing mechanics – pen, paper, ink etc.

The work of George Meyer was mainly restricted to what he considered the most important factors – extension, sideways, upwards and downwards movement, speed and pressure – i.e. the relationship between writing movement and the emotions (psychomotor functioning).

It was Dr Meyer who first discovered the significance of beginning and ending strokes in words, along with the slope of the line in the subconscious act of writing. He conducted experiments with patients while they were in states of manic elation and depression. Meyer maintained that you cannot examine a mental condition without considering the character of the person concerned.

Dr Klages and Hans Borse founded the German Graphological Society in 1897–1908 and produced a monthly magazine which helped to bring together all the serious workers in the field, who then pooled their research findings.

In 1904 Dr Klages, a philosopher and psychologist, criticised many former graphologists and caused a split between the German school and the French with their system of 'signs', although for practical purposes the work of Crepieux Jamin was still considered very important. Dr Klages was more penetrating than the others of his time and stated that every movement is composed of three main phases: speed, spacing and pressure, the importance being in the intensity and variation within the manuscript. He presumed there are two forces within us, the Mind, which inhibits, and the Soul, which frees the development of creativity. These two forces, being at variance dynamically, are projected into expressive motion, and handwriting rhythm should be intuitively understood, rather than defined scientifically.

Rudolph Pophal, Professor of Neurology at the University of Hamburg, undertook the study of the physical factors of the writing act, to which very little attention had been previously given. He established a system which helped to classify personality types through microscopic examination of the actual stroke quality – clear, muddy, weak, disintegrating or tremulous – which relates to the neuromuscular system, i.e. the interplay between nerves and muscles.

Robert Saudek came from Czechoslovakia and finished his main work in England around 1925. His research included handwriting styles of different nationalities and their divergence from the copybook characteristics. He made a special study in English handwriting at that time in relation to speed – to him, a very important factor. He also founded the first British journal of graphology, *Character and Personality*, which brought the study of graphology to the attention of many psychologists, as well as increasing knowledge of the science to other handwriting analysts of the day.

Max Pulver (1889–1952), the Swiss graphologist and an associate of Dr Carl Jung, linked handwriting with the psychology of the unconscious and what the writing space symbolised in the writer's mind – how it applied to freedom of expression. It was he who first recognised that writing was the pathway leading from 'I to you', a bridge of communication between the writer and the recipient. He also studied the handwriting of criminals.

Although graphology received most of its early foundations from the Continent, America also had its serious-minded enthusiasts. In the early 1900s June Downey, of the University of Iowa, became fascinated by handwriting analysis and contested the theory of single trait analysis. She experimented with handwriting styles based upon expressive movements, i.e. gesture and body movement. This was followed by an investigation in 1930 by Gordon Allport and Philip Vernon of the Harvard Clinic of Psychology. They considered external movement as an expression of personality to be a very important factor. Their extensive experiments were scientifically correlated to speed, size of script, and pressure of movement. This was later continued by Thea Lewinson.

Graphology began to make headway in England from 1936, when H.J. Jacoby arrived from Germany and published his work *Analysis of Handwriting: An Introduction into Scientific Graphology*, in 1939. This was the first graphology book to contain actual photographic reproductions of handwriting. To stress the usefulness of the science in an everyday context he dealt with samples relating to situations in industry, marriage, child problems, criminology and vocational guidance.

In 1942 Thea Lewinson and Joseph Zubin (USA) did much work to extend the general knowledge of handwriting factors including pressure. In 1945, after participating in these experiments, the American Rose Wolfson privately published her work which dealt mainly with the handwriting of delinquents. Another important contribution was made by Werner Wolff, who, in 1948, after twenty years' research, published his book *Diagrams of the Unconscious*. He created a method of analysis based on the study of the signature, of which he found the movements to be a result of natural expression rather than accidental. This was a theory already expressed by Dr Wilhelm Meyer in his earlier work.

In 1950 Ulrich Sonnemann, Professor at the New School for Social Research in New York, presented his work showing how graphology could be used as a 'psychodiagnostic tool', a serious contribution to clinical psychology. He made an extensive study of schizophrenics and their handwriting along with other anxiety states, to which other graphologists had made only tentative suggestions where graphic evidence was concerned. Also at the New School was Klara Roman, a Hungarian, who in 1952 published her second book, *Handwriting, a Key to Personality*. She had presented earlier a paper on muscular tension in handwriting after years of experiments mainly with children, using an instrument she had designed which recorded changes of speed and pressure during writing. This piece of equipment was an improvement on the first model constructed in 1931.

The history of graphology cannot be comprehensive without mention of the valuable work of Dr Alfred Kanfer, who researched for thirty years into the study of cancer detection, beginning at the City Hospital of Vienna, then at the Hospital for Joint Diseases in New York and subsequently at the Preventative Medicine Institute – Strang Clinic, also in New York. Born in Vienna in 1901, after leaving school he spent most of his time involved in handwriting work with insurance companies, major banks, and the Ministry of Justice. His work eventually led him to the individual differences and the measurement of neuromuscular changes, which in turn produced a factor to determine the pressure or absence of cancer characteristics. Dr Kanfer died in the 1970s, and his research notes were inadvertently destroyed.

Alfred O. Mendel, an American consultant and lecturer, devoted a chapter to Kanfer's work in his book *Personality in Handwriting*, published in 1946. However his main contribution was in factors leading to the detection of lying. He also researched extensively into the horizontal stroke and its implications in pressure.

Louise Rice, an American, founded the American Graphological Society in 1927. She wrote articles and analysed newspaper readers' letters throughout the USA using Crepieux Jamin's method of overall graphic examination. This brought graphology to many people who had hitherto been unaware of its existence. One of her assistants whom she had instructed in the science was Dorothy Sara who, in her own right, became a very popular handwriting analyst, but who did no research.

It is from the work of these early practitioners that modern graphology methods have evolved and are still used today.

There have been noteworthy graphologists since, whose books are still available to date. The most outstanding of these is Eric Singer, a doctor of law at Vienna University, who settled in England in 1938 and set up a graphology practice in London. He was concerned with what he termed 'guiding image', its sources and interpretation, along with Ego symbols such as the personal pronoun 'I'. He related these to Rudolph Pophal's study of the actual stroke and made a detailed study of the effects of ink colour in relation to personality types.

The history of graphology cannot be completely up to date without mention of the late Joan Cambridge, my tutor, who died in February 1989. She was Chairman of the professional organisation, Scientific Graphologists (England) and a member of the Scientific Council, the European Society for Handwriting Psychology. Her work involved many research projects and investigation into physically handicapped childrens' handwriting problems. She was recognised as one of the leading handwriting consultants in Europe.

In the bibliography I have included authors and titles I consider worthy of your attention.

Bibliography

Allport, Gordon and Vernon, Philip.
Studies in Expressive Movement, Macmillan, New York. 1933

Beauchataud, Gabrielle. Translated by Alex Tulloch.
Learn Graphology, Scriptor Books, London. First English Edition, 1988

Brooks, Harry C.
Your Character from your Handwriting, George Allen & Unwin, London. 1930

Cambridge, Joan and Anderson, Elizabeth.
The Handwriting of Spina Bifida Children,
Association for Spina Bifida and Hydrocephalus, London. 1979

Casewit, Curtis W.
Graphology Handbook, Para Research Inc, Massachusetts. 1980

Friedenhain, Paula.
Write and Reveal, Peter Owen, London. 1959

Green, James and Lewis, David.
The Hidden Language of your Handwriting, Souvenir Press, London. 1980

Green, Jane Nugent.
You and your Private 'I',
Llewelyn Publications, St Paul, Minnesota, USA. 1983

Gullan-Whur, Margaret.
The Graphology Workbook, Aquarian Press. 1986

Hartford, Huntington.
You are What you Write, Peter Owen, London. 1975

Heal, Jeanne.
You and your Handwriting, Pelham Books, London. 1973

Hearns, Rudolph S.
Handwriting, an Analysis through its Symbolism (American Institute of Handwriting Analysts), Vantage Press, New York. 1973

Jacoby, H.J.
Analysis of Handwriting, George Allen & Unwin, London. 1939

Koran, Anna.
The Secret Self, Adama Books, New York. 1987

Marne, Patricia.
Crime and Sex in Handwriting,
Constable & Co, London. 1981
Graphology, Hodder & Stoughton, London. 1980
The Secret's in their Signature, W. Foulsham & Co. Ltd., London. 1986

Mendel, Alfred O.
Personality in Handwriting,
Stephen Daye Press, New York, 1947. 5th Printing, 1975

Myer, Oscar N.
The Language of Handwriting, Peter Owen, London. 1951

Nezos, Renna.
Graphology. The Interpretation of Handwriting,
Century Hutchinson Ltd (Rider & Company), London. 1986

Olyanova, Nadya.
Handwriting Tells, Peter Owen, London. 1959
The Secrets of Handwriting Analysis,
Sterling Publishing Co., California, USA. Date unknown. Out of print

Paterson, Jane.
Interpreting Handwriting, Macmillan, London. 1976

Roman, Klara.
Encyclopaedia of the Written Word, Ungar Publishing Co., New York. 1968
Handwriting, a Key to Personality, Ungar Publishing Co., New York. 1952

Sara, Dorothy.
Handwriting for the Millions, Bell Publishing Co., New York.

Saudek, Robert.
Experiments with Handwriting, George Allen & Unwin, London. 1928
The Psychology of Handwriting, George Allen & Unwin, London. 1925

Singer, Eric.
A Manual of Graphology, Gerald Duckworth & Co., London. 1969
Personality in Handwriting, Gerald Duckworth & Co., London. 1954

Sonnemann, Ulrich.
Handwriting Analysis as a Psychodiagnostic Tool,
Grune & Stratton, New York. 1950

Victor, Frank.
Handwriting: A Personality Projection, Charles C. Thomas, Illinois, USA.
1952

Wolff, Werner.
Diagrams of the Unconscious, Grune & Stratton, New York. 1948

Index